Expert SQL Server 2008 Encryption

T0254598

Michael Coles and Rodney Landrum

Apress®

Expert SQL Server 2008 Encryption

ISBN-13 (pbk): 978-1-4302-2464-8

ISBN-13 (electronic): 978-1-4302-2465-5

Lead Editor: Jonathan Gennick
Technical Reviewer: Steve Jones
Editorial Board: Clay Andres, Steve Anglin, Mark Beckner, Ewan Buckingham, Tony Campbell, Gary Cornell, Jonathan Gennick, Michelle Lowman, Matthew Moodie, Jeffrey Pepper, Frank Pohlmann, Ben Renow-Clarke, Dominic Shakeshaft, Matt Wade, Tom Welsh
Project Managers: Beth Christmas and Debra Kelly
Copy Editor: Katie Stence
Compositor: folio 2
Indexer: Carol Burbo
Artist: April Milne

Distributed to the book trade worldwide by Springer-Verlag New York, Inc., 233 Spring Street, 6th Floor, New York, NY 10013. Phone 1-800-SPRINGER, fax 201-348-4505, e-mail orders-ny@springer-sbm.com, or visit http://www.springeronline.com.

For information on translations, please e-mail info@apress.com, or visit http://www.apress.com.

Apress and friends of ED books may be purchased in bulk for academic, corporate, or promotional use. eBook versions and licenses are also available for most titles. For more information, reference our Special Bulk Sales–eBook Licensing web page at http://www.apress.com/info/bulksales.

The source code for this book is available to readers at http://www.apress.com.

For Devoné and Rebecca
—Michael Coles

Contents at a Glance

Contents

Foreword

"What do you think of encryption?" Michael Coles asked me this question at the Microsoft MVP Summit.

This began a discussion of public keys, private keys, symmetric keys, and encryption algorithms. When Michael asked me if I had ever used database encryption in my career, I had to say no. He suggested that I should not underestimate the power of encryption and suggested I might want to explore the possibilities of it. Since then, I have implemented database encryption for many of my clients—who are now much safer from unauthorized access to their data.

Every age creates its own methods of implementing information security. In simpler times, kings sealed important letters with wax containing an impression of the royal seal. If the letter was opened the seal would break, making it easy to determine that the message had been compromised. Presently, this same concept has evolved into cryptographic hashing.

In the courier example, it is quite possible that even if the letter is properly sealed and safe with us, once we send it along the courier can be compromised. SQL Server 2008 allows you to encrypt communications between server and client.

To be quite honest, not many people know much about encryption beyond the usual public key and private key story. Few database experts talk about symmetric and asymmetric keys, which are just the tip of the iceberg. SQL Server has come a long way in this respect, with encryption taking on a whole new meaning in SQL Server 2008. There are many new features to secure your data, like Extensible Key Management, Transparent Data Encryption, cryptographic hashing, and access to SQL CLR cryptographic functions.

In the case of Transparent Data Encryption, the whole database is encrypted, adding security at the cost of some overhead to your SQL Server box. For the greatest efficiency, SQL Server allows you to offload data encryption, decryption, and encryption key management to third-party hardware devices with Extensible Key Management.

As I mentioned, data is everywhere—in fact, talking in Terabytes (TB) is a current reality. There are two major challenges when large data is dealt with. First, encrypting it takes a good amount of resources. Using it once it's encrypted is another big challenge. Searching TB data takes a long time in a regular database anyway—think about how much time it will take in an encrypted database.

Security is definitely one of the most important aspects of life in the Information Era. In fact, information security is one of the most vital pillars of our Information Age. As an example of the importance, consider the following questions: Do you leave the house unlocked when you have many valuables at home? Or, more specifically, how much time, money, and effort would it take to undo the damage if your identity was stolen? What kind of damage would it do to your customers if their information was compromised?

Michael always touches on uncommon subjects. I think his background of serving as a sergeant in the Army gives him the spirit to explore areas that have not been explored. I have not previously read a single book that addresses the subject of encryption for SQL Server 2008. Looking back, I do not know of another book written specifically on this subject for SQL Server until this one.

Michael and I discussed all of the above when we were at the summit. I have always known him as an excellent author. His expertise in XML and Full-Text Search is well known in the industry. He is an expert who puts complex subjects into simple words. No matter how complicated and complex the topic he is addressing, the outcome is always sweet like chocolate.

I especially like the manner in which the authors have explained the significance of encryption. There are many concepts that are domain specific, but there are few topics which are common to all. The book's appendixes are a must read for anyone who is in the planning state of their security strategies. What makes this book special is that each module is written independently, so one can just start creating solutions by reading each one of them.

I am a hands-on developer, and I only like the books that have lots of workable examples. Besides the first chapter, pretty much all of the chapters contain excellent examples and hands-on experiments. Chapter 1 is kind of unique because it not only gives introduction to encryption but also covers the very interesting history of encryption. Overall, the non-technical reader will enjoy this book as well.

It is my great pleasure to welcome this one of kind book into the SQL Server world. There is no doubt that it is exceptional and can wake up the inner soul of everyone who is ready to take their current security mechanism to the next level using encryption.

Pinal Dave
Founder http://blog.SQLAuthority.com

About the Authors

Michael Coles has over 15 years of experience in SQL database design, T-SQL development, and client-server application programming. He has consulted in a wide range of industries, including the insurance, financial, retail, and manufacturing sectors, among others. Michael's specialty is developing and performance-tuning high-profile SQL Server-based database solutions. He currently works as a consultant for a business intelligence consulting firm. He holds a degree in Information Technology and multiple Microsoft and other certifications.

Michael is a Microsoft MVP (SQL) and has published dozens of highly rated technical articles online and in print magazines, including *SQL Server Central, ASP Today*, and *SQL Server Standard* magazines. Michael is the author of the books *Pro T-SQL 2008 Programmer's Guide* (Apress, 2009) and *Pro SQL Server 2008 XML* (Apress, 2008).

Rodney Landrum, SQL MVP, has been architecting solutions for SQL Server for over 10 years. He has worked with and written about many SQL Server technologies, including Integration Services, Analysis Services, and Reporting Services. He has authored three books on Reporting Services for Apress, the latest being *Pro SQL Server 2008 Reporting Services* (2008). He is a regular contributor to SQL Server magazine, sqlservercentral.com, and Simple-talk.com. His three past articles in SQL Server magazine on building a DBA repository with SSIS and SSRS have been well received and implemented widely by DBAs around the world. Rodney's most recent book is *SQL Server Tacklebox: Essential Tools and Tips for the Day–to-Day DBA*. Rodney also speaks regularly on SQL topics at such events as SQL Saturday and a local SQL user group. His day job finds him overseeing the health and well-being of a large SQL Server infrastructure as manager of database administration in Pensacola, Florida.

About the Technical Reviewer

 **Steve Jones** is the founder and editor of SQLServerCentral. He has been working with and writing about SQL Server since 1991.

Acknowledgments

The authors would like to start out the acknowledgments by thanking the team at Apress, beginning with our editor Jonathan Gennick and our coordinating editor Debra Kelly. Thanks to our copyeditor Katie Stence. And a special thank you to our technical reviewer, Microsoft MVP Steve Jones.

Michael would also like to say a special thank you to Microsoft MVP Erland Sommarskog and author Alastair Aitchison of *Beginning Spatial with SQL Server 2008* (Apress, 2009) for their invaluable insights. I would also like to thank Microsoft's own SQL Server security guru, SQL Database Security Team Manager Il-Sung Lee for his patience and help. A very special thanks to SafeNet, Inc., for their support in helping us develop the Extensible Key Management portions of the book, featuring the Luna hardware security module.

Thank you to my family, Donna, Mom, Eric, Jennifer, Chris, Desmond, and Deja. Most importantly, thank you to my angels, Devoné and Rebecca.

Introduction

Information security is the new Wild West. It's full of bandits in black hats trying to rob the stagecoaches at every turn. Your job, as the town sheriff, is to keep these bad guys at bay. SQL Server 2008 provides much-needed encryption tools to help assist you in this task.

I've spoken with quite a few database professionals who don't understand the role of encryption in the database. Many have misconceptions about what encryption provides, and how it provides its services. A great number aren't concerned with encryption at all and see it as one more administrative task imposed by some faceless government agency somewhere.

While encryption is no security panacea, it is a valuable tool in the overall security toolbox. When used in support of a solid security strategy, encryption fulfills the role of a goalkeeper—it acts as a potent last line of defense against adversaries. As with the other pieces of a good security strategy, offense makes the best defense. That is to say, it is much easier and safer to build security into your databases and software products from the ground up than it is to try to retrofit legacy systems with proper security.

In this book, we'll cover the complete range of encryption tools available to SQL Server developers and DBAs to help keep the bad guys out of your data. We'll discuss the reasons for encrypting your data, the options available, and we'll talk about integrating encryption into your overall security strategy.

Who This Book Is For

This book was written by a SQL developer and a SQL DBA for security-minded developers and DBAs. We've designed this book to be useful for any data stewards whose responsibilities include maintaining the security of data stored in the database.

To help you effectively take advantage of the full range of SQL Server encryption tools available, we discuss the wide range of encryption features available. We also discuss how encryption can be used as part of your overall security strategy and the various levels of regulations and industry standards that specifically require encryption of data at rest. In order to take advantage of SQL Server 2008's encryption functionality, you will need to have knowledge of T-SQL. Most of the numerous code samples provided in this book are in SQL Server's native language. In addition, there are a few code samples written in C#, a .NET Framework-based language. While deep knowledge of C# and .NET is not required to use these samples, an understanding of the C# language will only help in understanding how the code performs its tasks.

How This Book Is Structured

This book is structured for use by two types of readers, namely:

- SQL developers who need to write code that takes advantage of SQL Server's built-in encryption functionality.

- DBAs who may not write a lot of code, but who need to understand how SQL Server's encryption functionality works.

Each chapter of the book addresses a different encryption-related topic, making it easy to locate specific information if the book is used as a reference guide. In many chapters, we build on concepts presented in prior chapters, so that reading the book from beginning to end will prove an engaging exercise. Following are brief summaries for each chapter in the book.

Chapter 1: Introduction to Encryption

Chapter 1 is an introduction to encryption, including a very short history of encryption and a discussion of cryptography and cryptanalysis. This chapter is designed to answer questions like "What is encryption?" and "Do I need encryption?" Even for advanced readers who are well-versed in cryptography, this chapter provides some interesting historical information and questions to ask and answer when preparing to implement an encryption solution.

Chapter 2: Encryption Key Management

Encryption key management is one of the hardest tasks in encryption. In Chapter 2, we describe how SQL Server handles encryption key management, with an introduction to the encryption key hierarchy. We also discuss the T-SQL statements, catalog views, and dynamic management views and functions available to manage encryption keys under the hierarchy.

Chapter 3: Symmetric Encryption

Symmetric encryption is the basic model that most people think of first when they hear the word "encryption." You have a piece of plaintext, you encrypt it with a key, and later you can decrypt it with the same key. In Chapter 3, we begin the discussion of SQL Server's cell-level encryption by demonstrating symmetric encryption functionality.

Chapter 4: Asymmetric Encryption

Asymmetric encryption is the type of encryption used to securely transmit your credit card number to remote web sites when you shop online. More complex and significantly slower than symmetric encryption, asymmetric encryption is used primarily in the SQL Server model to protect symmetric keys. In Chapter 4, we discuss asymmetric encryption functionality available in SQL Server.

Chapter 5: Extensible Key Management

In previous chapters we've discussed encryption functionality that is common to both SQL Server 2005 and SQL Server 2008. In Chapter 5, we begin the discussion of a SQL Server 2008-specific feature, Extensible Key Management (EKM). EKM allows you to use third party hardware to manage your encryption keys. You can also offload encryption and decryption functionality from your SQL Server box to the third party hardware, which can free up considerable resources on the server itself.

Chapter 6: Transparent Data Encryption

Another SQL Server 2008-only feature is Transparent Data Encryption (TDE). TDE allows you to encrypt an entire database at once, in a completely transparent fashion. You can use TDE to encrypt your databases with no changes to the applications that use them. In Chapter 6, we demonstrate the use of TDE to encrypt databases.

Chapter 7: Hashing

In addition to encryption and decryption functionality, SQL Server provides built-in access to closely-related cryptographic hashing functionality. In Chapter 7, we look at how cryptographic hashing allows you to "fingerprint" your data, to securely store and detect changes in passwords and other data.

Chapter 8: SQL CLR Cryptography

The SQL Common Language Runtime (SQL CLR) provides an unprecedented opportunity to expand on SQL Server's native encryption functionality. In Chapter 8, we show how to use SQL CLR functionality to overcome some of the limitations imposed on SQL Server's native encryption functions.

Chapter 9: Indexing Encrypted Data

Searching encrypted data is not an efficient proposition. Good encryption removes patterns from data that are necessary for efficient indexing and searching. In Chapter 9, we discuss some strategies you can use to make searches of encrypted data more efficient, to help give your applications a more user-friendly experience.

Chapter 10: Encrypting Connections to SQL Server 2008

In the previous chapters, we focused exclusively on protecting your data "at rest" in the database. But hackers are creatures of opportunity, and they have no qualms about grabbing your data in transit if it's easier for them. In Chapter 10, we explain how to set up SQL Server communications encryption, to secure your data "over the wire," between client applications and your SQL Server.

Chapter 11: Regulatory Requirements

In Chapter 11, we give a high-level view of regulatory and contractual requirements, any of which may drive a database encryption project. We provide a brief survey of selected privacy and data protection regulations and laws that pertain to a wide range of industries.

Appendix A: SQL Server 2008 Encryption Glossary

Throughout this book we've introduced a large number of domain-specific terminology. Although we've defined them along the way, we find it is sometimes useful to have a glossary of terms compiled in one place. Appendix A is the SQL Server encryption glossary, with definitions for many encryption-specific terms we've used in this book.

Appendix B: Encryption Checklist

Appendix B expands on some of the concepts, such as the comprehensive security strategy and threat modeling, which we presented in Chapter 1. This appendix will prove particularly useful for those who are in the planning stages of their security and encryption strategies.

Appendix C: Luna EKM Setup

In Chapter 5, we discussed EKM and demonstrated its use with the SafeNet Luna hardware security module (HSM). In Appendix C, we talk about how to set and configure the SafeNet Luna appliance. This appendix is specific to the Luna appliance used in the book.

Conventions

To help make reading this book a more enjoyable experience, and to help you get as much out of it as possible, we've used standardized formatting conventions throughout the book.

T-SQL source code is shown in code font, with keywords capitalized. Data types in the T-SQL code are consistently lowercased to help improve readability. Other portions of the T-SQL statements are generally in mixed-case.

```
DECLARE @string nvarchar(max);
```

C# code is shown in code font as well. Note that C# code is case-sensitive.

```
while (i < 100)
```

XML is shown in code font, with attribute and element content shown in boldface for readability. Some of the XML code samples and results in the book may have been reformatted for purposes of readability. XML ignores insignificant whitespace, so the significant content of these samples and results have not been altered.

```
<book publisher = "Apress">Expert SQL Server 2008 Encryption</book>
```

■Note   Notes, tips, and warnings are displayed in a special font with solid bars placed over and under the content.

Sidebars

Sidebars include additional information relevant to the current discussion, and other interesting facts. Sidebars are shown on a gray background.

Prerequisites

To make the most of this book you should have access to SQL Server 2008 and SQL Server Management Studio (SSMS). Alternatively, you can use the SQLCMD utility to execute the sample code provided in this book, but we find that SSMS provides a superior user experience for running samples.

Unless otherwise stated, all of the code samples in this book were designed to run against the official SQL Server 2008 AdventureWorksLT 2008 sample database, available for free download at http://www.codeplex.com. We highly recommend downloading and installing the AdventureWorksLT 2008 sample database if you would like to test the sample code in the book.

To run any sample client code, and to compile and deploy SQL CLR samples, you will need C# 2008. Note that you will need the professional editions of Visual Studio to compile and deploy database projects, such as SQL CLR stored procedures and user-defined functions. For the best user experience we highly recommend using Visual Studio 2008 to compile and deploy sample C# code in this book.

Downloading the Code

We provide numerous code samples throughout this book to demonstrate the concepts and syntax discussed in each section. All of these code samples are available for download in a single compressed ZIP file from the Source Code section of the Apress website. To get the ZIP file, go to http://www.apress.com, click on the Books option on the menu at the top, and then click on the Source Code option of the pop-up menu.

Contacting the Authors

The authors and the Apress team have made every effort to ensure that this book is free from errors and defects. Unfortunately, the occasional error does slip past us, despite our best efforts. In the event that you find an error in the book, please let us know! You can submit errors to Apress by visiting http://www.apress.com, locating the book page for this book, and clicking Submit Errata. Alternatively, feel free to drop a line directly to the lead author, Michael Coles, at michaelco@optonline.net.

CHAPTER 1

■ ■ ■

Introduction to Encryption

SQL Server 2008 provides the most comprehensive set of encryption technologies of any SQL Server release to date. The newest release of SQL Server implements encryption features that cover the spectrum from column-level encryption to database-level encryption, with support for external hardware security modules. In addition, Windows Vista and Windows Server 2008 provide encryption support via Encrypting File System and BitLocker encryption. This combination of options provides a complete toolset for securing your data at any storage granularity—cell-level, database-level, or an entire volume. In this book, I'll discuss all of these features for securing your SQL Server-based data.

Before I dive into the specific encryption tools available to SQL Server administrators and developers, I'll discuss the concept of encryption and put modern encryption in perspective by exploring historical encryption technologies.

What Is Encryption?

Encryption is the process of obscuring information (known as *plaintext*) using an algorithm (a *cipher*) in such a way that the information can only be recovered by someone possessing special knowledge (a *key*).

The plaintext consists of the raw data that you want to encrypt. This might be a document, a message, or personal/confidential data stored in a database table. There are a wide variety of ciphers available, from the extremely simple and insecure Caesar-shift style of cipher to the highly secure, modern Advanced Encryption Standard (AES) cipher. The choice of cipher has a direct impact on the security of your encryption, which is why I'll discuss several ciphers throughout this book.

The key (or multiple keys, in some instances) is used to both encrypt your plaintext and to decrypt your encrypted text. Modern encryption recognizes that, while a secure cipher is important, the complete security of your encrypted data rests with the key. In fact, encryption key management and distribution is one of the most complex problems in the world of encryption. I'll discuss encryption key management and distribution in Chapter 2 as well.

Do I Need Encryption?

The question, "Do I need encryption?" starts an investigative process that begins with your business requirements. To answer this question, your organization must first answer other related questions. For instance, you have to determine the level of confidentiality of the data you're storing and whether you're subject to any laws concerning data privacy. The following sections describe some of the major questions that have to be answered when deciding whether or not you need encryption.

1

Are You Storing Confidential or Sensitive Business Information in Your Databases?

If you are storing confidential information in your database, like social security numbers or credit information, encryption is very likely a business requirement. Not encrypting this type of data could potentially expose your organization to legal liability. If you are storing sensitive business information, like high security business documents, not encrypting your data could open up your organization up to hackers and industrial espionage.

According to a report issued by the California security firm McAfee, the damage caused by data theft topped *one trillion dollars* in 2008. As an example of the damage compromised data can result in, TJX Co. (the parent company of T.J. Maxx, Marshalls, and other department stores), reported in 2007 that their systems were hacked. Reports indicated that data was stolen from unencrypted wireless network transmissions as well as from their databases. The data stolen from TJX included 94 million credit and debit card numbers and 455,000 customer return records. The customer return records included driver's license numbers, military ID numbers, and social security numbers, as well as name and address information.

The fallout from TJX's failure to secure its data included dozens of lawsuits from banks and hundreds of millions of dollars in settlements with banks and state attorneys general. The total estimated cost of failing to secure TJX customer data has been estimated between $500 million and $1 billion. In addition, TJX received a lot of bad publicity over the theft and they achieved the dubious record of the worst data breach ever, until 2009 when Heartland Payment Systems set a new world record. Properly securing confidential consumer data would have helped TJX prevent, or limit, the damage caused by hackers.

Are You Subject to Laws and Regulations That Require You to Encrypt YourData?

Since the 1990s, a flurry of laws, state and federal regulations, and rules have been put in place to protect consumer data. Other countries have enacted tough legislation to protect confidential consumer information. This includes credit information, medical records, and a wide array of personal consumer data. Failure to comply with these laws and regulations, which generally involve taking steps like encryption to protect the data, can result in bad publicity, criminal action, and civil liability.

One such regulation,: the Fair and Accurate Credit Transaction Act (FACTA), requires implementation of appropriate information security as part of an identity theft prevention program. Forcompanies that fall under the purview of FACTA, data encryption is one of the most basic tools of compliance.

Are You Under Contractual or Professional Obligation to Protect Your Data?

As the numbers of attacks on private and confidential data increases, industries and individual companies have begun including data protection as part of their standard contracts. It is not uncommon for credit providers, credit card processing companies, and credit bureaus to spell out very specific encryption requirements for the storage of confidential credit and consumer data. These contracts may spell out, in excruciating detail, the specific encryption algorithms allowed, the minimum key size, and other details surrounding security.

As an example, I recently reviewed the technical criteria in a standard contract between a credit card processor and a credit provider. Over the course of ten pages, the credit provider specified the types of security the credit card processor had to implement. The contract detailed which data had to be encrypted, the encryption algorithm to be used, the minimum encryption key lengths, and acceptable methods of encryption key management, rotation, and distribution. The credit provider spelled out a wide array of penalties if the credit card processor did not implement all of the security protocols spelled out in the contract. The penalties included everything up to (and including) denying the credit card processor the ability to perform their most basic function—processing credit card payments!

A Security Mind-Set

After you've decided you have a business need to implement encryption as part of your overall encryption strategy, it's time to get into a security mind-set. A strong security mind-set really borders on the paranoid: as an information officer or technician you have to assume that your organizational data is constantly under attack. Threats are all around—hackers on the outside trying to break in, disgruntled employees on the inside trying to sneak information out, and a host of barbarians banging on the gates of your network. The most effective security strategies begin with this most basic assumption.

Another aspect to keep in mind when getting into a security mind-set is that hackers, just like other criminals, gravitate toward easy targets. The whole point of stealing (and most criminal activity) is to maximize gain while minimizing work.

Picture an average house with a wooden door and a deadbolt lock. Will this keep a determined thief out? Probably not—if you've ever watched an episode of COPS, you've probably seen wooden doors kicked in and knocked down by the Sheriff's office with relative ease. However, thieves like easy targets and they'll skip the house with the dead-bolted door in favor of the house where the door is wide open.

Every layer of security that you implement as part of your overall security plan acts as an additional deterrent. This makes your organizational data less appealing to hackers. Even the most basic security measures tend to keep honest people honest, quickly deter those who are looking for a quick and easy score, and completely eliminate would-be hackers with inadequate skills from the equation.

I'll discuss the implementation of encryption as part of a total security plan in greater detail in Appendix B.

Why Encrypt the Database?

Network and database administrators generally recognize that highly secure and sensitive data should be encrypted over the wire. Secure Sockets Layer (SSL), and its successor Transport Layer Security (TLS), are often used to secure network communications. This is generally considered adequate to protect your data while it's in transit between clients and servers.

To make the difference between data in transit and data at rest a little more concrete, picture thousands of prospectors panning for tiny gold nuggets along a fast-flowing river. Those prospectors are hackers, and the gold nuggets are the packets of data you're sending over your network and across the Internet. Now that this image is firmly in your mind, picture your corporate databases— mountains made of solid, pure gold. Believe me when I say this is not an overstatement of the value of your corporate data. Many organizational databases represent well-organized collections of confidential corporate information. Think about the types of data you store in your databases: customer contact and credit information, contracts, purchase orders, confidential employee data, sales forecasts, production plans, financials, and much more.

Corporate databases are well-defined, highly structured, substantial repositories of critical business information. Consider the damage that would result if your competitors got their hands on all that sensitive data you keep stored on your corporate network. Protecting your data in its transient form as it zips around the network, but failing to properly protect it at its origin or its destination can represent a serious flaw in your security policy.

This is not to give the impression that database encryption is the only security measure you should implement. In fact, database encryption is your last line of defense—your fail-safe in the event that a hacker actually defeats your front-line security measures to gain access to your database.

Threat Modeling

Threat modeling is a formalized process of describing security aspects of a system. The threat modeling process often begins with a diagram of the system being modeled. For purposes of this book, I'll start with a very simple diagram of a single SQL Server instance on a network, as shown in Figure 1-1.

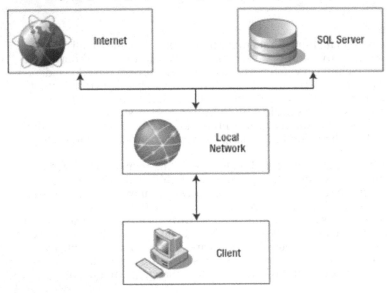

Figure 1-1. SQL Server on a network

This simplified diagram shows the network assets (like the SQL Server and clients) and their interfaces to the local network and to the Internet. In a real-world threat modeling exercise, you would model all individual hardware and software components that must be managed and their interfaces, both internal and external.

As you can see in this simplified representation, SQL Server can be accessed on the local network via network clients. The local network on which the SQL Server resides is also connected to the Internet. This figure shows two potential threat origins: from clients on the local network and from external sources on the Internet.

The next step is to identify threats that can cause harm to the identified assets. In identifying threats, you should identify their type, origin, and potential targets. For this example, we'll identify selected threats to with the target being the data stored on the SQL Server instance. These threats include the following intentional threats:

- *Databa*se Administrators (DBAs): Rogue DBAs are an internal threat. DBAs hold the "keys to the kingdom," with full access to everything within their area of responsibility. DBAs often have access to other network resources outside of the servers for which they are responsible—network shares, files, hardware, and applications. Database encryption, when combined with other measures like auditing, can act as a defense against a rogue DBA by making it difficult for him to access sensitive information that is outside of the scope of his duties.

- Business users: Business users are another internal threat. The primary defense against threats from business users is to strictly limit their access to only the information they need to do their jobs. Database encryption provides additional security against so-called "power users" who are given greater access for specific purposes and against normal business users who somehow acquire greater access than they need.

- Developers: Rogue developers, like rogue DBAs, represent a threat that originates internally. Developers design and implement applications that interact with the database management system (DBMS). Your developers have detailed knowledge of your databases and applications. Database encryption, combined with strict access policies and audit controls, can help limit the damage that can be done by a developer gone bad.

- Internet hackers: Hackers represent an external threat. Hackers have thousands of tools at theirdisposal to help them find weaknesses in their target systems, and the most experienced hackers know how to use them well. Strict access policies, network communications encryption, protection of network interfaces (firewalls), and database encryption can all be used to significantly reduce the risk of a successful external attack.

■ **Note** This list of threats is not a comprehensive list, but rather an abbreviated list that highlights a few of the most common types of threats.

You can use the intent of the threat to help determine what information to encrypt. The intent of internal threats is generally quite simple: financial gain or to "get even" for some perceived slight. External threats, however, have a wider range of intentions. A hacker might attack for financial gain, as retribution for a grievance, to make a political statement, to gain notoriety, or possibly even just self-edification. The goals of the threat, internal or external, might include stealing confidential corporate information, destroying information, or possibly just manipulating corporate data without cutting an easily detectible swath of destruction in the database.

Once you've identified the threats and the threatened assets, you can use that information to create threat matrices. A *threat matrix* is a tool you can use to assess the severity of threats against your assets in a summarized form. Figure 1-2 shows a simple threat matrix for the SQL Server instance in the previous diagram.

Threat	Source	Estimated Threat	Capabilities	Data Arsenal	Remediation	Remedial Threat Level
DBAs	Internal	High	4.0	4.5	Security screening at time of hire Limit access to scope of duties; regular access review Encrypt highly sensitive data; limit DBA access	Moderate
Developers	Internal	Moderate	3.8	3.9	Security screening at time of hire No access to production data Encrypt sensitive data; limit Developer access	Limited
Business Users	Internal	Limited	2.2	1.9	Security screening at time of hire No direct access to any databases Limit network/internet access	Low
Hackers	External	Significant	5.0	5.0	Firewall internet connection Strong passwords; password change policy Encrypt network traffic (SSL); encrypt sensitive data	Limited

Figure 1-2. Sample threat matrix

The threats themselves are listed in rows and the seven columns in this threat matrix represent the following:

Threat: The threat is the type of expected threat.

Source: The source of the threat can be internal to the company or it can originate from an external source.

Estimated threat: The estimated threat indicates the amount of damage a threat can inflict on the organization. I used the following scale (in order of increasing threat level):

- *Low*: The odds of a threat accessing an asset and causing harm is extremely unlikely.

- *Limited*: The threat may be able to access an asset and could potentially cause limited damage. Most often this would occur through means that are beyond your control, such as flaws in off-the-shelf software or invention of new technologies.

- *Moderate*: The threat has some access to an asset and could potentially cause damage. Often, this is the result of an inability to limit access to assets due to job function.

- *High*: A high threat level indicates the threat can access an asset and could cause a considerable amount of damage.

- *Significant*: A significant threat is one that has the means, motive, and opportunity to access assets and cause severe or potentially crippling damage to an organization. Your quickest route to remediation is to remove the opportunity by hardening your assets.

Capabilities: This is a combined measure of a threat's access to organizational assets and technical abilities. I've used a scale of 1.0 (extremely low) to 5.0 (extremely high).

Data arsenal: This is a measure of a threat's ability to obtain, install, and execute effective attacks using tools like viruses, keyloggers, and other malware or hacker hardware. As with Capabilities the scale is 1.0 (extremely low) to 5.0 (extremely high).

Remediation: Steps that can be taken to lower the threat level. In this example, I limited the sample to a few remediation steps per threat, but it's often easy to come up with dozens of remediation steps for most threats.

Remedial threat level: The estimated threat level after remediation steps have been implemented. In this example, the "Hackers" estimated threat level was lowered from a significant threat to a limited threat through a combination of securing the Internet connection, implementing a strong password policy, and encryption.

The threat matrix is a simple tool you can use to evaluate your overall security situation for each of your organization's assets. Notice in the example that encryption alone doesn't remediate threats, but when used in combination with other remediation steps it can help reduce the potential damage any given threat can inflict.

A Short History of Information Security

Encryption, codes, and ciphers have been the domain of militaries and governments for thousands of years. In fact, secure encryption technology has only been available to the public at large since the end of the 20th century.

Cryptology, the science of information security via codes and ciphers, consists of two major branches. The first branch, *cryptography*, is concerned with the creation of codes and ciphers to ensure information security. The second branch is *cryptanalysis*, which concerns itself with defeating the codes and ciphers created by cryptographers. Modern cryptology is a direct result of the constant struggle between cryptographers and cryptanalysts over the course of thousands of years.

To understand the current state of encryption technology it's important to understand its history. To that end, I'll review some of the major accomplishments and milestones in securing information over the past few thousand years.

The First Ciphers

One of the first known uses of a cipher to obscure messages dates to around 400 BCE. The Spartan scytale (pronounced "sit-uh-lee"; rhymes with *Italy*), was used to communicate critical information securely during military campaigns. The scytale was simply a rod around which a piece of leather was wrapped.

To encipher a message the sender wrapped a strap of leather around a scytale and wrote his message lengthwise across the bands of the leather. When unwrapped from the scytale, the leather looked like a simple leather strap with random letters and symbols written on it. Upon delivery of the message, the recipient simply wrapped the leather strap around a scytale of the same diameter as the sender's and the message was revealed.

Figure 1-3 shows a scytale in use, deciphering the message "_ ___ _ ___ ___." This particular message is attributed to Spartan mothers who admonished their sons going to war to come back either "with this or on this," victorious (with your shield) or dead (carried on your shield).

Figure 1-3. *Scytale used to decipher a message*

The scytale is an example of a simple transposition cipher in which the characters of the plaintext are simply methodically rearranged. The other prevalent method of enciphering information isvia substitution ciphers. A substitution cipher systematically replaces plaintext with encrypted text. Julius Caesar was recorded as having used a simple cipher, which has become known as the *Caesar Shift* cipher. Caesar simply replaced each letter of his plaintext with the letter that occurs three places to its right in the alphabet. Figure 1-4 shows an example of the Caesar Shift cipher in action.

Figure 1-4. *Encrypting a message with the Caesar Shift cipher*

As you can see in Figure 1-4, encrypting the message "ALEA IACTA EST" ("The die is cast," aquote attributed to Caesar himself) using the Caesar Shift cipher results in the ciphertext "DOHD LDFWD HVW." To decrypt the ciphertext, you simply replace each letter with the letter that occur three places to its left in the alphabet. The Caesar Shift is an example of the simplest form of *monoalphabetic substitution cipher*, since it relies on a simple one-for-one replacement strategy within the alphabet.

Variations on Caesar Shift, including other monoalphabetic substitution ciphers, were used effectively for over 800 years.

The Rise of Cryptanalysis

While monoalphabetic substitution ciphers proved effective against the largely uneducated adversaries against whom Caesar fought, they proved no match for the Arab polymath al-Kindi. ::Around 850 CE, al-Kindi published his monograph *A Manuscript on Deciphering Cryptographic Messages*, in which he described a method for defeating monoalphabetic substitution ciphers. A scholar of many languages and an expert in many different fields, al-Kindi is widely regarded as the founder of the science of cryptanalysis. In his manuscript, al-Kindi exploits the weakness of monoalphabetic substitution ciphers—namely, the frequency distribution of letters in the target language.

In the case of the monoalphabetic substitution cipher, al-Kindi realized that certain letters inany given language will occur more frequently than others. The letters *E*, *T*, *H*, *A*, and *O*, for example, account for nearly 50 percent of all written text in English. For a sufficiently lengthy text (al-Kindi suggested a length of one sheet of text or more), the frequency of letter occurrences tend to approach thenormal frequency distribution for the language in which it was written.

To test al-Kindi's theory, I chose to analyze the King James Version (KJV) Bible. Containing more than 3.2 million letters, the KJV Bible is of sufficient length to adequately test the frequency distribution theory. Figure 1-5 shows a side-by-side comparison of the occurrences of letters in the KJV Bible text and the normal frequency distribution of letters in English. Notice how close the distributions are, particularly for letters whose occurrences are at the extremes; that is, letters that occur most frequently and those that occur least frequently.

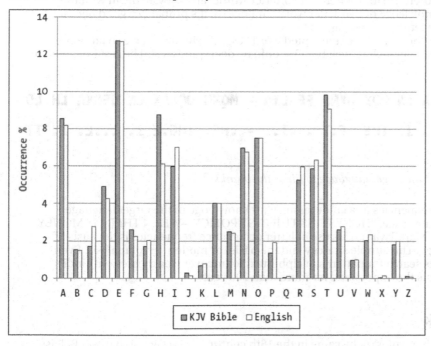

Figure 1-5. Frequency distribution of letters in the English language and the Bible (KJV)

This revelation exposes the flaw in simple monoalphabetic substitution ciphers. In the Caesar Shift, letters in the plaintext are replaced by other letters to obscure the information, but the frequency distribution is not obscured. If you replace the letter *E* in your plaintext with the letter *Z*, for instance, you can expect that *Z* will occur more frequently than any other letter. This makes it easy for a cryptanalyst to attack your ciphertext. The cryptanalyst will quickly surmise that the letter *Z* occurs mostfrequently in the ciphertext and will replace it with *E*. Likewise, other letters in the ciphertext will be replaced according to the frequency of occurrence until the cryptanalyst uncovers some intelligible information.

Consider the ciphertext "QEHXNOA LN OQX UXNO FESLIA—MQXH OQXDX LN GEHXA LH LO." In this short ciphertext, the letter *X* occurs most frequently, followed by the letter *O*. Frequency analysis indicates we should replace these letters in the ciphertext with the most frequently occurring plaintext letters, *E* and *T*, respectively. The result of this initial substitution is shown in Figure 1-6.

Ciphertext: **QEHXNOA LN OQX UXNO FESLIA - MQXH OQXDX LN GEHXA LH LO**

Plaintext: **...E.T. .. T.E .E.T ...... - ..E. T.E.E .. ...E. .. .T**

Figure 1-6. Initial steps of using frequency to recover an enciphered message

Shorter texts don't necessarily follow the normal distribution, so the cryptanalyst might make educated guesses of other enciphered letters based on his knowledge of the target language. In the enciphered text, for instance, there are four different two-letter words, and they all begin with the encrypted letter *L*. Based on knowledge of two-letter words in English, it's probably a good bet that theencrypted *L* represents the letter *I* in the plaintext.

There is also the matter of the three-letter encrypted word "OQX," which we have so far mapped to "T?E." Again it's probably safe to guess that the letter *Q* should be decrypted as *H*. The resultof applying these guesses is shown in Figure 1-7.

Ciphertext: **QEHXNOA LN OQX UXNO FESLIA - MQXH OQXDX LN GEHXA LH LO**

Plaintext: **H..E.T. I. THE .E.T ...I.. - .HE. THE.E I. ...E. I. IT**

Figure 1-7. Using knowledge of the target language to fill in the blanks

Continuing to use letter frequencies as a guide, along with knowledge of the target language, you'll eventually decipher the message: "HONESTY IS THE BEST POLICY—WHEN THERE IS MONEY INIT," a quote from humorist Mark Twain. This use of letter occurrence frequencies is the basis of al-Kindi's cryptanalysis strategy. This simple strategy laid the basis for modern cryptanalysis. Even inmodern times, cryptanalysts search for patterns in ciphertext to uncover weaknesses. Al-Kindi's methodology gave cryptanalysts the upper hand for more than 700 years.

Bellaso Strikes Back

The next major advancement in cryptography came in the 16th century when Giovan Battista Bellaso fully developed ideas from several sources into the first polyaphabetic substitution cipher. The polyalphabetic cipher known as the Vigenère cipher (it was misattributed to Blaise de Vigenère, who later modified Bellaso's original invention) improved on the monoalphabetic ciphers (like the Caesar

Shift) by applying multiple monoalphabetic cipher alphabets to encipher plaintext. This has the effect ofremoving the frequency patterns that al-Kindi's method of cryptanalysis depends on.

Bellaso's system defined polyalphabetic ciphers using what he called reciprocal tables. Bellaso's tables were later reformatted into the *tabula recta* by Vigenère. Figure 1-8 shows the tabula recta.

	A	B	C	D	E	F	G	H	I	J	K	L	M	N	O	P	Q	R	S	T	U	V	W	X	Y	Z
A	B	C	D	E	F	G	H	I	J	K	L	M	N	O	P	Q	R	S	T	U	V	W	X	Y	Z	A
B	C	D	E	F	G	H	I	J	K	L	M	N	O	P	Q	R	S	T	U	V	W	X	Y	Z	A	B
C	D	E	F	G	H	I	J	K	L	M	N	O	P	Q	R	S	T	U	V	W	X	Y	Z	A	B	C
D	E	F	G	H	I	J	K	L	M	N	O	P	Q	R	S	T	U	V	W	X	Y	Z	A	B	C	D
E	F	G	H	I	J	K	L	M	N	O	P	Q	R	S	T	U	V	W	X	Y	Z	A	B	C	D	E
F	G	H	I	J	K	L	M	N	O	P	Q	R	S	T	U	V	W	X	Y	Z	A	B	C	D	E	F
G	H	I	J	K	L	M	N	O	P	Q	R	S	T	U	V	W	X	Y	Z	A	B	C	D	E	F	G
H	I	J	K	L	M	N	O	P	Q	R	S	T	U	V	W	X	Y	Z	A	B	C	D	E	F	G	H
I	J	K	L	M	N	O	P	Q	R	S	T	U	V	W	X	Y	Z	A	B	C	D	E	F	G	H	I
J	K	L	M	N	O	P	Q	R	S	T	U	V	W	X	Y	Z	A	B	C	D	E	F	G	H	I	J
K	L	M	N	O	P	Q	R	S	T	U	V	W	X	Y	Z	A	B	C	D	E	F	G	H	I	J	K
L	M	N	O	P	Q	R	S	T	U	V	W	X	Y	Z	A	B	C	D	E	F	G	H	I	J	K	L
M	N	O	P	Q	R	S	T	U	V	W	X	Y	Z	A	B	C	D	E	F	G	H	I	J	K	L	M
N	O	P	Q	R	S	T	U	V	W	X	Y	Z	A	B	C	D	E	F	G	H	I	J	K	L	M	N
O	P	Q	R	S	T	U	V	W	X	Y	Z	A	B	C	D	E	F	G	H	I	J	K	L	M	N	O
P	Q	R	S	T	U	V	W	X	Y	Z	A	B	C	D	E	F	G	H	I	J	K	L	M	N	O	P
Q	R	S	T	U	V	W	X	Y	Z	A	B	C	D	E	F	G	H	I	J	K	L	M	N	O	P	Q
R	S	T	U	V	W	X	Y	Z	A	B	C	D	E	F	G	H	I	J	K	L	M	N	O	P	Q	R
S	T	U	V	W	X	Y	Z	A	B	C	D	E	F	G	H	I	J	K	L	M	N	O	P	Q	R	S
T	U	V	W	X	Y	Z	A	B	C	D	E	F	G	H	I	J	K	L	M	N	O	P	Q	R	S	T
U	V	W	X	Y	Z	A	B	C	D	E	F	G	H	I	J	K	L	M	N	O	P	Q	R	S	T	U
V	W	X	Y	Z	A	B	C	D	E	F	G	H	I	J	K	L	M	N	O	P	Q	R	S	T	U	V
W	X	Y	Z	A	B	C	D	E	F	G	H	I	J	K	L	M	N	O	P	Q	R	S	T	U	V	W
X	Y	Z	A	B	C	D	E	F	G	H	I	J	K	L	M	N	O	P	Q	R	S	T	U	V	W	X
Y	Z	A	B	C	D	E	F	G	H	I	J	K	L	M	N	O	P	Q	R	S	T	U	V	W	X	Y
Z	A	B	C	D	E	F	G	H	I	J	K	L	M	N	O	P	Q	R	S	T	U	V	W	X	Y	Z

Figure 1-8. The tabula recta

Encrypting a message requires a key that was previously agreed upon by the sender and receiver. The sender matches each letter of the plaintext with a letter of the key. The sender then locatesthe letters at the intersection of each key letter and its associated plaintext letter. Figure 1-9 demonstrates the encryption of a plaintext with the tabula recta, using a key of "BATMAN."

Key: **BAT MANB AT MANBA TMANB ATMANB AT MAN BATMA**
Plaintext: **THE RAIN IN SPAIN FALLS MAINLY IN THE PLAIN**
Ciphertext: **VIY EBWP JH FQOKO ZNMZU NUVOZA JH GIS RMUVO**

Figure 1-9. A message encrypted with the tabula recta

To decrypt the message the receiver first matches each letter of the ciphertext with each letter ofthe key. Then the receiver must locate each key letter that begins a row and identify the associated ciphertext letter within that row. The letter that labels the column where the ciphertext letter appears is the plaintext letter.

The important thing to notice about the tabula recta is that it again represents several substitution ciphers. While it greatly increases the security of ciphers by eliminating simple frequency analysis attacks, the polyalphabetic cipher was ahead of its time and didn't gain widespread adoption until the advent of the electromagnetic telegraph and Morse code in the 19th century. Charles Babbage discovered a successful attack on the Vigenère cipher in 1854 (the same attack was independently discovered by Freidrich Kasiski in 1869), rendering this generation of the polyalphabetic cipher insecure, even as it had started gaining widespread acceptance.

War and Security

At the end of the 19th century and entering the early 20th century, several events conspired to push the limits of cryptography. During this time period Italian inventor Guglielmo Marconi developed radio, proving it a viable communications system. As governments and militaries began adopting radio communications for increasing volumes of sensitive communications, increased security became imperative.

Code making and code breaking became increasingly important as the world entered "the warto end all wars," World War I. The Germans' infamous Zimmerman telegram underscored the importance of cryptology during World War I. The Zimmerman telegram, an encrypted message from the German empire, appealed to the Mexican government to form an alliance and declare war on the United States. The Germans promised Mexico military support and reclamation of the former Mexican territory that comprises the states of Texas, Arizona, and New Mexico. The interception and decryption of the Zimmerman telegram, which was subsequently turned over to the US government, was a major factor in the United States' declaration of war against Germany in 1917.

World War I also ushered in the only perfectly secure encryption system known, the *one-time pad*. A one-time pad contains random keys that are at least as long as the plaintext. The random keys are combined with the plaintext via modulo arithmetic functions. The sender and receiver of the messages must both have a copy of the same one-time pads, and they must agree in advance as to which key will be used; possibly via a previously agreed-upon key schedule. The major problem with one-time pads is distribution, which amounts to a massive logistical undertaking for large organizations like governments and armies. It's nearly impossible for small and midsized companies. The classic Hollywood image of trusted secret agents with tamper-proof briefcases handcuffed to their wrists, as they deliver one-time pads to high-ranking officials around the world actually isn't too far from the truth.

World War II brought with it major advances in mechanical cryptography. The use of machines to encrypt messages increased the efficiency of secure war-time messaging. Major advances in mathematics, information theory, and engineering all contributed to great strides in the field of cryptanalysis as well. To crack codes like the German Enigma (generated by the Enigma machine shown in Figure 1-10), Lorenz ciphers, and the Japanese Purple cipher, cryptanalysts went back to their roots and once again looked for patterns.

Figure 1-10. German Enigma machine

Strict military message structure and basic human nature (using the same keys multiple times, for instance) provided the patterns that Allied cryptanalysts used during World War II to crack enemy codes. German soldiers, for example, were trained to transmit the enciphered message key twice at the beginning of each message. This procedure proved to be the first weakness that Polish cryptanalysts identified and exploited to decipher Enigma messages. The cryptanalysts who cracked enemy ciphers during World War II, including the Enigma, Lorenz, and Purple ciphers, are credited with saving tens of thousands of lives by providing intelligence that shortened the war by as much as four years.

Prior to World War II cryptography and cryptanalysis were largely considered the domain of linguists and lexicography experts. During the war, it was recognized that the search for patterns could be effectively carried forward by mathematicians, statisticians, engineers, and a wide assortment of problem solvers including Chess grandmasters and crossword puzzle enthusiasts. These problem solvers contributed their talents to make great advances in cryptanalysis. Progress made on several academic fronts during the war contributed greatly to the body of cryptologic knowledge.

How to Share a Secret

After World War II ended, the governments of the world were still digesting the cryptographic and cryptanalytic knowledge they acquired in the heat of battle. After the war was over, government and military interest in cryptology dropped back down to its prewar levels. However, there were still unresolved problems; the first (and toughest) of which was key distribution. Key distribution has long been a vexing problem, introducing several potential points of failure along the way.

   One of the modern principles of encryption, Kerckhoffs' Assumption, also known as Kerckhoffs' Principle, can be most simply stated (as it was by Claude Shannon, the Father of Information Theory) as"The enemy knows the system." This one statement represents a very basic assumption, and an extremely valid one: assume that all cryptanalysts have access to your cryptographic algorithm. In modern cryptography it's generally recognized that security rests with the encryption key, and the onlyassumption that's made is that the enemy does not know the key. By introducing a flawed key distribution model into an otherwise secure system you significantly increase the odds that the enemy will obtain the key—creating a critical vulnerability.

   In 1976, the team of Whitfield Diffie and Martin Hellman devised an ingenious solution to theproblem of key distribution. The Diffie-Hellman key exchange protocol relies on passing shared information in public to calculate secret keys. The strength of the protocol is in the formula used to generate the secret keys, which is a one-way function. A one-way function in math is one which is hard to reverse, such as a factoring function. The sidebar discusses Diffie-Hellman key exchange.

Alice Meets Bob

Using the classic example, assume Alice needs to send Bob a secure message. In order to decrypt Alice's message Bob needs her encryption key. How does Alice securely transfer the key to Bob? One option is for Alice to meet with Bob somewhere and give him the key at that point; this might not be feasible if Alice lives in New York and Bob is in California. Another option is for Alice to hire an agent to carry the key to Bob for her. Unfortunately, this can be a costly and insecure option. Can the agent be trusted not to sell the key or use it for his own nefarious purposes? Could the key be intercepted by a malicious third party without the agent's knowledge? What if Alice needs to send secure messages to 100 different people— does she have the resources to hire 100 agents to distribute keys? If Alice had doubts about the trustworthiness of one agent, 100 agents represents a security nightmare.

Whitfield Diffie had an epiphany one day while thinking about physical locks. Diffie's revelation was in the mind of a thought experiment. Diffie's experiment begins with a simple question, "Alice wants to send Bob a secret message securely; how can she do it?" Diffie's answer follows:

1. Alice puts her message in a secure box and places her padlock on the box, locking it. Then she sends the box to Bob. She keeps her key.

2. Bob receives the box and places his own padlock on it. Keeping his own key, he sends the box back to Alice.

Alice Meets Bob, *continued*

3. Alice receives the box and uses her key to take her padlock off it. She then sends the box, secured only by Bob's padlock, back to Bob.

4. Bob uses his key to unlock his padlock and retrieves the contents of the box.

Diffie's answer involved a lot of overhead in sending, securing, and resending the same message back and forth between Alice and Bob, but it proved that secret messages could be sent securely without sharing keys. This thought experiment was the basis for Diffie-Hellman key exchange, in which Alice and Bob both have their own secret keys. They can both calculate the same key using a one-way function. While some information needs to be communicated between Alice and Bob, the one-way function used is very difficult to reverse, making it secure. Consider the following scenario:

1. Alice and Bob both agree on a one-way function, Y^X *(mod P)*. Then Alice and Bob agree on shared values for Y and P, in this case $Y = 11$ and $P = 13$.

2. Our hacker, Eve, is listening in on the conversation and sees the values for Y and P being communicated back and forth. It doesn't matter that Eve sees these values, as we'll see.

3. Alice generates a secret value for X, let's say 9. Bob generates a secret value for X on his side, we'll say 19. Alice doesn't know Bob's secret X, Bob doesn't know Alice's secret X, and Eve doesn't know either secret value.

4. Alice plugs the shared values and her secret value into the one-way function and gets the answer 11^9 (mod 13) = 8. Bob does the same and comes up with 11^{19} (mod 13) = 2.

5. Alice and Bob share the results of their calculations with one another. Eve, ever vigilant, captures Alice's result of 8 and Bob's result of 2 in transit. Again, without knowledge of Alice's and Bob's secret keys this information is useless to Eve.

6. Alice plugs Bob's result and her secret key into the same function as before, but replacing the Y with her secret key and the X variable with Bob's result. Alice ends up with 9^2 (mod 13) = 3. Bob does the same, but uses his secret key for Y and Alice's result for X. Bob ends up with 19^8 (mod 13) = 3. Now Alice and Bob have both generated the same key that they can use to encrypt messages back and forth securely.

In this scenario, Eve was able to see snippets of the communication between Alice and Bob, but she is unable to determine what the encryption key is because of the one-way function used. The important thing to note is that Eve doesn't have access to Alice's or Bob's secret keys. Since Alice and Bob don't need to share this secret information, Eve never gets a chance to intercept it in transit.

Weapons of Mass Encryption

During the last few decades of the 20th century, :computers became commonplace for both business and home use. The launch of the Internet and its commercial application, the World Wide Web, prompted a huge push for commercial-grade security. Businesses needed a means to convince customers that they could securely transmit their credit card numbers and confidential information tomake online purchases. Due to the problems involved in secure key distribution for symmetric key algorithms, the market needed an efficient and secure method of communicating with customers.

In 1977, Ron Rivest, Adi Shamir,: and Leonard Adleman of MIT invented the most widely-adopted asymmetric encryption algorithm in the world, the RSA algorithm. RSA encryption requires theuse of very large prime numbers, the products of which are used to generate key pairs. The key pairs include a public key, which is exposed to the world, and a private key, which must be kept secret. The public key and private key have a mathematical relationship to one another, but one that is not easily derivable without knowledge of both.

If Alice wants to send Bob an encrypted message using RSA, Bob would first need to expose hispublic key. Alice could then encrypt her message using Bob's public key and send it to him. Upon receipt, Bob could use his private key to decrypt the message. RSA algorithm security is primarily based on the mathematical difficulty of factoring very large numbers.

Since its introduction RSA has become a mainstay of Web-based security. It is used to secure communications over the Internet and within corporate networks around the world. In 2000, RSA Security released the RSA algorithm to the public domain.

Asymmetric key encryption, using algorithms like RSA, are considered very secure. RSA, and other asymmetric key encryption algorithms, require a lot more processing power and are not as efficient as symmetric key algorithms. In 1991, Phillip Zimmerman application: released an encryption application known as PGP (Pretty Good Privacy). Zimmerman used the RSA algorithm to encrypt session keys, or symmetric keys generated for a single message. The message itself was encrypted using the session keys. PGP combined the strength of asymmetric encryption with the,: efficiency of symmetric encryption.

ARMS DEALERS

Throughout the 1990s, high security encryption algorithms were classified as munitions according to US export regulations. Phillip Zimmerman was investigated from 1993 to 1996 for "munitions export without a license" when PGP was obtained by individuals, governments, and groups outside of the United States. In response to the investigation, Zimmerman released the full source code to PGP in the form of a book. The Supreme Court had previously held that export of books was protected under the First Amendment right to free speech. The government dropped the case against Zimmerman and PGP was subsequently bought by Network Associates.

Official Ciphers of the US Government

During the Cold War in the early 1970s, the US government surveyed the state of security and determined that a modernized encryption standard was required. In 1976, the :National Institute of Standards and Technology or NIST (formerly the National Bureau of Standards or NBS), adopted a modified version of IBM's Lucifer cipher as the Data Encryption Standard (DES). The version of DES that was implemented came under scrutiny from many quarters because it featured a 56-bit encryption key, largely regarded as small enough for a government agency with high-powered computing resources (such as the National Security Agency, or NSA) to crack within a relatively short amount of time.

Nevertheless, DES was adopted as the official symmetric encryption algorithm of the US government for more than two decades, until 1998 when a brute force attack by networked computers demonstrated that cracking DES was practical. Theoretical attacks also began to spring up, and the DES algorithm began to show cracks.

In response, the US government took two major steps: first DES was deprecated and a variant known as Triple DES, with a larger effective key length, was authorized. Second, the government held a public competition for a DES replacement algorithm. The winner of the contest was a cipher known as Rijndael, produced by the Belgian team of Joan Daemen and Vincent Rijmen. Three encryption key length variants of Rijndael, one with 128-bit keys, one with 192-bit keys, and one with 256-bit keys, were formalized as the Advanced Encryption Standard (AES) in 2001. AES is authorized by the US government for securing both Secret and Top Secret information.

What is Triple DES?

Two-key and three-key Triple DES were implemented as countermeasures against the vulnerabilities found in the plain vanilla DES algorithm. The Triple DES variants were originally introduced to minimize the changes required to government computers. Two-key Triple DES uses two separate keys, possibly derived from the same keying material. The first key is used to encrypt data using DES; the second key is used to decrypt the data; and finally the first key is used to reencrypt the data. This method is known as the Encrypt-Decrypt-Encrypt (EDE) process.

Three-key Triple DES uses a similar methodology, but it extracts three separate keys from the keying material. The first key is used to encrypt, the second key to decrypt, and the third key to encrypt again.

The investment to upgrade government computers that were programmed to use DES was significantly less than it would have been to create a whole new algorithm and upgrade all government computers with the new software. Triple DES essentially provided a "quick fix" for the government and for other organizations that relied on DES for security. The two-key EDE methodology increases the key length of DES from 56 bits to 112 bits, although the effective key length of two-key Triple DES is estimated at only 80 bits. Three-key Triple DES increases the key length of DES to 168 bits, but the effective key length is estimated at around 116 bits. The National Security Agency (NSA) estimates that three-key Triple DES will be provide adequate security until the year 2030.

Both AES and DES (and its variants) are block ciphers, which operate on fixed-length bit strings known as *blocks*. DES operates on 64-bit blocks while AES is a 128-bit block cipher. All block ciphers must support two main properties: *confusion* and *diffusion*. Confusion is primarily achieved through theprocess of replacing plaintext symbols with other symbols, usually done with a so-called *S-box*. The S-box is implemented in both AES and DES as static lookup arrays or tables, consisting of values with statistically nonlinear properties. It's a well-constructed S-box that prevents simple algebraic-based attacks on a given block cipher.

Diffusion is the removal of statistical patterns from ciphertext during the encryption process. A structure known as a *P-box* is often used by block ciphers to shuffle and transpose bits across ciphertext during processing. This process of *permutation* results in diffusion of bits, and statistical patterns, across the ciphertext. The diffusion process protects ciphertext from pattern-based statistical cryptanalysis, including classic frequency analysis attacks.

SQL Server supports DES, Triple DES, and AES encryption, all of which will be discussed in detail in Chapter 3.

SQL Server Encryption Tools

As our discussion brings us to modern encryption technologies, it's time to take a look at what SQL Server 2008 offers in terms of encryption. Historically SQL Server didn't provide any built-in support for encryption. In fact, I had to create my own extended stored procedure (XP) based encryption functionality for SQL Server 2000 (the *DBA Toolkit*, available with source code at www.sqlservercentral.com). In the following sections, I'll quickly recount the history of SQL Server database encryption.

Encryption in SQL Server 2000

Built-in cryptographic encryption functionality was nonexistent in SQL Server 2000 and prior versions. In order to get server-side encryption in SQL Server you had to resort to purchasing or creating your own SQL Server XPs. Creating your own cryptographic XPs could be a daunting task owing to the fact that XPs had to be compiled as native DLLs (using a language like C or C++) and the XP application programming interface (API) was poorly documented. In addition there were always concerns around creating well-behaved XPs that "played nicely" with the SQL Server process.

Encryption in SQL Server 2005

Prior to the release of SQL Server 2005 there was a flurry of regulatory activity in response to accounting scandals and attacks on repositories of confidential consumer data. Much of this regulation centered onthe need for protecting and controlling access to sensitive financial and consumer information. With the release of SQL Server 2005 Microsoft responded to the increasing demand for built-in encryption byproviding the necessary tools to encrypt data at the column level. This functionality prominently featured the following:

- Support for column-level encryption of data using symmetric keys or passphrases. Chapter 3 details symmetric encryption methodologies.

- Built-in access to a variety of symmetric and asymmetric encryption algorithms, including AES, DES, Triple DES, RC2, RC4, and RSA. These algorithms are discussed in Chapters 3 and 4.

- Capability to create and manage symmetric keys. Key creation and management are discussed in Chapter 2.

- Ability to generate asymmetric keys and self-signed certificates, or to install external asymmetric keys and certificates. I will discuss asymmetric keys and certificates in Chapter 4.

- Implementation of hierarchical model for encryption key management, similar to the ANSI X9.17 standard model. I'll discuss ANSI X9.17 in Chapter 2.

- SQL functions to generate one-way hash codes and digital signatures, including SHA-1 and MD5 hashes. I'll discuss hashing and digital signatures in Chapter 6.

- Additional SQL functions to encrypt and decrypt data.

- Extensions to the SQL language to support creation, use, and administration of encryption keys and certificates.

- SQL CLR extensions that provide access to .NET-based encryption functionality. I'll cover SQL CLR extensions and .NET-based encryption functions in Chapter 9.

All of these features provided much-needed encryption support to SQL Server. They are all supported in SQL Server 2008 as well. While support for cell-level encryption is a very important feature, and a large portion of this book is devoted to cell-level encryption functionality, there was still a need for even more encryption features. To use cell-level encryption functionality, for instance, you might have to refactor significant portions of your existing SQL and client code. For new databases and applications you have to take cell-level encryption into consideration early in the process, during the requirements gathering and design phases.

Encryption in SQL Server 2008

Encryption demands have increased over the past few years. For instance, there has been a demand for the ability to store encryption keys "off-the-box," physically separate from the database and the data it contains. Also there is a recognized requirement for legacy databases and applications to take advantage of encryption without changing the existing code base. To address these needs SQL Server 2008 adds the following features to its encryption arsenal:

- *Transparent Data Encryption (TDE)*: Allows you to encrypt an entire database, including log files and the tempdb database, in such a way that it is transparent to client applications. I'll discuss TDE in detail in Chapter 5.

- *Extensible Key Management (EKM)*: Allows you to store and manage your encryption keys on an external device known as a hardware security module (HSM). I'll discuss EKM functionality in Chapter 7 with real examples that take advantage of the first shipping SQL Server-enabled HSM, the SafeNet® Luna HSM appliance.

- Cryptographic random number generation functionality.

- Additional cryptography-related catalog views and dynamic management views, which I'll cover in Chapter 10.

- SQL language extensions to support the new encryption functionality.

SQL Server 2008 represents the most advanced SQL Server encryption capability to date, and you can leverage even more encryption functionality using other tools. For example, you can encrypt an entire hard drive with SQL Server databases on it via Windows BitLocker technology. You can also use SSL to encrypt your SQL Server communications, protecting your data in transit. I'll discuss these features and functionality in Chapter 11.

Summary

Cryptology is the science of hidden information. Two major branches of cryptology that have evolved over thousands of years are cryptography, the science of obscuring information, and cryptanalysis, the science of recovering encrypted information without access to the secret key used to encrypt it.

The state of modern cryptology represents the evolution of the struggle between these two conflicting sciences. Over the centuries, cryptographers have created even more secure algorithms to encrypt data and cryptanalysts have found increasingly sophisticated methods to destroy that security.

Initially a code or cipher could be expected to provide security for hundreds of years. However, with the ever-increasing computing power available to anyone, the life expectancy of a typical encryption algorithm can be measured in mere decades or less.

Modern encryption algorithms include some of the most sophisticated to date. AES, Triple DES, RSA, and other algorithms are all included in SQL Server 2008. In addition, you can use EKM to take advantage of third-party HSM appliances. SQL Server 2008 provides answers for some of the toughest challenges facing any cryptographic security system, including key management and encryption of entire databases at a time.

While encryption alone is not the holy grail of security, it can be an indispensable tool in your total security arsenal. In this chapter, I discussed one method of assessing threats to your organizational assets. In the following chapters, you'll begin an exploration of the encryption features and functionality available. in SQL Server 2008 that will help you implement a total security solution.

CHAPTER 2

■■■

Encryption Key Management

SQL Server 2008 includes a comprehensive suite of modern encryption technologies. SQL Server provides access to encryption features, like cell-level encryption, database-level encryption, and built-in encryption key management. In this chapter, I'll introduce the basics of SQL Server encryption, including the encryption hierarchy and encryption key management.

SQL Encryption Key Hierarchy

SQL Server uses a hierarchical model to manage keys and secure data. Figure 2-1 shows the SQL Server 2008 encryption hierarchy.

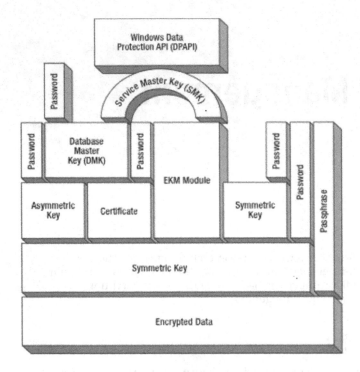

Figure 2-1. *SQL Server 2008 encryption hierarchy*

This model is similar to selected options from the ANSI X9.17 standard "Financial Institution Key Management (Wholesale)," which is published by the American National Standards Institute (ANSI).ANSI X9.17 describes a hierarchical structure for encryption key management. Figure 2-2 shows the ANSI X9.17 encryption hierarchy.

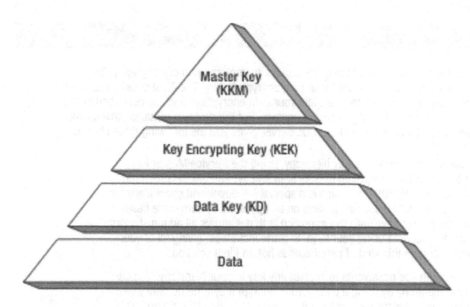

Figure 2-2. ANSI X9.17 encryption hierarchy

At the highest level of the X9.17 hierarchy is the Master Key (KKM), which maps to the top level of the SQL Server hierarchy. The KKM is roughly equivalent to the combination of the Windows Data Protection API (DPAPI), Service Master Key (SMK), and Database Master Key (DMK) in the SQL Server model. If you are using Extensible Key Management (EKM) then your Hardware Security Module (HSM) is managing your DMK.

The next level of encryption keys in the X9.17 standard consists of Key Encrypting Keys (KEKs). The KEKs are analogous to the middle layer of certificates, asymmetric keys, and symmetric keys in the SQL Server encryption hierarchy. Again, if you are using EKM then your KEKs are managed by the external HSM. The KEKs are encrypted by the KKM.

The final level of encryption keys in X9.17 consists of the Data Keys (KDs), equivalent to the symmetric keys at the lowest level of the SQL Server hierarchy. The KDs are encrypted by the KEKs above them in the hierarchy and they are used to encrypt user data, which sits below them in the hierarchy.

If you choose to use passwords to protect your keys or passphrases to protect your data directly you assume the responsibility for key management yourself. I'll discuss using passwords to secure encryption keys and using passphrases to encrypt data in Chapter 3.

■ **Note** ANSI X9.17 was initially approved in 1985, reapproved in 1991 with no changes, and reapproved with some modification in 1995. It has since been withdrawn. The current ISO 16609:2004 standard is based largely on the ANSI X9.17 standard, though much of the literature available still references ANSI X9.17 because it is so widely adopted.

Key Security

Encryption key management is definitely one of the hardest tasks to implement in cryptography. The problem ishow to secure the key you use to encrypt your data encryption key. The ANSI standard, and the SQL Server implementation, use a key hierarchy to protect your data encryption keys, as described in this section. Essentially, you use one encryption key to secure another. But the problem remains, how do you secure the key that secures your data encryption key? SQL Server gives you the following three choices:

- SQL Server will encrypt your entire key hierarchy, using the Service Master Key (SMK) at the top to protect everything directly or indirectly. The SMK is protected by the Data Protection API (DPAPI), which is a special API developed specifically for Windows to securely protect encryption keys on an operating system-wide basis. One of the issues people have with this approach is that it allows all administrators to encrypt and decrypt data using your keys. In some instances, giving all of your database administrators this kind of permission is not an ideal solution.

- Alternatively, you can use passwords to encrypt any key in your hierarchy. You can short circuit the hierarchy by using a password to encrypt a symmetric data encrypting key directly below another key inthe hierarchy. Using this method, you can limit access only to users and applications that have the password. This lets you specifically exclude database administrators from encrypting and decrypting data using certain keys. The downside is that when you do this, you take on all the responsibility for ensuring the security of your passwords.

- Finally, you can use EKM to offload the responsibility of securing your keys to a third-party hardware appliance, an HSM. This has several advantages over the other methods, including storage and management of your encryption keys off-box and increased performance that comes from passing alongencryption responsibility to the appliance. EKM can act as a replacement for your encryption key hierarchy or it can work to supplement it. I'll discuss EKM in greater detail in Chapter 5.

The encryption key hierarchy is a relatively simple concept, but it can be confusing when you first encounter it. One of the questions that often comes up is how do you limit access to encrypt and decrypt data if SQL Server isautomatically encrypting and decrypting the data encrypting keys? The answer is simply "permissions." If you deny users permission to a data encrypting key, or to any key or certificate above it in the encryption hierarchy, they will not be able to encrypt or decrypt data with that key.

For example, assume you have a symmetric key called "DataKey1" that encrypts your data. Also assume that this key is protected by a certificate, which in turn is protected by the DMK. In order to decrypt data with "Data Key," your user must have access to the symmetric key, the certificate that protects it, and the DMK. Ifpermissions are denied on any of these, the user will not be able to decrypt data with "DataKey1." Keep theencryption key hierarchy in mind as we explore the keys that make up the hierarchy in greater detail in the following sections.

Key Management

Encryption key management is one of the toughest tasks in cryptography. You can have the most secure encryption algorithms in the world, but improperly managing your keys compromises your entire security strategy. The basics of encryption key management include the following:

- Limit encryption key access to only those who really need it. Only those users who actually need access to decrypt previously encrypted data should have access to the encryption key.

- Back up your encryption keys and secure them. Encryption keys should be backed up immediately after creation and secured in protected off-site storage. This is important for two reasons: (1) you may need to restore an encryption key due to corruption or other issue, and (2) in the event of a disaster you may need to restore encryption keys to alternate servers as part of a disaster recovery plan.

- Rotate your encryption keys on a regular basis. Key rotation based on a regular schedule should be part of every organization's IT policy. If you leave the same encryption key in place for lengthy periods of time, you give hackers and other miscreants time to attack it. By rotating your keys regularly your keys become a moving target—much harder to hit.

The ANSI X9.17 hierarchical model for key management has certain advantages over a flat single-tier model for encryption keys, particularly in terms of key rotation. Consider this example: If you have a terabyte of data encrypted by a given encryption key and you must change/rotate this encryption key every month, you will have to decrypt and reencrypt then entire terabyte of data every time you change the KD. The decryption and reencryption of all your data will take a considerable amount of processing power, storage, and time. In the X9.17 model, you can instead set up a monthly KEK rotation in which you simply change out the middle layer of KEKs. Since the KEKs only encrypt the KDs below them in the hierarchy, the process of swapping out KEKs requires decrypting and reencrypting an insignificantly small amount of symmetric key data. Using this model, you can relegate KD rotations to a yearly or other longer-term schedule without compromising the security of your encrypted data.

Key Distribution

ANSI X9.17 and equivalent ISO standards define a protocol for distribution of encryption keys. In the X9.17 model, the highest level of keys, KKMs, are distributed manually. Lower levels of keys are distributed securely in an automated fashion, over a network for instance. Using this standard as a basis, assuming you had two SQL Server instances set up in different physical locations you would manually transfer the SMK and DMK to the second instance. The middle and lower levels of keys (KKMs and KDs) would be distributed online in a secure manner.

■ **Note** The X9.17 standard defines two-key Triple DES as the algorithm of choice for securely transferring encryption keys. In practice, this method of distributing keys is being replaced with asymmetric algorithms, like the Diffie-Hellman key exchange algorithm.

Because of the hierarchical structure defined by X9.17, middle-level KEKs are generally replaced on a short and regular schedule. High-level KKMs and low-level KDs are replaced on much longer schedules. This makes changing keys much more efficient.

Service Master Key

The Service Master Key (SMK) is a server-wide encryption key that sits at the top of the SQL Server encryption hierarchy. The SMK is created automatically the first time it's needed to encrypt a Database Master Key or other secret. Because of this, there is no CREATE SERVICE MASTER KEY statement. SQL Server does provide ALTER, BACKUP, and RESTORE statements to manage the SMK, all of which I'll describe in the following section.

Backing Up the SMK

As soon as you first create a DMK, credential, or linked server, SQL Server will create the SMK. You should immediately make a backup of the SMK and secure the backup in a protected location. Listing 2-1 shows the BACKUP statement in action.

Listing 2-1. *Backing Up an SMK*

```
BACKUP SERVICE MASTER KEY TO FILE = N'C:\MyServiceMasterKey.key'
ENCRYPTION BY PASSWORD = N'$45^ZeF&u';
```

The BACKUP statement exports your SMK to a binary file. In this example, it is exporting it to a file named MyServiceMasterKey.key in the root directory of the C: drive on the server. Because it would be unsafe to expose your SMK unencrypted in a file, SQL Server encrypts it using the password you specify in the ENCRYPTION BY PASSWORD clause. When you secure the backup of the SMK, make sure you also secure the password you used to encrypt the backup. The password you supply is subject to the operating system password complexity requirements. You need to supply the same password at restore time.

Backup and restore of the SMK is particularly useful in an environment where you need identical SQL Server instances or when migrating your SQL Server instance to a new machine. You can back up your SMK and restore it to the new server to configure the servers identically. You must have CONTROL SERVER permissions on the server in order to back up the SMK, and the SQL Server service account must have access to the directory where you want to create the file.

■ **Caution** Even though SQL Server encrypts the SMK when you back it up, don't leave the backup file lying around on a hard drive. After running the example in Listing 2-1, I immediately burned the SMK onto a CD and deleted the binary file from the hard drive. Your organizational IT policy may require multiple backups of encryption keys for disaster recovery purposes—make sure they are all stored securely.

Restoring the SMK

If you find that you need to restore the SMK, you'll need to use the RESTORE SERVICE MASTER KEY statement. The RESTORE statement restores the SMK from a previously taken backup file. Listing 2-2 demonstrates the RESTORE statement that restores the previous backup of the SMK.

Listing 2-2. Restoring an SMK

```
RESTORE SERVICE MASTER KEY FROM FILE = N'C:\MyServiceMasterKey.key'
DECRYPTION BY PASSWORD = '$45^ZeF&u';
```

Notice that I had to specify the same password that I used in the BACKUP statement when restoring the SMK. When you perform a restore of an SMK, the DMK and any other keys protected by the SMK, are first decrypted and then reencrypted using the restored SMK. If any of the decryptions fails, theSMK restore operation will also fail. You can force an SMK restore to complete by using the FORCE option of the RESTORE statement. By adding the FORCE keyword you indicate to SQL Server that you want the operation to succeed, regardless of any decryption errors. You must have CONTROL SERVER permissions to restore an SMK on a server.

■ **Caution** Using the FORCE option could result in data loss, and it should be used only as a last resort.

Altering the SMK

When the SMK is created, a couple of things worth noting occur:

1. The SMK is tied to the SQL Server service account that created it. The DPAPI uses the Windows credentials of the service account to encrypt the SMK. This means only the service account, or an account with access to the service account credentials, can decrypt the SMK.

2. A copy of the SMK is encrypted using the local machine key and stored separately.

If you change the SQL Server service account username or password, you will need to also change the service account information protecting the SMK to match. SQL Server provides an ALTER SERVICE MASTER KEY statement that allows you to do this, as shown in Listing 2-3.

Listing 2-3. Changing the SMK Service Account

```
ALTER SERVICE MASTER KEY
WITH NEW_ACCOUNT = 'SQL2008Server\Michael',
  NEW_PASSWORD = '^&3h4l1xPr';
```

In this example, the SQL Server service account has already been changed, and the new service account username and password are used to retrieve the account credentials used to protect the SMK. Atsome point, you may have to rebuild a server. In that case, you can use the OLD_ACCOUNT and OLD_PASSWORD options to specify the old service account credentials.

■ **Note** Altering the SMK account credentials works only with Windows credentials of domain or local user accounts. The Local System, Local Service, and Network Service accounts cannot be used to recover the SMK after an SQL Server service account change.

ENCRYPTION BY MACHINE KEY?

As of this writing SQL Server 2008 (and the 2005 release) both document ALTER SERVICE MASTER KEY options to drop or add encryption by machine key. Theoretically this option would cause SQL Server to store a redundant copy of the service master key encrypted by the machine encryption key. This feature was designed to aid in rebuilding servers, allowing the service key to be recovered via the machine encryption key and the SQL Server service account. In both SQL Server 2008 and 2005, the syntax for these options is not recognized, and they may even be removed from SQL Server Books Online by the time this book goes to print.

Finally the ALTER statement allows you to regenerate the SMK with the REGENERATE keyword. If you encounter errors during regeneration, you can force it with the FORCE REGENERATE keywords. Listing 2-4 regenerates the SMK.

Listing 2-4. Regenerating the SMK

```
ALTER SERVICE MASTER KEY REGENERATE;
```

As with the RESTORE statement, SQL Server has to decrypt and reencrypt all keys, certificates, and other secrets protected by the SMK when you regenerate. If you encounter decryption errors during the regeneration, you can use the FORCE REGENERATE clause. If you have to use FORCE you could be faced with data loss, due to the inability to decrypt.

You must have CONTROL SERVER permissions on the server to alter the SMK. To use the OLD_ACCOUNT and OLD_PASSWORD options, you must have knowledge of the old SQL Server service account logon username and password. To use the NEW_ACCOUNT and NEW_PASSWORD options, you must know the new SQL Server service account username and password. After regeneration of an SMK, you should immediately take a backup and secure it in a protected off-site storage facility.

Database Master Key

The second level of the SQL Server encryption hierarchy includes the Database Master Key. This key is encrypted by the SMK and it is used to encrypt the certificates, asymmetric keys, and symmetric keys beneath it in the hierarchy. Just as the SMK is limited to one per SQL Server instance, SQL Server limits you to one DMK per database. In the following section, I'll discuss the statements that SQL Server provides to create, alter, backup, restore, and drop DMKs.

Creating a DMK

The DMK is created via the CREATE MASTER KEY statement. You must be in the target database when you create a DMK. The CREATE statement is shown in Listing 2-5.

Listing 2-5. Create a DMK

```
CREATE MASTER KEY ENCRYPTION BY PASSWORD = 'aO*Ui)4x-f';
```

The CREATE statement includes a BY PASSWORD clause that causes the DMK to be encrypted by the password supplied. The password supplied is used to encrypt the DMK using Triple DES. When you create a DMK it is not only encrypted using the password you supplied, it is also encrypted by the SMK and stored in the master database and the target database. The copy of the DMK stored in the master database is automatically decrypted when issue an OPEN MASTER KEY statement to open the DMK without supplying a password. You can turn off this behavior with the ALTER statement, which I'll describe in the next section.

■ **Note** The OPEN MASTER KEY statement is described in the *Opening a DMK* section of this chapter.

To create a DMK you must have CONTROL permission on the target database. Because you cannot specify the database in the statement itself, you must execute a USE statement to switch to the target database before creating a DMK.

Altering a DMK

Once you've created a DMK, you can use the ALTER statement to modify its properties. For example, you can turn off the automatic decryption feature and force users to supply a password to open the DMK with the DROP ENCRYPTION BY SERVICE MASTER KEY clause of the ALTER statement, as shown in Listing 2-6.

Listing 2-6. Removing DMK Automatic Decryption Feature

```
ALTER MASTER KEY DROP ENCRYPTION BY SERVICE MASTER KEY;
```

You can also add or drop encryption by password with ADD and DROP ENCRYPTION BY PASSWORD = 'password' clauses, respectively. The DMK must be encrypted by at least one password, so you can't remove all password encryptions from a given DMK. Listing 2-7 demonstrates both adding and removing DMK encryption by password. You might want to add additional passwords to the DMK so that different users, or different groups of users or applications, don't have to share a single password between them. You may also prefer to just use encryption by the SMK and avoid managing SMK passwords yourself.

Listing 2-7. Adding and Removing DMK Encryption By Password

```
-- Add encryption by password
ALTER MASTER KEY ADD ENCRYPTION BY PASSWORD = '9(%^jQ!@#d';
GO
-- Remove encryption by password
ALTER MASTER KEY DROP ENCRYPTION BY PASSWORD = '9(%^jQ!@#d';
GO
```

You can also use the ALTER statement to regenerate a DMK in accordance with your key rotation schedule. When you regenerate a DMK, all keys secured by the DMK are first decrypted, the DMK is regenerated, and all of the keys it secures are then reencrypted. Listing 2-8 regenerates the DMK. The regenerated DMK is protected by the password you specify in the REGENERATE WITH ENCRYPTION BY PASSWORD clause of the statement.

■ **Tip** If you regenerate a DMK that has the SMK encryption option turned off, the SMK encryption option will remain off after the regeneration is complete. Likewise, if the SMK encryption option was turned on for the DMK it will remain on after regeneration. You can always execute an additional ALTER MASTER KEY statement to turn this option on or off to suit your needs. If you used ALTER MASTER KEY to create additional DMK decryption passwords, those passwords are lost after DMK regeneration. The newly regenerated DMK is protected only by the single password you specify in the REGENERATE clause and the SMK (if that option was turned on).

Listing 2-8. Regenerating a DMK

```
ALTER MASTER KEY REGENERATE WITH ENCRYPTION BY PASSWORD = '$4yAxU%t7';
```

During the regeneration if a decryption error occurs, the ALTER statement will fail. You can use the FORCE REGENERATE clause to force the regeneration. As with other FORCE options, if you use the FORCE REGENERATE clause you may suffer data loss.

Altering a DMK requires CONTROL permission on the target database. If the DMK is protected by password only, you also need to know the password to decrypt the DMK.

Backing Up a DMK

As with the SMKs, as soon as a DMK is created or altered you need to immediately get a backup of it andstore it in a secure location. You can use the BACKUP MASTER KEY statement to back up your DMKs. The syntax is similar to that of the SMK BACKUP statement. Listing 2-9 shows the DMK BACKUP statement.

Listing 2-9. Backing Up a DMK

```
BACKUP MASTER KEY TO FILE = N'C:\MyDatabaseMasterKey.key'
ENCRYPTION BY PASSWORD = N'O-!t4=Rtr=,';
```

The BACKUP statement backs up your DMK to a file. In this example, the file is MyDatabaseMasterKey.key on the C: drive. As with the SMK BACKUP statement, make sure you store the password used to encrypt the DMK in a secure location. You will need to supply this password again at restore time.

Backing up a DMK requires CONTROL permission on the database. The SQL Server service account must also have access to the destination directory where the output file will be created.

Restoring a DMK

You may have a need to restore your DMK at some point. If you experience a hardware failure, need to recover from a disaster, or want to move a database to a new instance, you may need to restore a DMK. The DMK RESTORE MASTER KEY statement is similar to, but slightly different from, the SMK RESTORE statement. Listing 2-10 shows the RESTORE statement in action.

Listing 2-10. Restore a DMK

```
RESTORE MASTER KEY FROM FILE = 'C:\MyDatabaseMasterKey.key'
DECRYPTION BY PASSWORD = 'O-!t4=Rtr=,'
ENCRYPTION BY PASSWORD = 'p#v8AO@+|';
```

The DECRYPTION BY PASSWORD = 'password' clause requires you to supply the same password you used when you took the backup. The ENCRYPTION BY PASSWORD = 'password' clause is used to specify the password you want SQL Server to use to encrypt the DMK when it is stored in the database.

■ **Tip** As with the ALTER MASTER KEY statement's REGENERATE clause, the restored DMK is protected by the single password you specify and is only protected by the SMK if the current DMK is protected by SMK. Any additional passwords you created to protect the DMK previously are lost when you perform a restore operation.

When you restore the DMK, all keys encrypted by the DMK are decrypted and reencrypted. As with other encryption DDL statements, if the decryption process fails you can use the FORCE option to force SQL Server to restore the DMK despite these errors. Again, if you have to use the FORCE option you may suffer data loss.

You must have CONTROL permission on the target database when you restore a DMK. Also, you must have knowledge of the password used to encrypt the DMK file you are importing.

■ **Note** You must specify a new password to encrypt the DMK on the server once it's restored (via the ENCRYPTION BY PASSWORD = 'password' clause). Make sure you record this new password and store it in a secure location immediately after a restore operation.

Dropping a DMK

You can choose to drop a DMK with the DROP MASTER KEY statement, as shown in Listing 2-11. The DROP statement will fail if there are any keys protected by the DMK in the database. You can use the sys.certificates and sys.asymmetric_keys to determine if the DMK is being used to encrypt any private keys.

Listing 2-11. Drop a DMK

```
DROP MASTER KEY;
```

Dropping a DMK requires CONTROL permission on the target database.

Opening a DMK

Before you can use a key or certificate that is secured by the DMK, you must first open the DMK. The standard encryption usage pattern is shown in Figure 2-3. Notice the DMK must be opened before the data-encrypting symmetric key it protects is opened.

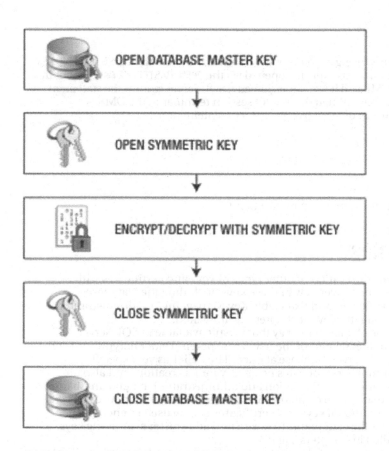

Figure 2-3. Standard encryption key usage pattern in SQL Server 2008

You have two options for opening your DMK: (1) since the DMK is always protected by a password you can supply the password in the OPEN MASTER KEY statement, or (2) if the DMK is also optionally protected by the SMK, the DMK will automatically be opened and decrypted by the SMK on an as-needed basis. An example of the OPEN MASTER KEY statement is shown in Listing 2-12.

Listing 2-12. Opening a DMK

```
OPEN MASTER KEY DECRYPTION BY PASSWORD = '$4yAxU%t7';
```

The OPEN MASTER KEY statement requires CONTROL permission on the target database. The OPEN MASTER KEY statement always requires a password. You don't need to issue OPEN MASTER KEY statements if you're using SMK protection for your DMK, and therefore won't need the password. You also need to know the password used to encrypt the DMK. I'll demonstrate automatic opening of a DMK protected by SMK in Chapter 3.

Closing a DMK

After you've opened a DMK and have finished using it, you should close the DMK with the CLOSE MASTER KEY statement. You can only close the DMK when it was explicitly opened via the OPEN MASTER KEY statement in the current session. If you try to close the DMK and it's not open already, SQL Server ignores the statement and returns without generating an error message. When the current session terminates, the DMK is automatically closed. Listing 2-13 is an example of the CLOSE MASTER KEY statement.

Listing 2-13. Closing a DMK

```
CLOSE MASTER KEY;
```

The CLOSE MASTER KEY statement has no permission requirements.

Other Keys and Certificates

SQL Server 2008 supports creation and administration of other types of keys and certificates with different purposes. This section provides a brief overview of these keys, including the Database Encryption Key, Encryption Keys and Certificates, and Extensible Key Management. Administration and use of each of these is described in detail in relevant chapters, as indicated.

SQL Server 2008 introduces a new type of encryption key that wasn't available in SQL Server 2005. The Database Encryption Key (DEK) is an integral part of the new Transparent Data Encryption (TDE) functionality, used to encrypt an entire SQL Server database at once. The DEK has very specific functionality in relation to TDE, has additional prerequisites necessary for its creation, and also for implementation of TDE functionality. I'll discuss DEK creation and administration in detail in Chapter 6.

The remaining certificates and keys that can be created in SQL Server include symmetric keys, asymmetric keys, and certificates. These additional keys and certificates can be used to encrypt still other keys and data. The specific syntax for the statements to create and administer symmetric keys, asymmetric keys, and certificates is detailed in Chapters 3 and 4.

EKM utilizes external hardware security modules to create, store, and manage keys and certificates. The HSM appliance is integrated with SQL Server through SQL language extensions and HSM vendor-supplied software drivers. Chapter 5 details EKM configuration and use with examples shown on the SafeNet Luna appliance.

Permissions

You have to have specific permissions to create and administer keys and certificates. Table 2-1 lists the permissions required to perform administrative actions on keys and certificates on SQL Server 2008.

Table 2-1. Encryption Administrative Task Permissions

Secret Type	Action	Permissions
Asymmetric Key	ALTER	CONTROL (Asymmetric Key)
--	CREATE	CREATE ASYMMETRIC KEY (Database)

--	DROP	CONTROL (Asymmetric Key)
Certificate	ALTER	ALTER (Certificate)
--	BACKUP	CONTROL (Certificate)
--	CREATE	CREATE CERTIFICATE (Database)
--	DROP	CONTROL (Certificate)
Database Encryption Key	ALTER	CONTROL (Database)
--	CREATE	CONTROL (Database)
--	DROP	CONTROL (Database)
Database Master Key	ALTER	CONTROL (Database)
--	BACKUP	CONTROL (Database)
--	CLOSE	None
--	CREATE	CONTROL (Database)
--	DROP	CONTROL (Database)
--	OPEN	CONTROL (Database)
--	RESTORE	CONTROL (Database)
Service Master Key	ALTER	CONTROL SERVER
--	BACKUP	CONTROL SERVER
--	RESTORE	CONTROL SERVER
Symmetric Key	ALTER	ALTER (Symmetric Key)
--	CREATE	ALTER ANY SYMMETRIC KEY (Database)
--	DROP	CONTROL (Symmetric Key)

Some administrative actions require additional permissions on other objects. For example, if you want to issue an ALTER statement against a symmetric key, and that symmetric key is protected by a certificate, you must have VIEW DEFINITION permissions on the certificate. You may also need access to the password used to protect the certificate.

If you're importing or restoring a certificate or key from an external file, the SQL Server service account must have permissions to access the file.

Opening, closing, and encrypting keys or data with symmetric keys, asymmetric keys, and certificates requires additional permissions, which I'll discuss in detail in Chapters 3 and 4.

Catalog Views

SQL Server 2008 provides several encryption-specific catalog views that provide information that's useful for key and certificate administration. The information about keys, certificates, and cryptographic providers returned by these catalog views is useful for many management tasks. You can use these catalog views to perform automated or manual comparisons of cryptographic configurations between two databases, to keep a log of changes to cryptographic settings, or even to write cryptographic administration applications. In this section, I'll discuss these system views and how you can use them tomanage your keys and certificates.

sys.asymmetric_keys

The sys.asymmetric_keys catalog view returns information about asymmetric keys in the current database. This catalog view returns one row per asymmetric key. The information available includes the name and GUID of the asymmetric key, the integer ID of the key, the public key of the asymmetric key pair, key length, and algorithm and cryptographic provider information. Listing 2-14 queries the sys.asymmetric_keys catalog view. Results are shown in Figure 2-4. There are additional columns returned by this catalog view, which are not shown in the following sample.

Listing 2-14. Retrieving a List of Asymmetric Keys in the Current Database

```
SELECT
  name,
  asymmetric_key_id,
  pvt_key_encryption_type_desc,
  thumbprint,
  algorithm_desc,
  key_length,
  public_key
FROM sys.asymmetric_keys;
```

	name	asymmetric_key...	pvt_key_encryption_type_desc	thumbprint	algorithm_de...	key_len...	public_key
1	AsymKey1_Accounting	256	ENCRYPTED_BY_MASTER_KEY	0xBBD5E568C3B21934	RSA_2048	2048	0x0602000000240...
2	AsymKey1_HumanResources	257	ENCRYPTED_BY_MASTER_KEY	0xE5E74B9FB306732A	RSA_1024	1024	0x0602000000240...

Figure 2-4. Asymmetric keys in the current database

sys.certificates

The sys.certificates catalog view retrieves information about certificates in the current database. This catalog view consists of a single row for each certificate. The information returned includes the nameand GUID of the certificate, certificate serial number, and certificate metadata, like subject and expiration date. Listing 2-15 demonstrates how to retrieve certificate information, with results shown inFigure 2-5. This catalog view returns additional columns that are not shown in the sample query.

Listing 2-15. Retrieving a List of Certificates Installed in the Current Database

```
SELECT
  name,
  certificate_id,
  pvt_key_encryption_type_desc,
  subject,
  cert_serial_number,
  start_date,
  expiry_date,
  thumbprint
FROM sys.certificates;
```

	name	certificate...	pvt_key_encryption_type_desc	subject	cert_serial_number	start_date	expiry_date	thumbprint
1	Cert1_InfoTech	256	ENCRYPTED_BY_PASSWORD	Corporate IT Certificate	23 e6 31 03 c0 37 9...	2009-03-21 ...	2012-01-01...	0x4E6D3E3A5EEB4539CD1F0F8D...
2	Cert1_Production	257	ENCRYPTED_BY_PASSWORD	Corporate Production Certificate	1f 01 bf 75 ed ab 1d ...	2009-03-21 ...	2011-10-15...	0x3E72B1A241EE01839D7C2D00...

Figure 2-5. Certificates installed in a database

sys.credentials

The sys.credentials catalog view returns information about EKM provider credentials. The view returns one row per credential. Information returned includes credential ID, credential name, and identity name and information about the associated cryptographic provider. This view only returns information if you have an EKM provider registered with SQL Server. Listing 2-16 retrieves credentials of EKM providers that are registered with an instance of SQL Server. The results in Figure 2-6 show the credentials of an EKM provider that I've registered with my development SQL Server instance.

Listing 2-16. Retrieving EKM Provider Credentials

```
SELECT
  credential_id,
  name,
  credential_identity,
  create_date,
  modify_date,
  target_type,
  target_id
FROM sys.credentials;
```

	credential...	name	credential_identity	create_date	modify_date	target_type	target_id
1	65542	LunaCredential	LunaUser	2009-02-20 08:43:42.920	2009-03-15 01:33:03.773	CRYPTOGRAPHIC PROVIDER	65536

Figure 2-6. EKM provider credentials list

sys.cryptographic_providers

When you register an EKM cryptographic provider with SQL Server 2008 you have to install, and register, a Dynamic Link Library (DLL) file with your SQL Server instance. The sys.cryptographic_providers catalog view returns information about installed EKM cryptographic providers, with one row per cryptographic provider. Information includes provider ID and name, provider GUID, version, DLL path, and a flag indicating whether the provider is enabled or disabled. Listing 2-17 uses the sys.cryptographic_providers catalog view to return information about registered cryptographic providers. Results from my development SQL Server instance are shown in Figure 2-7.

Listing 2-17. Querying Registered Cryptographic Providers

```
SELECT
  provider_id,
  name,
  guid,
  version,
  dll_path,
  is_enabled
FROM sys.cryptographic_providers;
```

	provider_id	name	guid	version	dll_path	is_enabled
1	65536	lunaekmprovider	3E16C4F9-1B3F-46FE-B740-F19C75670347	1.0.0.1	c:\lunasa\ekm\lunaekm.dll	1

Figure 2-7. Registered cryptographic provider list

sys.crypt_properties

The sys.crypt_properties catalog view returns one row for each cryptographic property associated with securables, with one row per property per securable. Results include whether the property exists on an object or column, encryption type, and the property itself. Listing 2-18 demonstrates one possible use of this catalog view by retrieving a list of all database columns and objects. Figure 2-8 shows that two database objects—SQL Server stored procedures—were digitally signed using certificates installed in the database.

Listing 2-18. Retrieving Cryptographic Properties for Database Objects and Columns

```
SELECT
  o.name AS object_name,
  SCHEMA_NAME(o.schema_id) AS object_schema,
  cp.major_id,
  cp.class_desc,
  cp.crypt_type_desc,
  cp.thumbprint
FROM sys.crypt_properties cp
INNER JOIN sys.all_objects o
  ON cp.major_id = o.object_id;
```

	object_name	object_schema	major_id	class_desc	crypt_type_desc	thumbprint
1	CalculateLossTriangles	Accounting	5575058	OBJECT_OR_COLUMN	SIGNATURE BY CERTIFICATE	0x442D4E0B26E91B...
2	CalculateWrittenPremium	Accounting	2137058649	OBJECT_OR_COLUMN	SIGNATURE BY CERTIFICATE	0x442D4E0B26E91B...

Figure 2-8. List of stored procedures that are digitally signed by certificate

sys.key_encryptions

When a symmetric key is created with the CREATE SYMMETRIC KEY statement's ENCRYPTION BY clause, a reference is added to this view. The sys.key_encryptions catalog view returns information about all keys and certificates used to encrypt symmetric keys. The information returned includes the ID of the encrypted key and the type of the encryption. The sample query in Listing 2-19 returns a list of installed symmetric keys that are encrypted by certificates. These symmetric keys, and the certificates that encrypt them, are shown in the results in Figure 2-9.

Listing 2-19. Retrieving Symmetric Keys That are Encrypted By Certificates

```
SELECT
  sk.name AS key_name,
  ke.crypt_type_desc,
  ke.crypt_property,
  c.name AS cert_name,
  sk.algorithm_desc AS key_algorithm_desc,
  sk.key_length,
  ke.thumbprint
FROM sys.key_encryptions ke
INNER JOIN sys.symmetric_keys sk
  ON sk.symmetric_key_id = ke.key_id
INNER JOIN sys.certificates c
  ON ke.thumbprint = c.thumbprint;
```

	key_name	crypt_type_desc	crypt_property	cert_name	key_algorithm_desc	key_length	thumbprint
1	SymKey1_Accounting	ENCRYPTION BY CERTIFICATE	0x5ED734EDADE...	Cert1_Accounting	TRIPLE_DES_3KEY	192	0x442D4E0B26E...
2	SymKey2_Accounting	ENCRYPTION BY CERTIFICATE	0x31E6135A7205...	Cert1_Accounting	AES_192	192	0x442D4E0B26E...

Figure 2-9. List of symmetric keys and the certificates that encrypt them

sys.symmetric_keys

The sys.symmetric_keys catalog view retrieves information about symmetric keys that exist in the current database. The view returns one row per symmetric key and the information returned includes symmetric key name and GUID, key length, and encryption algorithm. The previous example in Listing 2-19 uses the sys.symmetric_keys catalog view to return the list of symmetric keys that are encrypted by certificate.

Dynamic Management Views and Functions

Dynamic management views (DMVs) and functions (DMFs) return internal SQL Server state data. The SQL Server state data is transient and often exists only for the length of a single SQL statement or until the service is cycled. The information returned by the encryption-specific DMVs and DMFs is useful for diagnosing cryptographic problems. Like the catalog views discussed in the previous section, DMVs and DMFs provide extremely useful troubleshooting and administrative information. This section discusses the cryptographic DMVs and DMFs available on SQL Server 2008.

sys.dm_cryptographic_provider_algorithms

The sys.dm_cryptographic_provider_algorithms DMF accepts the integer ID of an EKM provider as a parameter. The DMF returns algorithm and key type information. You need to have an EKM provider registered in order to use this DMF. Listing 2-20 uses the sys.dm_cryptographic_provider_algorithms DMF toretrieve information about all the algorithms supported by a registered EKM provider. The registered EKM provider in this example has a provider_id of 65536. Figure 2-10 shows the results of this query.

Listing 2-20. Retrieving Algorithms Supported By a Registered Cryptographic Provider

```
SELECT
    algorithm_id,
    algorithm_tag,
    key_type,
    key_length
FROM sys.dm_cryptographic_provider_algorithms (65536);
```

	algorithm_id	algorithm_tag	key_type	key_length
1	1	RSA_512	ASYMMETRIC KEY	512
2	2	RSA_1024	ASYMMETRIC KEY	1024
3	3	RSA_2048	ASYMMETRIC KEY	2048
4	4	RC2	SYMMETRIC KEY	128
5	5	RC4	SYMMETRIC KEY	40
6	6	RC4_128	SYMMETRIC KEY	128
7	7	DES	SYMMETRIC KEY	64
8	8	Triple_DES	SYMMETRIC KEY	128
9	9	TRIPLE_DES_3KEY	SYMMETRIC KEY	192
10	10	AES_128	SYMMETRIC KEY	128
11	11	AES_192	SYMMETRIC KEY	192
12	12	AES_256	SYMMETRIC KEY	256

Figure 2-10. List of encryption algorithms supported by a registered EKM provider

sys.dm_cryptographic_provider_keys

The sys.dm_cryptographic_provider_keys DMF also accepts the ID of an EKM provider as a parameter. This DMF returns information about the keys available via an EKM provider, as shown in Listing 2-21. The information returned includes key ID, name, algorithm, and key length information (see Figure 2-11).

Listing 2-21. Querying the Keys Exposed By the EKM Provider

```
SELECT
  keyid,
  key_name,
  algorithm_tag,
  key_type,
  key_length,
  key_thumbprint
FROM sys.dm_cryptographic_provider_keys (65536);
```

	keyid	key_name	algorithm_tag	key_type	key_length	key_thumbprint
1	1	EKM_SymKey3_Accounting	AES_256	SYMMETRIC KEY	256	0x0E532AA6AF58...
2	2	EKM_SymKey2_Auditing	AES_192	SYMMETRIC KEY	192	0xD26385D0CF0D...

Figure 2-11. Keys available through the sample EKM provider

sys.dm_cryptographic_provider_properties

The sys.dm_cryptographic_provider_properties DMV retrieves information about registered cryptographic providers. The information returned includes provider ID and GUID, version, authentication type, and flags indicating support for asymmetric and symmetric key functionality. Listing 2-22 retrieves the EKMprovider properties and feature support flags with results shown in Figure 2-12. This DMV returns additional flags not shown in the sample query.

Listing 2-22. Getting Properties and Feature Support Flags of the EKM Provider

```
SELECT
  provider_id,
  provider_version,
  sqlcrypt_version,
  friendly_name,
  authentication_type,
  symmetric_key_support,
  asymmetric_key_support
FROM sys.dm_cryptographic_provider_properties;
```

	provider_id	provider_version	sqlcrypt_versi...	friendly_name	authentication_type	symmetric_key_support	asymmetric_key_support
1	65536	1.00.0000.01	1.01.0000.00	SafeNet EKM Provider	BASIC	1	1

Figure 2-12. Properties and selected feature set for the EKM provider

sys.dm_cryptographic_provider_sessions

The sys.dm_cryptographic_provider_sessions DMF returns the set of current cryptographic provider sessions. The DMF accepts a single parameter, which can be one of the following two values:

0 = Return session information for the current cryptographic connection only

1 = Return session information for all cryptographic connections

This information is useful for determining who has an open EKM session at any given point in time. The information returned includes the provider ID, a cryptographic session handle, the identity used to authenticate with the EKM, and the Server Process ID (SPID). The sample query in Listing 2-23 returns information about all open cryptographic provider sessions. Results are shown in Figure 2-13.

Listing 2-23. Retrieving a List of Cryptographic Provider Sessions

```
SELECT
  provider_id,
  session_handle,
  identity,
  spid
FROM sys.dm_cryptographic_provider_sessions(1);
```

	provider_id	session_handle	identity	spid
1	65536	0x9000DF42	LunaUser	54
2	65536	0xE000DF42	LunaUser	56

Figure 2-13. Current cryptographic provider sessions

sys.dm_database_encryption_keys

The sys.dm_database_encryption_keys DMV retrieves a list of database encryption keys and the databases they protect using Transparent Data Encryption (TDE). Listing 2-24 queries the list of database encryption keys, returning their current state, algorithm, key length, and the names of the databases they protect. Figure 2-14 shows the results. The DMV and catalog view I used in this example have additional columns that aren't returned by the code sample.

Listing 2-24. Querying the List of Database Encryption Keys

```
SELECT
  d.name AS db_name,
  dbek.encryption_state,
  dbek.key_algorithm,
  dbek.key_length,
  dbek.percent_complete
FROM sys.dm_database_encryption_keys dbek
INNER JOIN sys.databases d
  ON dbek.database_id = d.database_id;
```

	db_name	encryption_state	key_algorithm	key_length	percent_complete
1	tempdb	3	AES	256	0
2	Crypto	3	AES	256	0

Figure 2-14. Databases protected by database encryption keys (TDE)

In this example, TDE is turned on in a database named Crypto. TDE automatically encrypts the tempdb database when any database on the SQL Server instance is encrypted. I'll discuss this feature of TDE in greater detail in Chapter 6. Another notable feature of this DMV is the encryption_state column. It can be any of the following values:

0 = No database encryption key is present; the database is not encrypted.

1 = Database is unencrypted.

2 = Database encryption is currently in progress.

3 = Database is encrypted.

4 = Database encryption key change is in progress.

5 = Database decryption is currently in progress.

The percent_complete column signal how far along the current database encryption change has proceeded. This might return 50 when the database encryption process has reached the halfway point. This column will be set to zero when no change is in progress.

Summary

SQL Server 2008 provides a comprehensive set of encryption tools to protect your data within the database. One of the hardest problems in encryption is the issue of encryption key management. SQL Server implements an encryption key hierarchy similar to the ANSI X9.17 standard to help simplify key management. To help administer encryption keys and certificates, the SQL Server team has added dozens of new extensions to T-SQL, SQL Server's native tongue. Using the new extensions to the language you can create, modify, and remove every type of encryption key SQL Server supports. In addition, SQL Server 2008 provides several system views (catalog views, DMFs, and DMVs) to help monitor and troubleshoot your database encryption.

In this chapter, I described the SQL Server encryption hierarchy and how it helps you to implement an efficient encryption key rotation. I discussed the top layers of the encryption key hierarchy—the master keys and key encrypting keys—and how to use T-SQL statements to administer them. I also discussed the system views available to help you monitor encryption on your server.

In the next chapter, I'll begin a deep dive into the internals of SQL Server's implementation of symmetric encryption.

CHAPTER 3

■ ■ ■

Symmetric Encryption

Symmetric encryption is the class of encryption that involves using the same key (or two keys that are trivially related, mathematically speaking) for encryption and decryption. SQL Server provides support for symmetric encryption via a variety of algorithms, including AES, DES, Triple DES, RC2, and RC4. The SQL Server encryption hierarchy uses symmetric encryption algorithms to encrypt both keys and data. In this chapter, I'll discuss how to create symmetric encryption keys and use symmetric encryption to secure your data and other encryption keys.

Note Trivially related keys are keys whose relationship can be defined in simple mathematical terms. For example, assume you have two keys, *x* and *y*. If the relationship between the two keys can be defined in terms of a simple relationship, such as $y = x + 1$, the keys are trivially related.

Symmetric Keys

SQL Server 2008 supports the creation and management of symmetric keys to encrypt data. Symmetric keys are protected by asymmetric keys, certificates, passwords, or even other symmetric keys. I discussed the encryption hierarchy, and where symmetric keys fit into it, in Chapter 2. In this chapter, I'll discuss the symmetric encryption algorithms that SQL Server supports and describe how to encrypt data and other keys using symmetric keys.

For purposes of demonstration, I'll be creating a table called SalesLT.EncryptedCustomer in the AdventureWorksLT database. Listing 3-1 is the CREATE TABLE statement that creates this table.

Note You can download and install the sample AdventureWorksLT 2008 sample database from http://msftdbprodsamples.codeplex.com to run the samples in the following sections and throughout the rest of the book.

Listing 3-1. Create SalesLT.EncryptedCustomer Table

```
CREATE TABLE SalesLT.EncryptedCustomer
(
  CustomerID    int NOT NULL PRIMARY KEY,
  FirstName     varbinary(200),
  MiddleName    varbinary(200),
  LastName      varbinary(200),
  EmailAddress  varbinary(200),
  Phone         varbinary(150),
  rowguid       uniqueidentifier
);
GO
```

Creating and Protecting Symmetric Keys

Before you create a symmetric key to protect your data you first need to create an asymmetric key or certificate to protect the symmetric key. Listing 3-2 shows how to create a self-signed certificate on SQL Server to protect your symmetric keys.

> ■ **Tip** Instead of creating self-signed certificates, you can install an existing certificate or asymmetric key from an external source. I'll discuss this option in Chapter 4.

Listing 3-2. Creating a Certificate to Protect Symmetric Keys

```
CREATE CERTIFICATE Cert1_Sales
WITH SUBJECT = N'Sales Certificate',
START_DATE = N'2009-01-01',
EXPIRY_DATE = N'2018-12-31';
GO
```

This example creates a certificate named Cert1_Sales. Once the certificate is created, you can use it to protect symmetric keys you create. Listing 3-3 creates an AES 256-bit symmetric key and uses the certificate to protect it.

Listing 3-3. Creating the AES 256-Bit Symmetric Key

```
CREATE SYMMETRIC KEY SymKey1_Sales
WITH ALGORITHM = AES_256,
  IDENTITY_VALUE = N'Barbarians at the Gate',
  KEY_SOURCE = N'We will leave the light on for you'
ENCRYPTION BY CERTIFICATE Cert1_Sales;
GO
```

The WITH ALGORITHM clause specifies which encryption algorithm the symmetric key will be used with. This clause assigns an encryption algorithm to the symmetric key. The key length can be either explicit in the algorithm name, as in AES_256, or implied as in RC4. Once you've created a symmetric encryption key, it is stored permanently within the database (except in the case of temporary symmetric keys, which are described later in this section). The IDENTITY_VALUE and KEY_SOURCE options allow you to re-create the exact same key at a later time. I'll discuss these options in the "Duplicating Symmetric Keys" section of this chapter. For now it's enough to know that you'll generally want to use these options since there is no way to back up or export a symmetric key.

Encrypting Data

Once you've created a symmetric key you have to open it to encrypt and decrypt data with it. Listing 3-4 uses the SymKey1_Sales key to create an encrypted copy of a table of contact information. If the upstream DMK is protected by the SMK you don't need to open the DMK. The sample in Listing 3-4 automatically opens the DMK without an explicit OPEN MASTER KEY statement.

Listing 3-4. Encrypting Contact Data with a Symmetric Key

```
-- First wipe out the target table
TRUNCATE TABLE SalesLT.EncryptedCustomer;
GO

-- Open the key that's protected by certificate
OPEN SYMMETRIC KEY SymKey1_Sales
DECRYPTION BY CERTIFICATE Cert1_Sales;
GO

-- Encrypt the data
INSERT INTO SalesLT.EncryptedCustomer
(
  CustomerID,
  FirstName,
  MiddleName,
  LastName,
  EmailAddress,
  Phone,
  rowguid
)
SELECT
  CustomerID,
  EncryptByKey(Key_Guid(N'SymKey1_Sales'), FirstName),
  EncryptByKey(Key_Guid(N'SymKey1_Sales'), MiddleName),
  EncryptByKey(Key_Guid(N'SymKey1_Sales'), LastName),
  EncryptByKey(Key_Guid(N'SymKey1_Sales'), EmailAddress),
  EncryptByKey(Key_Guid(N'SymKey1_Sales'), Phone),
  rowguid
FROM SalesLT.Customer;
GO

-- Close the key
CLOSE SYMMETRIC KEY SymKey1_Sales;
GO
```

The first step in the SQL Server symmetric encryption process is to open the symmetric key. Because the symmetric key is protected by the Cert1_Sales certificate you have to specify this certificate in the DECRYPTION BY clause of the OPEN SYMMETRIC KEY statement, as shown in the following code snippet.

```
OPEN SYMMETRIC KEY SymKey1_Sales
DECRYPTION BY CERTIFICATE Cert1_Sales;
GO
```

Keep in mind that every symmetric key has to maintain an internal state mechanism. This state is subject to change during the encryption and decryption process. Therefore, it's not technically feasible for multiple users to use the same single symmetric key at the same time. However, SQL Server is able to work around this limitation. When you open a symmetric key, SQL Server makes a copy of it and ties that copy to your session. What this means for you is that several users can use the same key to encrypt and decrypt data simultaneously. The amount of state information maintained internally by a symmetric key depends entirely on the algorithm chosen, with some algorithms requiring a lot more state storage than others.

■ **Note** There's no easy way to quantify exactly how much memory SQL Server uses for state storage since it's all handled internally. However, based on the definitions of the algorithms themselves you can estimate it's not more than a few kilobytes to store substitution boxes (S-boxes), permutation boxes (P-boxes), and additional state information for any given instance of a symmetric key.

After you open a symmetric key, the next step is to actually use that symmetric key to encrypt your data. This task is performed with the EncryptByKey function. The basic no-frills version of the EncryptByKey function accepts two parameters, the GUID of the symmetric key and the plaintext you wish to encrypt. EncryptByKey returns a varbinary(8000) value, meaning the encrypted text can be no longer than 8,000 bytes. If the ciphertext result of a symmetric encryption will be longer than 8,000 bytes, EncryptByKey returns a null.

As you can see in the following code snippet taken from the previous listing, I've used the Key_Guid system function to return the GUID for the symmetric key. Simply pass the Key_Guid function the name of your symmetric key and it will do the work of retrieving the GUID for you. This is much simpler than the alternative, which involves querying the sys.symmetric_keys table.

```
INSERT INTO SalesLT.EncryptedCustomer
(
  CustomerID,
  FirstName,
  MiddleName,
  LastName,
  EmailAddress,
  Phone,
  rowguid
)
```

```
SELECT
  CustomerID,
  EncryptByKey(Key_Guid(N'SymKey1_Sales'), FirstName),
  EncryptByKey(Key_Guid(N'SymKey1_Sales'), MiddleName),
  EncryptByKey(Key_Guid(N'SymKey1_Sales'), LastName),
  EncryptByKey(Key_Guid(N'SymKey1_Sales'), EmailAddress),
  EncryptByKey(Key_Guid(N'SymKey1_Sales'), Phone),
  rowguid
FROM SalesLT.Customer;
GO
```

The final step, of course, is to close the symmetric key as shown in the following code.

```
CLOSE SYMMETRIC KEY SymKey1_Sales;
GO
```

It's a good idea to manually close your symmetric keys, but if you're disconnected before you can close open symmetric keys for some reason, don't worry. All open symmetric keys are automatically closed as soon as the current session is disconnected.

You can query the SalesLT.EncryptedCustomer table after populating it with encrypted data, using a query like the one in Listing 3-5. Essentially, the results will look like binary gibberish as shown in the partial results of Figure 3-1. Note that when your run the sample on your server, your ciphertext will be different from that shown in the figure.

Listing 3-5. Querying the Binary Encrypted Contact Data

```
SELECT
  CustomerID,
  FirstName
FROM SalesLT.EncryptedCustomer;
```

	CustomerID	FirstName
1	1	0x009A59501F240D4DBB7343619B6EED5C01000000BF2678F0ACF3FFE7B10E8B5027B0C8D771EB5CBA228A6498A4C48B08DB3CE846...
2	2	0x009A59501F240D4DBB7343619B6EED5C01000000694C1BA361AC99FC7C57148C8B87FE3089801BCE1ACD9775FE09435E8C4ABA88...
3	3	0x009A59501F240D4DBB7343619B6EED5C010000005AA25B5D1ADC03B7782F69298528993F65DE52A2827840853372A1F5EE738DD9...
4	4	0x009A59501F240D4DBB7343619B6EED5C01000000B4BFF070A5F4C5A6821F0DDAAFE1C2D0824DBB8AAF928D97ADF39B9E77F2F340...
5	5	0x009A59501F240D4DBB7343619B6EED5C01000000CE8CEF714F5169B1F7E9CFC71F2A1885A3BE3F4A80B93C8C710809A2C878A4848...
6	6	0x009A59501F240D4DBB7343619B6EED5C01000000957BE2554B35E4911D98A06AE64E5FD7CBA1FD2F68F98A26D3957F306492E556...
7	7	0x009A59501F240D4DBB7343619B6EED5C01000000F0BAF7C03154536F2BB12DE2EEE1A8093D24ECFB977344083BF97C8782EE76775...
8	10	0x009A59501F240D4DBB7343619B6EED5C01000000D7A7C1F3D7B54C41288C2EB312683F350CDEB68A8E8E49B4FC9CCDA99DA35E2...
9	11	0x009A59501F240D4DBB7343619B6EED5C01000000063B87BC82C16233F696137494DCA1D80B7E478329B30DBFBB5A79CBD5A4BAF...
10	12	0x009A59501F240D4DBB7343619B6EED5C010000009E750B9E313314C14A9E894A152DC45DF2435E808D3F7F91077B1C8B7396AB25...
11	16	0x009A59501F240D4DBB7343619B6EED5C01000000537774A1A34B921C8EAAA66EA09A1217E53A609F50147DCD286CAD6EFA82C1E1...
12	18	0x009A59501F240D4DBB7343619B6EED5C010000009FB7DE32321A5FF17AEEF4E2341B8003B6C9139B86E1755817303E78266A2921F...
13	19	0x009A59501F240D4DBB7343619B6EED5C010000000F293CB67BEEA366115EA8F4139F4B5843D3DBF74F7CF73C16FB9C9AD01F35672...
14	20	0x009A59501F240D4DBB7343619B6EED5C010000004B1081DCFCEBB45E9317D545FE39C495C33698C0439CA0FD49F52F34365AE91A...
15	21	0x009A59501F240D4DBB7343619B6EED5C0100000011825ABA39F25A7ACC800745ED164EC675FEA929C033CD4EB95825BA6A00AF9A...

Figure 3-1. Looking at encrypted data stored in a table

The Structure of Chaos

As mentioned, the encrypted data looks like a bunch of `binary` data type gibberish. From the perspective of trying to secure your data, this is a good thing. When you look at the encrypted data, as you did in Figure3-1, however, you might notice a pattern in the ciphertext. Specifically, the first several bytes of binary data appear to be the same in every single row. In Chapter 1, I spent a good deal of time talking about how cryptanalysts use patterns to attack your data, so the question you might be asking right now is "Does this pattern compromise my encryption security?" The short answer is no, this particular pattern does not pose a security risk.

To explain why this is, I need to describe the structure SQL Server imposes on encrypted data. Put simply, SQL Server stores additional metadata with every encrypted value. This metadata includes information about the version of SQL Server encryption being used, the GUID of the key used to encrypt the data, and various other information. The encrypted data value can actually be viewed as an encrypted data record with an exact structure. The encrypted data record structure for AES and other 128-bit block ciphers is shown in the illustration below.

GUID of Symmetric Key	Version	Random Initialization Vector (IV)	Encrypted Data
0x00C8EE9A16724442845C285BBC06AF95	01000000	191E78D433B80C78543CD8566FB9D79C	2167E755D6DC6295DFFC8386D49437E0
16 bytes	4 bytes	16 bytes	Up to 7,964 bytes

As you can see, the encrypted data record begins with a 16-byte reference to the GUID of the key used to encrypt the data. This is followed by the 4-byte version, which in the current version of SQL Server is hardwired as 0x01000000. Next is a 16-byte randomly generated initialization vector (IV). I'll discuss the purpose of the IV in the "Encryption Algorithms" section of this chapter. The final field, which can be up to 7,964 bytes in length, is the actual encrypted data. This encrypted data record structure is indicative of 128-bit block ciphers, like AES. For a 64-bit block cipher, like DES or Triple DES, the random IV will actually be 8 bytes in length and the encrypted data can be 7,972 bytes.

There is one more variable that can affect the length of the final encrypted data record. If you use the authenticator option, which I'll describe in the "Adding an Authenticator" section of this chapter, SQL Server will add an extra 32 bytes of metadata to your encrypted data when using a 128-bit block cipher (24 bytes are added when using a 64-bit block cipher).

This additional metadata is placed between the random IV and your encrypted data. It consists of additional header information plus a hash of your authenticator value. When the authenticator is used, the maximum length of your encrypted data is reduced to 7,932 bytes for AES and other 128-bit block ciphers, and 7,944 bytes for 64-bit block ciphers like DES.

Decrypting Data

Once you've encrypted your data using a symmetric key, you can use the DecryptByKey system function to decrypt it on an as-needed basis. Listing 3-6 uses DecryptByKey to decrypt the first names of the contacts that I previously encrypted in Listing 3-4. Partial results are shown in Figure 3-2.

Listing 3-6. Decrypting Previously Encrypted Data

```
-- Open the key that's protected by certificate
OPEN SYMMETRIC KEY SymKey1_Sales
DECRYPTION BY CERTIFICATE Cert1_Sales;
GO

-- Decrypt the data
SELECT
  CustomerID,
  CAST(DecryptByKey(FirstName) AS nvarchar(100)) AS DecryptedFirstName,
  FirstName
FROM SalesLT.EncryptedCustomer;
GO

-- Close the key
CLOSE SYMMETRIC KEY SymKey1_Sales;
GO
```

	ContactID	DecryptedFirstName	FirstName
1	1	Gustavo	0x007FC1BF631F9346BB88584B9D5F90...
2	2	Catherine	0x007FC1BF631F9346BB88584B9D5F90...
3	3	Kim	0x007FC1BF631F9346BB88584B9D5F90...
4	4	Humberto	0x007FC1BF631F9346BB88584B9D5F90...
5	5	Pilar	0x007FC1BF631F9346BB88584B9D5F90...
6	6	Frances	0x007FC1BF631F9346BB88584B9D5F90...
7	7	Margaret	0x007FC1BF631F9346BB88584B9D5F90...
8	8	Carla	0x007FC1BF631F9346BB88584B9D5F90...
9	9	Jay	0x007FC1BF631F9346BB88584B9D5F90...
10	10	Ronald	0x007FC1BF631F9346BB88584B9D5F90...
11	11	Samuel	0x007FC1BF631F9346BB88584B9D5F90...
12	12	James	0x007FC1BF631F9346BB88584B9D5F90...
13	13	Robert	0x007FC1BF631F9346BB88584B9D5F90...
14	14	François	0x007FC1BF631F9346BB88584B9D5F90...
15	15	Kim	0x007FC1BF631F9346BB88584B9D5F90...

Figure 3-2. Decrypted sample data

As with the encryption process, the first step in decryption is to open the symmetric key. This is shown in the code snippet that follows.

```
OPEN SYMMETRIC KEY SymKey1_Sales
DECRYPTION BY CERTIFICATE Cert1_Sales;
GO
```

Next the DecryptByKey function is called to decrypt a column of data. The DecryptByKey function call is shown in the following code snippet.

```
SELECT
  ContactID,
  CAST(DecryptByKey(FirstName) AS nvarchar(100)) AS DecryptedFirstName,
  FirstName
FROM SalesLT.EncryptedCustomer;
GO
```

Notice that, unlike EncryptByKey, the DecryptByKey system function requires only one parameter: the encrypted data. You don't have to supply the GUID of the key used to encrypt the data—but why this difference? Recall from the previous section that the GUID of the symmetric key is stored with the encrypted data itself (see the sidebar *The Structure of Chaos* in the previous section). The DecryptByKey function simply retrieves the symmetric key's GUID from the encrypted data record itself.

Of course, to decrypt the data you still need permissions to the symmetric key used to encrypt the data, permissions to the asymmetric key or certificate used to encrypt the symmetric key (or you need to know the password used to encrypt the symmetric key), and permissions to the DMK if it wasused to encrypt the asymmetric key or certificate protecting the symmetric key. If you don't have permissions to all of the necessary keys and certificates, and knowledge of the passwords if passwords were used to protect them, you won't be able to decrypt previously encrypted data. Also, this is all predicated on your having permissions to access the table containing the encrypted data.

Notice also that I wrapped the DecryptByKey function inside a CAST function call. This is because DecryptByKey returns a varbinary result. Because I started with nvarchar data, I have to explicitly cast the result back to nvarchar.

■ **Caution** If you initially encrypted nvarchar data, you must cast it back to nvarchar. If you cast it back to varchar instead, you could lose data.

Adding an Authenticator

So far I've talked about the basic parameters that symmetric encryption functions accept: The EncryptByKey function takes a symmetric key GUID and plaintext to encrypt, and the DecryptByKey function accepts the encrypted ciphertext. In addition to the basic parameters, these functions can accept an additional authenticator flag and authenticator string value. When the authenticator flag issetto 1 the encryption and decryption functions apply the authenticator value to further obfuscate yourciphertext.

Consider Figure 3-3, which represents a table of bank account information, but with account balance information encrypted.

Name		Account Balance
Ballmer	Steve	0x158D0402AB080E02
Gates	Bill	0x1256D5D32EBF508A
Page	Larry	0xC5DE7C6EB2DD95F5
Brin	Sergey	0xBEDE882F1AA5BC67
Smith	John	0x92AB34E12B010D51

Figure 3-3. Table with encrypted bank account balances

For this example, we'll just say that our hacker, John Smith, has accessed this information. He recognizes some of the names on the other accounts and realizes that there's a very high probability that their account balances are larger than his (which currently sits at a hefty $3.99). John decides to copy Bill Gates' encrypted account balance over to his account balance. This is a whole-value substitution attack, and authenticators help mitigate this risk.

The purpose of the authenticator is to prevent this type of whole-value substitution attacks onyour data, in which an attacker replaces an encrypted value with another encrypted value. The authenticator can be used to tie your encrypted ciphertext value to a given row, so the encrypted data can't be copied to another row. You'll generally want to use a different authenticator for every row (probably a value from another column in the same row).

Listing 3-7 modifies the code in Listing 3-4 to encrypt the same data, but with the addition of an authenticator, which is the fourth parameter passed to the EncryptByKey function.

Listing 3-7. Encrypting with an Authenticator

```
-- First wipe out the target table
TRUNCATE TABLE SalesLT.EncryptedCustomer;
GO

-- Open the key that's protected by certificate
OPEN SYMMETRIC KEY SymKey1_Sales
DECRYPTION BY CERTIFICATE Cert1_Sales;
GO

-- Encrypt the data with authenticator
INSERT INTO SalesLT.EncryptedCustomer
(
  CustomerID,
  FirstName,
  MiddleName,
  LastName,
  EmailAddress,
  Phone,
  rowguid
)
```

```
SELECT
  CustomerID,
  EncryptByKey(Key_Guid(N'SymKey1_Sales'), FirstName, 1,
    CAST(rowguid AS nvarchar(100))),
  EncryptByKey(Key_Guid(N'SymKey1_Sales'), MiddleName, 1,
    CAST(rowguid AS nvarchar(100))),
  EncryptByKey(Key_Guid(N'SymKey1_Sales'), LastName, 1,
    CAST(rowguid AS nvarchar(100))),
  EncryptByKey(Key_Guid(N'SymKey1_Sales'), EmailAddress, 1,
    CAST(rowguid AS nvarchar(100))),
  EncryptByKey(Key_Guid(N'SymKey1_Sales'), Phone, 1,
    CAST(rowguid AS nvarchar(100))),
  rowguid
FROM SalesLT.Customer;
GO

-- Close the key
CLOSE SYMMETRIC KEY SymKey1_Sales;
GO
```

To decrypt the data, you'll need to apply the same authenticator you used to encrypt it, as shown in Listing 3-8. The DecryptByKey function accepts the authenticator as its third parameter.

Listing 3-8. Decryption with an Authenticator

```
-- Open the data key that's protected by certificate
OPEN SYMMETRIC KEY SymKey1_Sales
DECRYPTION BY CERTIFICATE Cert1_Sales;
GO

-- Decrypt the data with authenticator
SELECT
  CustomerID,
  CAST
  (
    DecryptByKey(FirstName, 1, CAST(rowguid AS nvarchar(100))
  ) AS nvarchar(100)) AS DecryptedFirstName,
  FirstName
FROM SalesLT.EncryptedCustomer;
GO

-- Close the symmetric key
CLOSE SYMMETRIC KEY SymKey1_Sales;
GO
```

Automatic Key Management

My examples of encryption and decryption so far have assumed that the Database Master Key (DMK) is encrypted by the Service Master Key (SMK). This is referred to by Microsoft as *automatic key management*. It simply means that you don't have to manually open the DMK when you want to use the keys and certificates protected by it.

When you have automatic key management turned on, all your database administrators (DBAs) have access to decrypt all data encrypted by the keys and certificates that are in turn protected by the DMK. In some cases, you might want to limit the access DBAs have to encrypted data. You can turn off automatic key management by using the ALTER MASTER KEY statement, as shown in Listing 3-9.

Listing 3-9. Turning Off Automatic Key Management

```
ALTER MASTER KEY
DROP ENCRYPTION BY SERVICE MASTER KEY;
```

Now, to encrypt and decrypt data using certificates and keys that are protected by the DMK you first have to issue an OPEN MASTER KEY statement. After turning off automatic key management, you'll get an error like the following if you try to encrypt or decrypt data without first manually opening the DMK.

```
Msg 15581, Level 16, State 3, Line 1

Please create a master key in the database or open the master key in the

session before performing this operation.



(847 row(s) affected)

Msg 15315, Level 16, State 1, Line 2

The key 'SymKey1_Sales' is not open. Please open the key before using it.
```

Listing 3-10 revises the encryption example in Listing 3-6 to properly decrypt the data without automatic key management. Notice the DMK must be opened first, as indicated in bold text in Listing 3-10.

Listing 3-10. Decrypting Data Without Automatic Key Management

```
-- Open the DMK that's protected by password; necessary because
-- the certificate is protected by the DMK
OPEN MASTER KEY
DECRYPTION BY PASSWORD = N'ao*Ui)4x-f';
GO

-- Open the symmetric key that's protected by certificate
OPEN SYMMETRIC KEY SymKey1_Sales
DECRYPTION BY CERTIFICATE Cert1_Sales;
GO
```

```
-- Decrypt the data
SELECT
  CustomerID,
  CAST(DecryptByKey(FirstName) AS nvarchar(100)) AS DecryptedFirstName,
  FirstName
FROM SalesLT.EncryptedCustomer;
GO

-- Close the key and DMK
CLOSE SYMMETRIC KEY SymKey1_Sales;
GO
```

CLOSE MASTER KEY;
```
GO
```

You can also protect your certificates, asymmetric keys, and symmetric keys with passwords instead of the DMK. If you've been executing the samples as you read the chapter, then you've already removed automatic key management from your DMK.

In Listing 3-11, I'll take it a step farther. In this listing, I'll add password encryption to, and remove certificate encryption from, the SymKey1_Sales symmetric key. This removes the symmetric key from the scope of SQL Server's built-in key management hierarchy, effectively shifting the responsibility for key management back to you. Note that if you want to alter the symmetric key you have to open it first, as I've done in the example.

Listing 3-11. Using Encryption By Password to Protect a Symmetric Key

```
-- Open the DMK that's protected by password
OPEN MASTER KEY
DECRYPTION BY PASSWORD = N'aO*Ui)4x-f';
GO

-- Open the data encrypting key
OPEN SYMMETRIC KEY SymKey1_Sales
DECRYPTION BY CERTIFICATE Cert1_Sales;
GO

-- Add encryption by password to the key
ALTER SYMMETRIC KEY SymKey1_Sales
ADD ENCRYPTION BY PASSWORD = N'~@~*&a1B4!';
GO

-- Drop certificate protection from the key
ALTER SYMMETRIC KEY SymKey1_Sales
DROP ENCRYPTION BY CERTIFICATE Cert1_Sales;
GO

-- Close the key and DMK
CLOSE SYMMETRIC KEY SymKey1_Sales;
GO

CLOSE MASTER KEY;
GO
```

After this change, whenever you want to use the symmetric key SymKey1_Sales, you'll need to specify the password in the DECRYPTION BY clause of the OPEN SYMMETRIC KEY statement. This is shown in Listing3-12, which modifies Listing 3-4 yet again.

Listing 3-12. Decrypting Data with a Symmetric Key, Protected By Password

```
-- Open the symmetric key that's protected by password
OPEN SYMMETRIC KEY SymKey1_Sales
DECRYPTION BY PASSWORD = N'~@~*&a1B4!';
GO

-- Decrypt the data
SELECT
  CustomerID,
  CAST(DecryptByKey(FirstName) AS nvarchar(100)) AS DecryptedFirstName,
  FirstName
FROM SalesLT.EncryptedCustomer;
GO

-- Close the symmetric key
CLOSE SYMMETRIC KEY SymKey1_Sales;
GO
```

Taking Over Key Management

Now that I've shown you how to remove your symmetric keys from the standard SQL Server key hierarchy, I'd like to address the "why." That is, why would you want to do this? As mentioned, when you remove the encryption by certificate (or by asymmetric key) you shift the responsibility for key management from SQL Server to yourself.

While it's not necessarily easy to manually manage your symmetric keys, there could be valid reasons for doing so. You might have an organizational IT policy that requires symmetric keys to be managed manually, for instance. Or you might already have a key management infrastructure in place and the SQL Server key management hierarchy might not fit into your structure. For example, you might need to manually manage your keys for security reasons—to guarantee a strict separation of access by DBAs and developers.

If you find that you need to protect your symmetric keys by password, for whatever reason, ensure that you have the proper safeguards and policies in place to keep them secure.

Duplicating Symmetric Keys

When you create a symmetric key using the syntax I've shown so far, SQL Server randomly generates the key material—the base data from which the key is built. An important point to mention here is that there is no way to back up a symmetric key. You can't make a backup and restore it later, or export it and import it to another machine. So how do you reinstall a symmetric key after a server rebuild, or duplicate it on another machine?

The answer is to duplicate it through re-creation with the KEY_SOURCE and IDENTITY_VALUE options. You can use KEY_SOURCE to specify a passphrase that will be used as the source key material that SQL Server uses to generate the encryption key. The IDENTITY_VALUE option is used by SQL Server to generate the GUID for the key.

When you create two or more symmetric keys with the same KEY_SOURCE passphrase, IDENTITY_VALUE and encryption algorithm SQL Server guarantees it will generate identical keys. This means you can generate duplicates of a key on multiple servers, or regenerate a key from scratch, by specifying the same KEY_SOURCE, IDENTITY_VALUE, and algorithm. Listing 3-13 demonstrates how to create a 192-bit AES key with the KEY_SOURCE and IDENTITY_VALUE options.

Listing 3-13. Creating an AES Key with the KEY_SOURCE Option

```
CREATE SYMMETRIC KEY SymKey5_Sales
WITH ALGORITHM = AES_192,
KEY_SOURCE = N'She sells sea shells by the seashore.',
IDENTITY_VALUE = N'My identity is a shared secret.'
ENCRYPTION BY CERTIFICATE Cert1_Sales;
GO
```

If you needed to re-create this key in the future you could by executing the CREATE SYMMETRIC KEY statement, specifying the exact same options. When you don't specify a KEY_SOURCE SQL Server generates a random key. If you don't specify an IDENTITY_VALUE SQL Server generates a random GUID. If you specify KEY_SOURCE and IDENTITY_VALUE when creating a symmetric key, be sure to record and store this information securely so you can re-create the same key in the future. It's critical to secure this information since anyone with these values can re-create your symmetric keys on their own servers.

Temporary Keys

In addition to permanent symmetric encryption keys, you can also create temporary symmetric encryption keys. You use the CREATE SYMMETRIC KEY statement, just like when you create any other symmetric key. The difference is that you prefix the symmetric key name with a pound sign (#) as you would when creating a temporary table. While a permanent encryption key is accessible to all sessions connected to your SQL Server instance, a temporary key is accessible only on the connection on which it was created.

The business uses for a temporary symmetric key might include situations in which you can'tstore permanent symmetric keys in the database for security reasons, or when you only need totemporarily encrypt data that's being stored for the duration of your session. When you create a temporary key that will be used to encrypt and decrypt data that's stored permanently you need to create it with the KEY_SOURCE and IDENTITY_VALUE options to ensure you can re-create it later. Listing 3-14 demonstrates creation of a temporary symmetric key in the database.

Listing 3-14. Creating a Temporary Symmetric Key

```
CREATE SYMMETRIC KEY #TempAESKey
WITH ALGORITHM = AES_128,
KEY_SOURCE = N'I am the very model of a modern major general',
IDENTITY_VALUE = N'I think therefore I am'
ENCRYPTION BY CERTIFICATE Cert1_Sales;
GO
```

As with permanent symmetric keys you can use the Key_GUID function to retrieve the GUID for a temporary key. You can use the DROP SYMMETRIC KEY to dispose of a temporary symmetric key, or you can simply disconnect your session. As soon as the current session which owns the temporary key is closed, the temporary key is closed and dropped.

Layering Symmetric Keys

Another feature of the SQL Server encryption key hierarchy is the ability to protect symmetric keys withother symmetric keys. You can use symmetric keys to create multiple levels of key encrypting keysin the middle layer of your encryption key hierarchy. This could prove very useful in an enterprise environment where large amounts of data are protected by your lowest-level data keys. The advantage oflayering symmetric keys is that you can significantly lengthen your key rotation schedule for several layers of keys, and maximize the efficiency of your key rotations.

Before I go on, I want to turn automatic key management back on using the script in Listing 3-15, just to make things simpler in the samples that follow.

Listing 3-15. Turning Automatic Key Encryption Back On

```
-- Open the DMK
OPEN MASTER KEY
DECRYPTION BY PASSWORD = 'aO*Ui)4x-f';
GO

-- Add encryption by SMK
ALTER MASTER KEY
ADD ENCRYPTION BY SERVICE MASTER KEY;
GO

-- Close the DMK
CLOSE MASTER KEY;
GO
```

Now that automatic key management is turned on, I'll use the SQL Server encryption hierarchy to encrypt multiple levels of symmetric keys with other symmetric keys in Listing 3-16. The multiple levels of symmetric keys encrypting other keys are shown in Figure 3-4.

Listing 3-16. Layering Symmetric Keys

```
-- Create a symmetric key, protect it with a certificate
CREATE SYMMETRIC KEY SymKey2_Sales
WITH ALGORITHM = AES_256
ENCRYPTION BY CERTIFICATE Cert1_Sales;
GO

-- Open top-level symmetric key
OPEN SYMMETRIC KEY SymKey2_Sales
DECRYPTION BY CERTIFICATE Cert1_Sales;
GO

-- Create the next symmetric key, protect it with the top-level symmetric key
CREATE SYMMETRIC KEY SymKey3_Sales
WITH ALGORITHM = AES_192
ENCRYPTION BY SYMMETRIC KEY SymKey2_Sales;
GO

-- Open the previously created symmetric key
OPEN SYMMETRIC KEY SymKey3_Sales
DECRYPTION BY SYMMETRIC KEY SymKey2_Sales;
GO

-- Create the bottom-level symmetric key, protect it with the previous key
CREATE SYMMETRIC KEY SymKey4_Sales
WITH ALGORITHM = AES_128
ENCRYPTION BY SYMMETRIC KEY SymKey3_Sales;
GO

-- Close all open keys
CLOSE SYMMETRIC KEY SymKey3_Sales;
GO

CLOSE SYMMETRIC KEY SymKey2_Sales;
GO
```

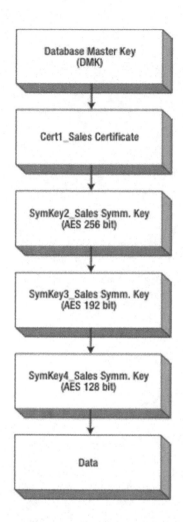

Figure 3-4. Layered symmetric keys in the SQL Server encryption key hierarchy

In this example, the SymKey4_Sales symmetric key is the data encrypting key. This key is encrypted by the SymKey3_Sales symmetric key, which is in turn protected by the SymKey2_Sales symmetric key. The SymKey2_Sales key is protected by a certificate, and so on up the key management hierarchy.

You may notice that all the symmetric keys in this example use the AES encryption algorithm. The higher-level symmetric keys are more secure than the lower-level keys. The SymKey2_Sales key uses a 256-bit key, for instance, while the lower-level SymKey4_Sales key uses a 128-bit key. Best practices indicate that you should use an algorithm and a key that are as strong as, or stronger than, the keys theysecure.

The downside of layering symmetric keys is that you have to open all levels of keys to encrypt or decrypt your data. Listing 3-17 demonstrates the encryption process.

Listing 3-17. Encrypting Data with Layered Symmetric Keys

```
-- First wipe out the target table
TRUNCATE TABLE SalesLT.EncryptedCustomer;
GO

-- Open the multiple levels of symmetric keys
OPEN SYMMETRIC KEY SymKey2_Sales
DECRYPTION BY CERTIFICATE Cert1_Sales;
GO

OPEN SYMMETRIC KEY SymKey3_Sales
DECRYPTION BY SYMMETRIC KEY SymKey2_Sales;
GO

OPEN SYMMETRIC KEY SymKey4_Sales
DECRYPTION BY SYMMETRIC KEY SymKey3_Sales;
GO

-- Encrypt the data
INSERT INTO SalesLT.EncryptedCustomer
(
  CustomerID,
  FirstName,
  MiddleName,
  LastName,
  EmailAddress,
  Phone,
  rowguid
)
SELECT
  CustomerID,
  EncryptByKey(Key_GUID(N'SymKey4_Sales'), FirstName),
  EncryptByKey(Key_GUID(N'SymKey4_Sales'), MiddleName),
  EncryptByKey(Key_GUID(N'SymKey4_Sales'), LastName),
  EncryptByKey(Key_GUID(N'SymKey4_Sales'), EmailAddress),
  EncryptByKey(Key_GUID(N'SymKey4_Sales'), Phone),
  rowguid
FROM SalesLT.Customer;
GO

-- Close the symmetric keys
CLOSE ALL SYMMETRIC KEYS;
GO
```

You might have noticed the introduction of a new statement in the sample code. The CLOSE ALL SYMMETRIC KEYS statement closes all currently open symmetric keys and the DMK (in the current session) at once. As with encryption, decryption requires you to open all levels of symmetric keysas demonstrated in Listing 3-18. Partial results are shown in Figure 3-5.

Listing 3-18. Decrypting Data with Layered Symmetric Keys

```
-- Open the top-level symmetric key that's protected by certificate
OPEN SYMMETRIC KEY SymKey2_Sales
DECRYPTION BY CERTIFICATE Cert1_Sales;
GO

-- Open the key that's protected by the top-level key
OPEN SYMMETRIC KEY SymKey3_Sales
DECRYPTION BY SYMMETRIC KEY SymKey2_Sales;
GO

-- Open the data encrypting key that's protected by the previous key
OPEN SYMMETRIC KEY SymKey4_Sales
DECRYPTION BY SYMMETRIC KEY SymKey3_Sales;
GO

-- Decrypt the data
SELECT
  CustomerID,
  CAST(DecryptByKey(FirstName) AS nvarchar(100)) AS DecryptedFirstName,
  FirstName
FROM SalesLT.EncryptedCustomer;
GO

-- Close all the keys
CLOSE ALL SYMMETRIC KEYS;
GO
```

	CustomerID	DecryptedFirstNa...	FirstName
1	1	Orlando	0x00E9324149CA324A8606B520ED9AB12A01000000CC8ADF...
2	2	Keith	0x00E9324149CA324A8606B520ED9AB12A010000001925C0A...
3	3	Donna	0x00E9324149CA324A8606B520ED9AB12A01000000C58C736...
4	4	Janet	0x00E9324149CA324A8606B520ED9AB12A01000000E257DB...
5	5	Lucy	0x00E9324149CA324A8606B520ED9AB12A010000005885F0E...
6	6	Rosmarie	0x00E9324149CA324A8606B520ED9AB12A0100000027E3EF2...
7	7	Dominic	0x00E9324149CA324A8606B520ED9AB12A010000000BF13C9...
8	10	Kathleen	0x00E9324149CA324A8606B520ED9AB12A01000000F38AD3...
9	11	Katherine	0x00E9324149CA324A8606B520ED9AB12A010000000FC82B9...
10	12	Johnny	0x00E9324149CA324A8606B520ED9AB12A010000003CFD26...
11	16	Christopher	0x00E9324149CA324A8606B520ED9AB12A01000000F3055CE...
12	18	David	0x00E9324149CA324A8606B520ED9AB12A010000007F1853B...
13	19	John	0x00E9324149CA324A8606B520ED9AB12A010000002E43FA5...
14	20	Jean	0x00E9324149CA324A8606B520ED9AB12A0100000054A5AB...
15	21	Jinghao	0x00E9324149CA324A8606B520ED9AB12A0100000092BCA4...

Figure 3-5. Results of decryption with layered symmetric keys

Encryption with Passphrases

You can also encrypt your data without encryption keys, using passphrases. A passphrase is essentially the same thing as a password, but you can use an entire phrase instead of a single word. SQL Server 2008 supplies two functions to support this feature: EncryptByPassPhrase and DecryptByPassPhrase.

The EncryptByPassPhrase function accepts a passphrase and your plaintext. It uses the passphrase to encrypt your plaintext, and returns a varbinary result. DecryptByPassPhrase accepts a passphrase and your previously encrypted ciphertext. The result is a varbinary representation of your decrypted ciphertext. Listing 3-19 encrypts a plaintext message using a passphrase. The result is shown in Figure 3-6.

Listing 3-19. Encrypting and Decrypting By Passphrase

```
-- Define the plaintext
DECLARE @plaintext nvarchar(100) = N'Four score and seven years ago our
fathers brought forth, upon this continent, a new nation...';

-- Encrypt the data with a passphrase
DECLARE @encryptedtext varbinary(300);

SET @encryptedtext = EncryptByPassPhrase(N'Quick brown fox', @plaintext);

-- Decrypt the data with the same passphrase
SELECT CAST
  (
    DecryptByPassPhrase(N'Quick brown fox', @encryptedtext) AS nvarchar(100)
  ) AS DecryptedData;
GO
```

	DecryptedData
1	Four score and seven years ago our fathers brought forth, upon this continent, a new nation...

Figure 3-6. Result of encryption and decryption by passphrase

Behind the scenes the EncryptByPassPhrase and DecryptByPassPhrase functions use the passphrase you supply to generate a symmetric encryption key. The Triple DES algorithm is used toencrypt or decrypt your data with the generated key. When you use these functions you take responsibility for your own key management, just like when you secure your symmetric keys with passwords.

Encryption Algorithms

SQL Server 2008 supports several symmetric encryption algorithms. Which one should you use? The answer to that depends partially on your requirements, which might be driven by regulatory agencies and laws, contractual obligations, or other business needs. One of the factors I'll address in this section is overall security—some algorithms are more secure than others. Figure 3-7 is a list of algorithms SQL Server supports (in order from most secure to least secure).

Keyword	Algorithm	Key Length
AES_256	AES	256
AES_192	AES	192
AES_128	AES	128
Triple DES 3Key	Triple DES (3-Key)	192^
Triple DES	Triple DES (2-Key)	128^
DES	DES	64*
RC2	RC2	128
RC4_128	RC4	128
RC4	RC4	40

* DES uses 56 bits of the 64 bit key
  Triple DES (2-Key) uses 112 bits of the 128 bit key
  Triple DES (3-Key) uses 168 bits of the 192 bit key

Figure 3-7. SQL Server supported symmetric encryption algorithms

■ **Caution** SQL Server also has a DESX keyword, which is misleading. The DESX algorithm was misnamed andactually represents the Triple DES (3-Key) algorithm in SQL Server. Avoid using the DESX keyword; it is deprecated and will be removed in a future version of SQL Server.

In the following sections, I'll explore each of these algorithms and explain why each is more (or less) secure than others.

AES Family

AES was selected by the National Institute of Standards and Technology (NIST) as a Federal Information Processing Standard (FIPS) in May 2002. It is generally regarded as one of the most secure symmetric encryption algorithms available today—with its 192-bit and 256-bit key lengths it is even authorized to secure government information classified as Top Secret.

AES is a 128-bit block cipher with key lengths of 128, 192, and 256 bits. SQL Server supports all three AES encryption key lengths. Input plaintext is padded out to a length that is a multiple of 16 bytes using PKCS #7 style padding. The data is encrypted using cipher block chaining mode (CBC), with a random initialization vector (IV, or sometimes referred to as "salt") generated prior to encryption.

Padding and Chaining Mode

Encryption algorithms require you to pad out your plaintext data to the block length of the algorithm. For a 128-bit block cipher like AES this means the plaintext must be padded to a multiple of 16 bytes. If the plaintext is already a multiple of 16 bytes another 16 bytes of padding are added to the plaintext. There are several standard methods of padding plaintext, but the method used by SQL Server is known as PKCS #7. This method is described in RFC 2315. PKCS #7 works by first determining how many bytes short of a block length multiple you are. If you're using AES (block length = 128 bits or 16 bytes) and your plaintext is 13 bytes long, PKCS #7 pads the remaining 3 bytes with the value 0x03. This is shown in the illustration below.

Character Number	1	2	3	4	5	6	7	8	9	10	11	12	13	14	15	16
Plaintext	a	c	c	e	p	t	a	b	i	l	i	t	y	/	/	/
Hex Byte Value	0x61	0x63	0x63	0x65	0x70	0x74	0x61	0x62	0x69	0x6c	0x69	0x74	0x79	0x03	0x03	0x03

When SQL Server decrypts the ciphertext it automatically strips the padding values from the end of the data.

Cipher block chaining mode (CBC) refers to the method SQL Server uses to further obfuscate your encrypted text. In CBC encryption mode, SQL Server combines the previously encrypted ciphertext block with the current plaintext block (using reversible exclusive-or operations) before it encrypts the current block. The first block doesn't have a previous block to be combined with; instead, the random IV is combined with the first block. CBC mode helps further obfuscate your ciphertext.

Although the CryptoAPI that SQL Server relies on offers several padding options and block chaining modes, you cannot override, or turn off, the default modes that SQL Server uses.

You can use the AES_256, AES_192, or AES_128 keywords in the ALGORITHM clause of the CREATE SYMMETRIC KEY statement to create AES 256, 192, or 128-bit keys, respectively. The AES algorithm is fast and operates efficiently in memory.

AES performs a variable number of transformation rounds that convert plaintext into ciphertext. Each round consists of combinations of the following processing steps:

- *AddRoundKey*: each byte of a 4×4 matrix of bytes (the *state*) is combined with the round key, which is derived from the key using a key schedule.

- *SubBytes*: each byte is replaced with bytes in a lookup table in a nonlinear fashion.

- *ShiftRows*: each row of the state is shifted cyclically a specified number of steps.

- *MixColumns*: an operation that combines the four bytes in each column of the state.

Figure 3-8 shows a high-level overview of AES algorithm encryption.

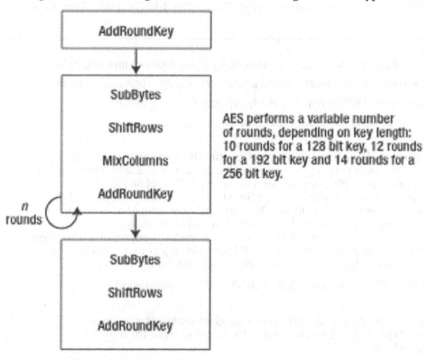

Figure 3-8. High-level AES encryption process

There are no known direct attacks on AES. In fact, the only successful attacks mounted against AES are so-called "side-channel" attacks. These attacks rely on information leaked by an AES implementation, such as timing information. Most known side-channel attacks require an intruder to install a virus or Trojan horse on your server to watch processes in real-time, or to have access to various metadata related to cache timings and so forth. To date, the integrity of the AES algorithm has not been compromised.

DES Family

The Data Encryption Standard (DES) algorithm was a US Government FIPS standard for nearly two decades, from 1976 to 2002. In the late 1990s, DES began to show its age as cryptanalysts began mounting successful attacks against it. DES is a 64-bit block cipher with a 56-bit key length—far shorter than the AES family of algorithms.

In 1999, Triple DES was introduced as a relatively quick fix for the flaws found in DES. Triple DES comes in two varieties, 2-key and 3-key. Triple DES implements an Encrypt-Decrypt-Encrypt pattern, in which the plaintext is first encrypted with a 56-bit key. Next, the ciphertext is decrypted with asecond 56-bit key. The final step is to encrypt the data again, with the first 56-bit key in the case of the 2-key algorithm, or with a third key when the 3-key variety is used.

You can use the TRIPLE_DES, TRIPLE_DES_3KEY, and DES keywords in the ALGORITHM clause of the CREATE SYMMETRIC KEY statement to choose the Triple DES 2-key, Triple DES 3-key, orDES algorithms.

■ **Caution** SQL Server also uses the keyword DESX, which is another DES variant algorithm invented by Ron Rivest of RSA fame. However, the keyword in SQL Server was misnamed, and actually represents Triple DES (3-key). The DESX keyword is deprecated and will be removed in a future version of SQL Server.

Triple DES 3-key has an actual key length of 168 bits, but its effective key security is estimated much lower, at around 112 bits. The 2-key version has an actual key length of 112 bits, but its effective key security is estimated at around 80 bits. Plain vanilla DES has a key length of 56 bits, but its effective key security has been estimated as low as 47 bits. Triple DES (2-key and 3-key) and DES all use CBC mode and PCKS #7 padding, as described in the *Padding and Chaining Mode* sidebar. DES and its variants operate quickly in hardware, but are less efficient in software implementations.

DES is a complex algorithm that relies on a Feistel function, which features encryption operations on alternating halves of a block of data in a crisscross fashion. DES processing consists of 16rounds of processing through the Feistel function. The Feistel function consists of the following steps:

- *Expansion*: a half-block (32-bits) is expanded to 48 bits using an *expansion permutation*.

- *Key mixing*: the result of the expansion step is combined with a subkey using a reversible exclusive-or operation. Sixteen 48-bit subkeys are derived from the main key using a key schedule.

- *Substitution*: the block is divided into eight 6-bit pieces and processed through the *substitution boxes*, or *S-boxes*. Each of the S-boxes replaces six input bits with four output bits via a nonlinear transformation.

- *Permutation*: the final step is to rearrange the 32 S-box outputs according to a fixed *permutation box*, or *P-box*.

Figure 3-9 provides a high-level overview of DES encryption processing. Triple DES requires three passes through the 16-round Feistel network.

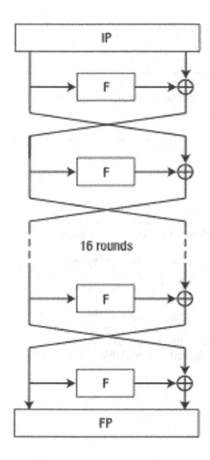

Figure 3-9. High-level DES encryption process

DES has proven vulnerable to direct attacks, including differential cryptanalysis, linear cryptanalysis, and even large-scale brute force attacks. I highly recommend avoiding plain old DES. TheTriple DES algorithms are considered much more secure. The NSA believes the 2-key variant willremain secure until 2030, and the 3-key variant beyond that date. If you must use a DES family algorithm, I highly recommend you use one of the Triple DES algorithms.

RC2 and RC4

The RC2 and RC4 algorithms were created by Ron Rivest of RSA Security in the late 1980s. RC2 is a 64-bit block cipher and RC4 is a stream cipher. You can specify these algorithms via the RC2, RC4, and RC4_128 keywords in the ALGORITHM clause of the CREATE SYMMETRIC KEY statement to choose RC2, RC4, or RC4 with a 128-bit key, respectively.

RC2 and RC4 are simple, and fast, encryption algorithms. Their speed does come with a price, however. RC4 is susceptible to a wide range of attacks and is not recommended for new development. In addition, the implementation of RC4 in SQL Server does not apply a random IV to each new encryption value, making it extremely vulnerable to attack. RC2 has proven vulnerable to related-key attacks. In light of the security considerations, I recommend avoiding the use of RC2 and RC4 encryption in your database.

■ **Caution** Microsoft has issued a warning not to use the RC4 and RC4_128 algorithms. These algorithms are currently deprecated and will be removed in a future version of SQL Server.

Summary

SQL Server 2008 provides access to several encryption algorithms, including support for AES, Triple DES,DES, and the RC2 and RC4 family of algorithms. The first step to using symmetric encryption in SQL Server is the creation of symmetric keys. In this chapter, I explained how to create and manage symmetric encryption keys.

SQL Server provides symmetric encryption functions, including EncryptByKey, DecryptByKey, EncryptByPassPhrase, and DecryptByPassPhrase. I spent most of the chapter discussing the use of these functions and their options to secure your data. In addition to protecting your data, I described how symmetric keys can be used to secure additional symmetric keys.

To round out the chapter, I discussed the various symmetric encryption algorithms available through SQL Server. I gave a brief history of each algorithm, provided an overview of the AES and DES algorithm processing, and explained the security concerns with using the RC2 and RC4 algorithms. In addition, I talked briefly about performance and security implications of the various algorithms available. . In the next chapter I'll begin an exploration of SQL Server asymmetric encryption

CHAPTER 4

■ ■ ■

Asymmetric Encryption

While symmetric encryption involves using the same key, or trivially related keys, for both encryption and decryption, asymmetric encryption uses two completely separate keys that are not trivially related. SQL Server supports asymmetric encryption through the widely used RSA algorithm. SQL Server implements asymmetric encryption through the use of asymmetric keys and certificates, both of which can be created on the server or created by an external source and then registered on the server. You can use asymmetric encryption to encrypt data, but Microsoft recommends the use of asymmetric keys and certificates to encrypt symmetric keys that encrypt data. In this chapter, I'll talk about how to create asymmetric keys and certificates to secure both your data and symmetric encryption keys.

Asymmetric Keys

SQL Server 2008 allows you to create and manage asymmetric keys to encrypt symmetric keys or data. Asymmetric keys, or more appropriately *asymmetric key pairs*, consist of two separate keys: a public key that is exposed to the world and a private key that is protected. The public key is the key that anyone can use to encrypt data with, while the mathematically-related private key is used to decrypt the same data. As I discussed in Chapter 1, the security of asymmetric encryption is dependent on the difficulty of calculating the relationship between the public and private keys. When you create an asymmetric key pair the private key is automatically protected by the DMK by default.

■ **Note** If the DMK does not exist, you must supply a password to protect the private key of the asymmetric key pair. If a DMK does exist, protection by password is optional.

Generating and Installing Asymmetric Keys

SQL Server allows you to install asymmetric key pairs that were generated outside of the server. You can install asymmetric keys from Strong-Name Key (SNK) files and executable files. As the first step to installing an asymmetric key on SQL Server, I'll generate an SNK file from the command-line using the sn.exe utility, as shown in Figure 4-1. The sn.exe utility is distributed with Visual Studio, and can be found in the bin subdirectory of the Visual Studio Software Development Kit (SDK).

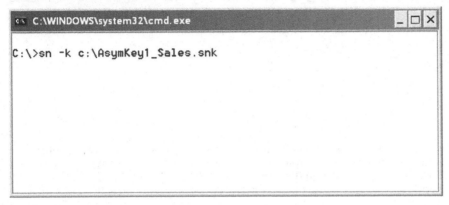

Figure 4-1. Creating a strong-name key file from the command-line

The SNK file generated by this statement at the command-line is named AsymKey1_Sales.snk. After you create this, the SNK file can use the CREATE ASYMMETRIC KEY statement to register its asymmetric key pair with SQL Server, as shown in Listing 4-1.

Listing 4-1. Creating an Asymmetric Key from an SNK File

```
CREATE ASYMMETRIC KEY AsymKey1_Sales
FROM FILE = N'c:\AsymKey1_Sales.snk';
```

■ **Tip** The CREATE ASYMMETRIC KEY statement in Listing 4-1 looks for the source file on the SQL Server box. That is to say the AsymKey1_Sales.snk file must exist on the same computer on which the SQL Server service is running.

Generating Asymmetric Keys on the Server

You can generate asymmetric keys directly on SQL Server, as shown in the code snippet below.

```
CREATE ASYMMETRIC KEY AsymKey2_Sales
WITH ALGORITHM = RSA_1024;
```

The WITH ALGORITHM clause allows you to specify RSA_512, RSA_1024, or RSA_2048, indicating the RSA algorithm with a private key length of 512, 1024, or 2048 bits, respectively. One interesting thing you'll notice about SQL Server asymmetric key functionality is the complete lack of statements to perform backups and restores of this type of key. Oddly, SQL Server provides no DML statements to export asymmetric keys generated on the server.

What this means is that using SQL Server DML to generate asymmetric keys on the server could conflict with your business interruption and disaster recovery plans. Why would you want to do this? The main reason would seem to be to allow developers to develop and test asymmetric key-based code without granting them direct access to your secure production asymmetric keys.

Because of this lack of ability to backup and restore individual asymmetric keys, I have to recommend against using SQL Server-generated asymmetric keys in a production environment or on any critical server. Registering externally-generated asymmetric key pairs with SQL Server is not a problem, however, since you can always backup the external asymmetric key pair source files.

■ **Tip** While you can't backup and restore individual asymmetric key pairs, you can backup and restore certificates. I'll discuss certificates in the Certificates section of this chapter. If you need to generate asymmetric key pairs within SQL Server for encryption, generate a certificate instead of an asymmetric key pair.

In addition to SNK files, you can register key pairs from executable files and public keys from registered CLR assemblies. Once the asymmetric key is created, you can use it to protect a symmetric key, as shown in Listing 4-2.

Listing 4-2. Protecting Symmetric Key with an Asymmetric Key

```
CREATE SYMMETRIC KEY SymKey6_Sales
WITH ALGORITHM = AES_256
ENCRYPTION BY ASYMMETRIC KEY AsymKey1_Sales;
```

As shown in Chapter 3, you can use the symmetric key to encrypt data. Listing 4-3 creates two sample tables that will hold customer credit card information—very important data to encrypt. The first table, SalesLT.CreditCardInfo, will be used to store unencrypted randomly generated credit card data. The second table, SalesLT.EncryptedCreditCardInfo, will hold encrypted versions of the same data.

Listing 4-3. Sample Table to Hold Credit Card Information

```
-- Nonencrypted credit card info
CREATE TABLE SalesLT. CreditCardInfo
(
  SalesOrderID int not null primary key,
  CreditCardNumber nvarchar(50),
  CreditCardExpirationDate datetime,
  TotalCharge money
);

-- Encrypted credit card info
CREATE TABLE SalesLT.EncryptedCreditCardInfo
(
  SalesOrderID int not null primary key,
  CreditCardNumber varbinary(150),
  CreditCardExpirationDate varbinary(150),
  TotalCharge varbinary(150)
);
```

Listing 4-4 populates the SalesLT.CreditCardInfo table with unencrypted randomly generated credit card data.

Listing 4-4. Generating Random Credit Card Information

```
WITH Generate4Digits /* Generate 4 random digits */
AS
(
  SELECT SUBSTRING
  (
    CAST
    (
      ABS(CHECKSUM(NEWID())) % 10000 AS NVARCHAR(4)
    ) + N'0000', 1, 4
  ) AS Digits
),
CardNum /* Generate a 16 digit random credit card number */
AS
(
  SELECT N'0999-' +
  (
    SELECT Digits
    FROM Generate4Digits
  ) + N'-' +
```

```
(
  SELECT Digits
  FROM Generate4Digits
) + N'-' +
(
  SELECT Digits
  FROM Generate4Digits
) AS CardNumber
),
AS
(
  SELECT ABS(CHECKSUM(NEWID()) % 700) AS Days
)
INSERT INTO SalesLT.CreditCardInfo
(
  SalesOrderID,
  CreditCardNumber,
  CreditCardExpirationDate,
  TotalCharge
)
SELECT
  SalesOrderID,
  CardNumber,
  DATEADD(DAY, Days, OrderDate),
  TotalDue
FROM SalesLT.SalesOrderHeader
CROSS APPLY CardNum
CROSS APPLY DaysToExpire;
```

The INSERT statement features common table expressions (CTEs) that use some interesting code to generate random sixteen digit credit card numbers and expiration dates. I won't dive deeply into the details of the CTEs, since they're just a vehicle to move the example forward. Just keep in mind that if you're interested in generating random test data, a combination of the CHECKSUM and NEWID functions is hard to beat. A quick query of the SalesLT.CreditCardInfo table shows that the confidential credit card data stored in it is not properly secured. Listing 4-5 queries the table and Figure 4-2 shows the unsecured result. Note that since this data is randomly generated your results from the following code samples will differ from those I produced.

Listing 4-5. Querying the Unsecured Credit Card Information

```
SELECT
  SalesOrderID,
  CreditCardNumber,
  CreditCardExpirationDate,
  TotalCharge
FROM SalesLT.CreditCardInfo;
```

	SalesOrderID	CreditCardNumber	CreditCardExpirationDate	TotalCharge
1	71774	0999-8034-9070-1442	2005-07-25 00:00:00.000	972.785
2	71776	0999-2999-9585-5790	2004-06-28 00:00:00.000	87.0851
3	71780	0999-8436-7205-8106	2006-01-15 00:00:00.000	42452.6519
4	71782	0999-7910-2449-4621	2005-08-09 00:00:00.000	43962.7901
5	71783	0999-3296-8427-4321	2005-07-30 00:00:00.000	92663.5609
6	71784	0999-8876-4235-4454	2005-10-01 00:00:00.000	119960.824
7	71796	0999-7683-7259-6143	2006-01-03 00:00:00.000	63686.2708
8	71797	0999-6151-1508-6591	2005-10-23 00:00:00.000	86222.8072
9	71815	0999-8535-8802-8219	2005-12-21 00:00:00.000	1261.444
10	71816	0999-2654-3820-6088	2005-05-22 00:00:00.000	3754.9733
11	71831	0999-2304-4508-2660	2004-08-16 00:00:00.000	2228.0566
12	71832	0999-9544-5887-5401	2005-03-11 00:00:00.000	39531.6085
13	71845	0999-8199-9484-6384	2004-09-10 00:00:00.000	45992.3665
14	71846	0999-4042-5079-7682	2005-05-25 00:00:00.000	2711.4098
15	71856	0999-5958-6826-5167	2005-12-18 00:00:00.000	665.4251

Figure 4-2. Unencrypted credit card data stored in the database

Now that I've registered the asymmetric key pair with SQL Server, created a symmetric key that is protected by this asymmetric key, and populated a table with random sample data it's time to secure the customers' sensitive credit card data.

Encrypting Data

After the setup in the previous section, it's time to encrypt the sample data. Listing 4-6 populates thesample table with encrypted random credit card information using the previously created SymKey6_Sales symmetric key, which is protected by the AsymKey1_Sales asymmetric key.

Listing 4-6. Populate the Table with Encrypted Credit Card Data

```
-- Wipe out the sample data in the table
TRUNCATE TABLE SalesLT.EncryptedCreditCardInfo;
GO

-- Open symmetric data encrypting key
OPEN SYMMETRIC KEY SymKey6_Sales
DECRYPTION BY ASYMMETRIC KEY AsymKey1_Sales;

-- Encrypt sample random credit card data
INSERT INTO SalesLT.EncryptedCreditCardInfo
```

```
(
  SalesOrderID,
  CreditCardNumber,
  CreditCardExpirationDate,
  TotalCharge
)
SELECT
  SalesOrderID,
  EncryptByKey(Key_Guid(N'SymKey6_Sales'), CreditCardNumber),
  EncryptByKey(Key_Guid(N'SymKey6_Sales'), CAST
    (
      CreditCardExpirationDate AS varbinary(10)
    )
  ),
  EncryptByKey(Key_Guid(N'SymKey6_Sales'), CAST
    (
      TotalCharge AS varbinary(10)
    )
  )
FROM SalesLT.CreditCardInfo;

-- Close data encrypting key
CLOSE SYMMETRIC KEY SymKey6_Sales;
```

This sample first truncates the target table and then opens the symmetric key I'm going to use to encrypt the test data, as shown in the following code snippet.

```
-- Wipe out the sample data in the table
TRUNCATE TABLE SalesLT.EncryptedCreditCardInfo;
GO

-- Open symmetric data encrypting key
OPEN SYMMETRIC KEY SymKey6_Sales
DECRYPTION BY ASYMMETRIC KEY AsymKey1_Sales;
```

■ **Note** Opening the encryption key before you attempt to use it is very important. If you don't first open the encryption key you won't get an error message, but you will get NULL as a result of every encryption or decryption performed with that key.

Next is the INSERT statement that encrypts the source credit card data and stores it in the SalesLT.EncryptedCardInfo table, as shown in the following code.

```
-- Encrypt sample random credit card data
INSERT INTO SalesLT.EncryptedCreditCardInfo
(
  SalesOrderID,
  CreditCardNumber,
  CreditCardExpirationDate,
  TotalCharge
)
SELECT
  SalesOrderID,
  EncryptByKey(Key_Guid(N'SymKey6_Sales'), CreditCardNumber),
  EncryptByKey(Key_Guid(N'SymKey6_Sales'), CAST
    (
      CreditCardExpirationDate AS varbinary(10)
    )
  ),
  EncryptByKey(Key_Guid(N'SymKey6_Sales'), CAST
    (
      TotalCharge AS varbinary(10)
    )
  )
)
FROM SalesLT.CreditCardInfo;
```

One important thing to notice about this query is that the EncryptByKey function cannot accept columns, variables, or values of the integer, money, or datetime data types for its second parameter (the plaintext to encrypt). Just keep in mind that the EncryptByKey function's second parameter is actually a varbinary parameter. If you want to encrypt data that is of a data type that cannot be implicitly converted to varbinary you must explicitly cast it to varbinary yourself, as shown in the sample.

In this example, I encrypted not only the credit card identifying information, but also the TotalCharge column. While you don't necessarily have to encrypt every column in a table, my purpose for encrypting this column is twofold. First, I wanted to demonstrate that you can encrypt almost any data type (in this case the money data type) by first casting it to varbinary. The second purpose was to demonstrate that in some cases you might want to encrypt additional columns that might "leak" information to cryptanalysts. A cryptanalyst might have knowledge of a particular credit card number and a specific total charge amount associated with it in advance. In this case, he would have a known plaintext and he could use the TotalCharge values to considerably narrow the potential ciphertexts he needs to attack. Whether the additional data in a table leaks useful information to a cryptanalyst is something that should be considered carefully when designing your encryption solution.

In the final step of the encryption example, the symmetric key is closed, as shown in the following code snippet.

```
-- Close data encrypting key
CLOSE SYMMETRIC KEY SymKey6_Sales;
```

After executing the sample code in Listing 4-6, you can query the table to see the encrypted data, as shown in Figure 4-3.

	SalesOrderID	CreditCardNumber	CreditCardExpirationD...	TotalCharge	
1	71774	0x00A9221F0644664C9F82F67A77E70D5B01000000960507931CCE8306...	0x00A9221F0644664...	0x00A9221F0644664...	
2	71776	0x00A9221F0644664C9F82F67A77E70D5B01000000584014E8718A4E6E...	0x00A9221F0644664...	0x00A9221F0644664...	
3	71780	0x00A9221F0644664C9F82F67A77E70D5B01000000EB8813FD8837AAF...	0x00A9221F0644664...	0x00A9221F0644664...	
4	71782	0x00A9221F0644664C9F82F67A77E70D5B010000002BB0B04B8206BA0...	0x00A9221F0644664...	0x00A9221F0644664...	
5	71783	0x00A9221F0644664C9F82F67A77E70D5B010000003E04B969EC90B7E...	0x00A9221F0644664...	0x00A9221F0644664...	
6	71784	0x00A9221F0644664C9F82F67A77E70D5B0100000036BAE86EF5D76B5...	0x00A9221F0644664...	0x00A9221F0644664...	
7	71796	0x00A9221F0644664C9F82F67A77E70D5B010000002F3D55AE1448AAC...	0x00A9221F0644664...	0x00A9221F0644664...	
8	71797	0x00A9221F0644664C9F82F67A77E70D5B010000005E8B2A8CA9BE70A...	0x00A9221F0644664...	0x00A9221F0644664...	
9	71815	0x00A9221F0644664C9F82F67A77E70D5B01000000F1FEF059316209F9...	0x00A9221F0644664...	0x00A9221F0644664...	
10	71816	0x00A9221F0644664C9F82F67A77E70D5B010000009741F91C25E8BE63...	0x00A9221F0644664...	0x00A9221F0644664...	
11	71831	0x00A9221F0644664C9F82F67A77E70D5B01000000DD8070CED8B8868...	0x00A9221F0644664...	0x00A9221F0644664...	
12	71832	0x00A9221F0644664C9F82F67A77E70D5B010000008DD209403BFBBA8...	0x00A9221F0644664...	0x00A9221F0644664...	
13	71845	0x00A9221F0644664C9F82F67A77E70D5B010000003F367DAA2C0F613...	0x00A9221F0644664...	0x00A9221F0644664...	
14	71846	0x00A9221F0644664C9F82F67A77E70D5B010000005CB8C2E1B1ECAF4...	0x00A9221F0644664...	0x00A9221F0644664...	
15	71856	0x00A9221F0644664C9F82F67A77E70D5B01000000CC51DC3371AF5DF...	0x00A9221F0644664...	0x00A9221F0644664...	

Figure 4-3. Encrypted credit card data

As you can see, the encryption process has rendered the sensitive credit card information unreadable. To decrypt the credit card information, you have to open the symmetric key again, specifying the asymmetric key in the DECRYPTION BY clause. Then, as in Chapter 3, simply use the DecryptByKey function (with some explicit data type casting) to decrypt the result and make it readable again. Listing 4-7 demonstrates the decryption process.

Listing 4-7. Decrypting Sensitive Credit Card Information

```
-- Open symmetric data encrypting key
OPEN SYMMETRIC KEY SymKey6_Sales
DECRYPTION BY ASYMMETRIC KEY AsymKey1_Sales;

-- Decrypt previously encrypted credit card data
SELECT
  SalesOrderID,
  CAST
  (
    DecryptByKey(CreditCardNumber) AS nvarchar(100)
  ) AS CreditCardNumber,
  CAST
  (
    DecryptByKey(CreditCardExpirationDate) AS datetime
  ) AS CreditCardExpirationDate,
  CAST
  (
    DecryptByKey(TotalCharge) AS money
  ) AS TotalDue
FROM SalesLT.EncryptedCreditCardInfo;

-- Close data encrypting key
CLOSE SYMMETRIC KEY SymKey6_Sales;
```

Protecting Asymmetric Keys with Passwords

By default when you create an asymmetric key, SQL Server uses the DMK to protect the private key of the asymmetric key pair. You can optionally add protection by password to your asymmetric key pair's private key, in the CREATE ASYMMETRIC KEY statement or with the ALTER ASYMMETRIC KEY statement. Listing 4-8 uses ALTER ASYMMETRIC KEY to add password encryption to the AsymKey1_Sales private key.

Listing 4-8. Adding Password Encryption to the Asymmetric Key

```
ALTER ASYMMETRIC KEY AsymKey1_Sales
WITH PRIVATE KEY (ENCRYPTION BY PASSWORD = N'%ui!@90~p');
```

Using Password-Protected Asymmetric Keys

If you add encryption by password to your asymmetric key, you can specify the password as a third parameter in calls to the DecryptByAsymKey function. You can't specify the password in calls to the EncryptByAsymKey function though. This means SQL Server still has to protect the private key of the asymmetric key pair with the DMK. It was an unusual choice to provide password protection for your asymmetric keys, yet disallow use of the password during the encryption process.

When you secure an asymmetric key by password you can use the DecryptByKeyAutoAsymKey function to decrypt data that is protected by symmetric key when the asymmetric key is protected by password. The DecryptByAutoKeyAsymKey function is like the DecryptByAsymKey function, except that it automatically opens and closes the necessary symmetric key for you. Listing 4-9 demonstrates the use of this function.

Listing 4-9. Decrypting By Symmetric Key with Auto Asymmetric Key

```
-- Decrypt previously encrypted credit card data
SELECT
  SalesOrderID,
  CAST
  (
    DecryptByKeyAutoAsymKey
      (
        AsymKey_ID(N'AsymKey1_Sales'),
        N'%ui!@90~p',
        CreditCardNumber
      ) AS nvarchar(100)
  ) AS CreditCardNumber
FROM SalesLT.EncryptedCreditCardInfo;
```

You can also remove the encryption by password by using the DECRYPTION BY PASSWORD clause of the ALTER ASYMMETRIC KEY statement, without the ENCRYPTION BY PASSWORD clause, as shown in Listing 4-10. When you use the DECRYPTION BY PASSWORD clause you specify the old password that was used to protect the private key. By not including a new ENCRYPTION BY PASSWORD clause, SQL Server removes password protection from the private key.

Listing 4-10. Removing Password Encryption from the Asymmetric Key

```
ALTER ASYMMETRIC KEY AsymKey1_Sales
WITH PRIVATE KEY (DECRYPTION BY PASSWORD = N'%ui!@90~p')
```

Encrypting Data Directly with Asymmetric Keys

Asymmetric keys are designed to protect symmetric keys, which in turn protect your data. As discussed in Chapter 1, the reason is that asymmetric encryption is resource intensive and relatively slow when compared with symmetric encryption. Encrypting large chunks of data with asymmetric encryption can be a long and slow process. For completeness in its encryption toolset, however, SQL Server does provide this capability. You may have reason to encrypt small amounts of data using asymmetric encryption, though it's recommended that you save asymmetric keys for protecting symmetric keys. Listing 4-11 modifies Listing 4-6 to use the EncryptByAutoAsymKey function to encrypt the random credit card data.

Listing 4-11. Encrypting Data with an Asymmetric Key

```
-- Wipe out the sample data in the table
TRUNCATE TABLE SalesLT.EncryptedCreditCardInfo;
GO

-- Encrypt sample random credit card data
INSERT INTO SalesLT.EncryptedCreditCardInfo
(
  SalesOrderID,
  CreditCardNumber,
  CreditCardExpirationDate,
  TotalCharge
)
SELECT
  SalesOrderID,
  EncryptByAsymKey(AsymKey_ID(N'AsymKey1_Sales'), CreditCardNumber),
  EncryptByAsymKey(AsymKey_ID(N'AsymKey1_Sales'), CAST
    (
      CreditCardExpirationDate AS varbinary(10)
    )
  ),
  EncryptByAsymKey(AsymKey_ID(N'AsymKey1_Sales'), CAST
    (
      TotalCharge AS varbinary(10)
    )
  )
FROM SalesLT.CreditCardInfo;
```

When comparing this code to Listing 4-6, one of the first things you might notice is the lack of OPEN and CLOSE statements for the asymmetric key. They're not necessary. The partial code snippet that follows is the SELECT query that performs the actual encryption.

```
...
SELECT
  SalesOrderID,
  EncryptByAsymKey(AsymKey_ID(N'AsymKey1_Sales'), CreditCardNumber),
  EncryptByAsymKey(AsymKey_ID(N'AsymKey1_Sales'), CAST
    (
      CreditCardExpirationDate AS varbinary(10)
    )
  ),
  EncryptByAsymKey(AsymKey_ID(N'AsymKey1_Sales'), CAST
    (
      TotalCharge AS varbinary(10)
    )
  )
FROM SalesLT.CreditCardInfo;
```

You'll notice that Listing 4-11, unlike Listing 4-6, uses the EncryptByAsymKey function to encrypt the data directly using the asymmetric key. The EncryptByAsymKey function accepts the ID of the asymmetric key and the plaintext to encrypt. The asymmetric key ID is retrieved in the code sample by passing the name of the key to the Asymkey_Id function. As with the EncryptByKey symmetric encryption function, the second parameter of the EncryptByAsymKey function is the plaintext to encrypt in varbinary format.

SQL Server supplies the DecryptByAsymKey function to decrypt data that was previously encrypted by asymmetric key. Unlike the symmetric key DecryptByKey function where you only have to pass in the encrypted ciphertext to get a decryption, with DecryptByAsymKey you must pass in both the asymmetric key ID and the encrypted ciphertext, as shown in Listing 4-12 (modifying Listing 4-7).

Listing 4-12. Decrypting Sensitive Credit Card Data with an Asymmetric Key

```
-- Decrypt the credit card info with asymmetric key
SELECT
  SalesOrderID,
  CAST
  (
    DecryptByAsymKey
    (
      Asymkey_Id(N'AsymKey1_Sales'), CreditCardNumber
    ) AS nvarchar(100)
  ) AS CreditCardNumber,
  CAST
  (
    DecryptByAsymKey
    (
      Asymkey_Id(N'AsymKey1_Sales'), CreditCardExpirationDate
    ) AS datetime
  ) AS CreditCardExpirationDate,
  CAST
  (
    DecryptByAsymKey
```

```
(
    Asymkey_Id(N'AsymKey1_Sales'), TotalCharge
) AS money
) AS TotalCharge
FROM SalesLT.EncryptedCreditCardInfo;
```

Removing the Private Key

You can use the ALTER ASYMMETRIC KEY statement to remove the private key from your asymmetric key pair. The implication is that you'll be able to encrypt data with your asymmetric key, but you won't be able to decrypt it. Why would you want to do this? One scenario is if you want to encrypt data for storage on a server, but you don't want it decrypted on the same server. In those cases, you can use the same asymmetric key pair (with private key, of course) on a different server—possibly another SQL Server, web server, or application server—to decrypt the data away from the SQL Server where the data is actually stored. Listing 4-13 removes the private key from the previously created asymmetric key.

Listing 4-13. Removing the Private Key from an Asymmetric Key Pair

```
ALTER ASYMMETRIC KEY AsymKey1_Sales
REMOVE PRIVATE KEY;
```

■ **Tip** You can use the asymmetric key pair's public key, which is not encrypted by password or the DMK, to encrypt data. To encrypt data with the public key you don't even have to open the asymmetric key first. To decrypt the data, however, you have to access the private key of the asymmetric, which means you have to open the asymmetric key.

Certificates

A certificate is simply an asymmetric public key or public and private key pair with additional metadata attached. Certificates have a standardized format, as defined by the X.509 standard. SQL Server provides the ability to install certificates issued by a certification authority (CA) or to generate self-signed certificates. I've already used a self-signed certificate in sample code from Chapter 3 so now I'll discuss SQL Server certificate support in detail.

Creating Certificates

Before I begin the discussion of creating and registering certificates, I'll set up a table to hold encrypted customer address information. Listing 4-14 creates this table.

Listing 4-14. Create a Table to Hold Encrypted Address Information

```
CREATE TABLE SalesLT.EncryptedAddress
(
  AddressID int NOT NULL PRIMARY KEY,
  AddressLine1 varbinary(256) NOT NULL,
  AddressLine2 varbinary(256) NULL,
  City varbinary(256) NOT NULL,
  StateProvince varbinary(256) NOT NULL,
  CountryRegion varbinary(256) NOT NULL,
  PostalCode varbinary(256) NOT NULL,
  rowguid uniqueidentifier NOT NULL,
  ModifiedDate datetime NOT NULL
);
```

The next step is to create and register your certificate with SQL Server. You can register certificates issued from outside of SQL Server with a SQL Server instance. Figure 4-4 uses the Visual Studio makecert.exe utility to create a self-signed certificate from the command-line. Table 1-1 lists the command-line options I used with the utility to generate the certificate.

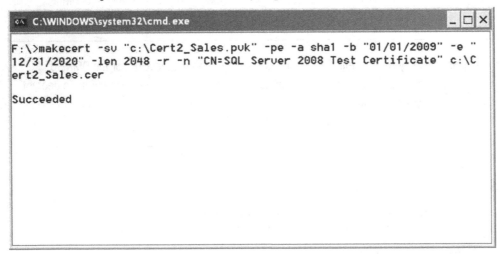

Figure 4-4. Using makecert.exe to create a self-signed certificate

Table 4-1. Commonly Used Options for makecert.exe

Option	Description
-sv	Specifies the private key file. If the private key file doesn't exist it is created automatically.
-pe	Makes the private key exportable.
-a	Specifies the signature algorithm. This must be sha1 or md5, with a default of md5.
-b	Sets the beginning or start date of the certificate's validity period.
-e	Sets the end date of the certificate's validity period.
-len	Specifies the generated private key length.
-r	Creates a self-signed certificate.
-n	Sets the certificate name (SQL Server uses this as the certificate subject).
filename	Name of the certificate file.

■ **Tip** The makecert utility is a separate .NET SDK utility, and its command-line options are subject to change without warning. For an up-to-date list of makecert options, see the "Certificate Creation Tool (Makecert.exe)" topic in the MSDN library at http://msdn.microsoft.com.

In the example makecert.exe call, I produced a self-signed certificate named Sales2_Cert.cer with its private key stored in a file named Sales2_Cert.pvk. When you create a certificate with makecert.exe and export a private key, the utility will ask you to enter a password. The password is used to encrypt the private key. For this example, I used a password of '*t$%0p}gl*'. You'll need the password you use to encrypt the private key again when you register the certificate with SQL Server.

Once you've created a self-signed certificate (or once you've had a certificate issued by a CA), you'll need to register it with SQL Server. Listing 4-15 is the CREATE CERTIFICATE statement needed to register the newly created certificate with SQL Server.

Listing 4-15. Registering a Certificate File with SQL Server

```
CREATE CERTIFICATE Cert2_Sales
FROM FILE = N'c:\Cert2_Sales.cer'
WITH PRIVATE KEY
(
  FILE = N'c:\Cert2_Sales.pvk',
  DECRYPTION BY PASSWORD = N't$%0p}gI'
);
```

This `CREATE CERTIFICATE` statement specifies the certificate file as the source for the publickey and certificate metadata (Cert2_Sales.cer) and the private key file (Cert2_Sales.pvk). The `DECRYPTION BY PASSWORD` clause contains the password previously entered to encrypt the private key file. Once you've created or acquired your certificate and private key files, you should immediately store a backup in a secure off-site facility.

■ **Tip** Private keys imported from external sources must have a length between 384 and 3,456 bits, in multiples of 64 bits.

Creating SQL Server Self-Signed Certificates

In addition to registering externally issued certificates with SQL Server, you can also create self-signed certificates directly inside SQL Server with the `CREATE CERTIFICATE` statement. SQL Server self-signed certificates are a much better option than SQL Server-generated asymmetric keys. Certificates provide all of the asymmetric encryption functionality of asymmetric keys, but have the advantage of backup and restore capabilities built right into T-SQL. To create a self-signed certificate on SQL Server you can issue a `CREATE CERTIFICATE` statement, like the one in Listing 4-16.

Listing 4-16. Creating a Self-Signed Certificate in SQL Server

```
CREATE CERTIFICATE Cert3_Sales
WITH SUBJECT = N'SQL Server 2008 Test Certificate 3',
START_DATE = '20090101',
EXPIRY_DATE = '20201231';
```

Self-signed certificates generated in this way always automatically have a 1024-bit private key. By default the private key is protected by the DMK, although you can override this behavior with the `ENCRYPTION BY PASSWORD` clause. If you don't have a DMK installed, you have to specify a password.

■ **Tip** You can set the start and expiration dates of the certificate, but the built-in encryption functions don't enforce these time limits. It's up to the administrators and developers to determine whether an encryption operation should or should not occur based on the specified time limits.

Encrypting Data

The primary need for certificates in SQL Server data encryption, as with asymmetric keys, is to secure symmetric keys. Listing 4-17 creates a symmetric key protected by the certificate I created in the previous section.

Listing 4-17. Protecting a Symmetric Key with a Certificate

```
CREATE SYMMETRIC KEY SymKey7_Sales
WITH ALGORITHM = AES_256
ENCRYPTION BY CERTIFICATE Cert2_Sales;
```

Using a symmetric key that's protected by a certificate is very similar to using one that's protected by asymmetric key. Listing 4-18 uses the SymKey7_Sales key to encrypt the random customer address data from the SalesLT.Address table.

Listing 4-18. Encrypting Data with a Symmetric Key Protected by Certificate

```
-- Wipe out the sample data in the table
TRUNCATE TABLE SalesLT.EncryptedAddress;
GO

-- Open symmetric data encrypting key
OPEN SYMMETRIC KEY SymKey7_Sales
DECRYPTION BY CERTIFICATE Cert2_Sales;

-- Encrypt sample random credit card data
INSERT INTO SalesLT.EncryptedAddress
(
  AddressID,
  AddressLine1,
  AddressLine2,
  City,
  StateProvince,
  CountryRegion,
  PostalCode,
  rowguid,
  ModifiedDate
)
SELECT
  AddressID,
  EncryptByKey(Key_Guid(N'SymKey7_Sales'), AddressLine1),
  EncryptByKey(Key_Guid(N'SymKey7_Sales'), AddressLine2),
  EncryptByKey(Key_Guid(N'SymKey7_Sales'), City),
  EncryptByKey(Key_Guid(N'SymKey7_Sales'), StateProvince),
  EncryptByKey(Key_Guid(N'SymKey7_Sales'), CountryRegion),
  EncryptByKey(Key_Guid(N'SymKey7_Sales'), PostalCode),
  rowguid,
  ModifiedDate
FROM SalesLT.Address;
```

```
-- Close data encrypting key
CLOSE SYMMETRIC KEY SymKey7_Sales;
```

As with the asymmetric key examples, you simply open the symmetric key that's protected by certificate and use the EncryptByKey function to encrypt the data. Listing 4-19 queries the encrypted data, so you can verify the encryption worked properly, as shown in Figure 4-5.

Listing 4-19. Querying the Encrypted Addresses

```
SELECT
  AddressID,
  AddressLine1,
  AddressLine2,
  City,
  StateProvince,
  CountryRegion,
  PostalCode,
  rowguid,
  ModifiedDate
FROM SalesLT.EncryptedAddress;
```

	AddressID	AddressLine1	AddressLin...	City	StateProvince
1	9	0x00488B2D3817D44BAA7A703D9E951...	NULL	0x00488B2D3817D44BAA7A703D9E9510...	0x00488B2D3817D44BAA7.
2	11	0x00488B2D3817D44BAA7A703D9E951...	NULL	0x00488B2D3817D44BAA7A703D9E9510...	0x00488B2D3817D44BAA7.
3	25	0x00488B2D3817D44BAA7A703D9E951...	NULL	0x00488B2D3817D44BAA7A703D9E9510...	0x00488B2D3817D44BAA7.
4	28	0x00488B2D3817D44BAA7A703D9E951...	NULL	0x00488B2D3817D44BAA7A703D9E9510...	0x00488B2D3817D44BAA7.
5	32	0x00488B2D3817D44BAA7A703D9E951...	NULL	0x00488B2D3817D44BAA7A703D9E9510...	0x00488B2D3817D44BAA7.
6	185	0x00488B2D3817D44BAA7A703D9E951...	NULL	0x00488B2D3817D44BAA7A703D9E9510...	0x00488B2D3817D44BAA7.
7	297	0x00488B2D3817D44BAA7A703D9E951...	NULL	0x00488B2D3817D44BAA7A703D9E9510...	0x00488B2D3817D44BAA7.
8	445	0x00488B2D3817D44BAA7A703D9E951...	NULL	0x00488B2D3817D44BAA7A703D9E9510...	0x00488B2D3817D44BAA7.
9	446	0x00488B2D3817D44BAA7A703D9E951...	NULL	0x00488B2D3817D44BAA7A703D9E9510...	0x00488B2D3817D44BAA7.
10	447	0x00488B2D3817D44BAA7A703D9E951...	NULL	0x00488B2D3817D44BAA7A703D9E9510...	0x00488B2D3817D44BAA7.
11	448	0x00488B2D3817D44BAA7A703D9E951...	NULL	0x00488B2D3817D44BAA7A703D9E9510...	0x00488B2D3817D44BAA7.
12	449	0x00488B2D3817D44BAA7A703D9E951...	NULL	0x00488B2D3817D44BAA7A703D9E9510...	0x00488B2D3817D44BAA7.
13	450	0x00488B2D3817D44BAA7A703D9E951...	NULL	0x00488B2D3817D44BAA7A703D9E9510...	0x00488B2D3817D44BAA7.
14	451	0x00488B2D3817D44BAA7A703D9E951...	NULL	0x00488B2D3817D44BAA7A703D9E9510...	0x00488B2D3817D44BAA7.

Figure 4-5. Previewing encrypted customer address data

Decrypting the encrypted data requires the DecryptByKey function, as shown in Listing 4-20. Results are shown in Figure 4-6.

Listing 4-20. Decrypting Customer Address Data

```
-- Open symmetric data encrypting key
OPEN SYMMETRIC KEY SymKey7_Sales
DECRYPTION BY CERTIFICATE Cert2_Sales;

-- Decrypt sample random credit card data
SELECT
```

```
AddressID,
CAST(DecryptByKey(AddressLine1) AS nvarchar(60)),
CAST(DecryptByKey(AddressLine2) AS nvarchar(60)),
CAST(DecryptByKey(City) AS nvarchar(30)),
CAST(DecryptByKey(StateProvince) AS nvarchar(50)),
CAST(DecryptByKey(CountryRegion) AS nvarchar(50)),
CAST(DecryptByKey(PostalCode) AS nvarchar(15)),
rowguid,
ModifiedDate
FROM SalesLT.EncryptedAddress;

-- Close data encrypting key
CLOSE SYMMETRIC KEY SymKey7_Sales;
```

	AddressID	(No column name)	(No column na...	(No column na...	(No column na...	(No column na...	(No column na...	rowguid
1	9	8713 Yosemite Ct.	NULL	Bothell	Washington	United States	98011	268AF621
2	11	1318 Lasalle Street	NULL	Bothell	Washington	United States	98011	981B3303
3	25	9178 Jumping St.	NULL	Dallas	Texas	United States	75201	C8DF3BD!
4	28	9228 Via Del Sol	NULL	Phoenix	Arizona	United States	85004	12AE5EE'
5	32	26910 Indela Road	NULL	Montreal	Quebec	Canada	H1Y 2H5	84A95F62
6	185	2681 Eagle Peak	NULL	Bellevue	Washington	United States	98004	7BCCF442
7	297	7943 Walnut Ave	NULL	Renton	Washington	United States	98055	52410DA4
8	445	6388 Lake City Way	NULL	Burnaby	British Columbia	Canada	V5A 3A6	53572F25
9	446	52560 Free Street	NULL	Toronto	Ontario	Canada	M4B 1V7	801A1DFC
10	447	22580 Free Street	NULL	Toronto	Ontario	Canada	M4B 1V7	88CEE379
11	448	2575 Bloor Street East	NULL	Toronto	Ontario	Canada	M4B 1V6	2DF6D0AI
12	449	Station E	NULL	Chalk Riber	Ontario	Canada	K0J 1J0	8B5A7729
13	450	575 Rue St Amable	NULL	Quebec	Quebec	Canada	G1R	5F3C345A
14	451	2512-4th Ave Sw	NULL	Calgary	Alberta	Canada	T2P 2G8	49644F1E

Figure 4-6. Decrypted customer address data

As with asymmetric keys, certificates also provide an auto-decryption function: DecryptByKeyAutoCert. This function accepts the certificate ID, plaintext, and a certificate password for certificates that are protected by password. The advantage of this function is that it eliminates the need to explicitly open and close your symmetric key.

Encrypting Data Directly with Certificates

You can use certificates to encrypt data directly, although it's not recommended. Because certificates implement asymmetric encryption, it's a costly operation on large quantities of data. However, as with asymmetric keys, SQL Server provides the option for those times when it might be necessary. Listing 4-21 encrypts the customer address data directly with the previously created certificate.

Listing 4-21. Encrypting Data Directly with a Certificate

```
-- Wipe out the sample data in the table
TRUNCATE TABLE SalesLT.EncryptedAddress;
GO
```

```
-- Encrypt sample random credit card data
INSERT INTO SalesLT.EncryptedAddress
(
  AddressID,
  AddressLine1,
  AddressLine2,
  City,
  StateProvince,
  CountryRegion,
  PostalCode,
  rowguid,
  ModifiedDate
)
SELECT
  AddressID,
  EncryptByCert(Cert_ID(N'Cert2_Sales'), AddressLine1),
  EncryptByCert(Cert_ID(N'Cert2_Sales'), AddressLine2),
  EncryptByCert(Cert_ID(N'Cert2_Sales'), City),
  EncryptByCert(Cert_ID(N'Cert2_Sales'), StateProvince),
  EncryptByCert(Cert_ID(N'Cert2_Sales'), CountryRegion),
  EncryptByCert(Cert_ID(N'Cert2_Sales'), PostalCode),
  rowguid,
  ModifiedDate
FROM SalesLT.Address;
```

The EncryptByCert function accepts a certificate ID and plaintext to encrypt. The Cert_ID function retrieves the ID of a certificate by name. As with encryption by asymmetric key, you don't have to open and close a certificate to perform encryption and decryption with it. The DecryptByCert function will decrypt the data for you, as shown in Listing 4-22.

Listing 4-22. Decryption by Certificate

```
SELECT
  AddressID,
  CAST
  (
    DecryptByCert(Cert_ID(N'Cert2_Sales'), AddressLine1) AS nvarchar(60)
  ),
  CAST
  (
    DecryptByCert(Cert_ID(N'Cert2_Sales'), AddressLine2) AS nvarchar(60)
  ),
  CAST
  (
    DecryptByCert(Cert_ID(N'Cert2_Sales'), City) AS nvarchar(30)
  ),
  CAST
  (
    DecryptByCert(Cert_ID(N'Cert2_Sales'), StateProvince) AS nvarchar(50)
  ),
  CAST
```

```
(
  DecryptByCert(Cert_ID(N'Cert2_Sales'), CountryRegion) AS nvarchar(50)
),
CAST
(
  DecryptByCert(Cert_ID(N'Cert2_Sales'), PostalCode) AS nvarchar(15)
),
rowguid,
ModifiedDate
FROM SalesLT.EncryptedAddress;
```

■ **Tip** You may notice when running the decryption query that it can take a considerable amount of time to decrypt just a few hundred rows of data. This is normal for asymmetric encryption and decryption, which is why it's not recommended for large amounts of data.

As with asymmetric keys, you can remove the private key from the certificate's asymmetric keypair with the ALTER CERTIFICATE statement. If you do this, you'll be able to encrypt data with the certificate, but you won't be able to decrypt the data with the same certificate on the same SQL Server. You'll have to decrypt data away from the SQL server, possibly in a client application or on another server with the private key.

You can also use ALTER CERTIFICATE to configure your certificate for use with SQL Server Service Broker with the WITH ACTIVE FOR BEGIN_DIALOG clause. You can also add encryption by password to your certificate with the ENCRYPTION BY PASSWORD clause.

Backing Up Certificates

From an administrative perspective, perhaps the biggest advantage that server-generated self-signed certificates have over asymmetric keys is the ability to perform backups and restores. SQL Server provides the BACKUP CERTIFICATE statement to export a self-signed certificate to a backup file. Listing 4-23 demonstrates how to backup the Cert3_Sales certificate previously created in this chapter.

Listing 4-23. Backing Up a Certificate

```
BACKUP CERTIFICATE Cert3_Sales
TO FILE = N'c:\Cert3_Sales.cer'
WITH PRIVATE KEY
(
  FILE = N'c:\Cert3_Sales.pvk',
  ENCRYPTION BY PASSWORD = N'@oo$k3-9!'
);
```

The BACKUP CERTIFICATE statement takes the name of the file to export the certificate public key and metadata to in the TO FILE clause. The WITH PRIVATE KEY clause allows you to specify a file to export the certificate's private key to. If you export the private key you must also specify the password you want to use to encrypt the file in the ENCRYPTION BY PASSWORD clause. You'll need to store this password securely since you'll need it to restore the certificate later.

After you make a backup of your certificate and private key, get it onto external backup media and store it in a secure off-site facility. Delete the backup files from your local computer immediately.

There is no dedicated restore statement for certificates, per se. To restore a previously backed-up certificate use the CREATE CERTIFICATE statement, as shown in Listing 4-24. The statement in this listing restores the previously backed-up certificate. In order for this certificate to be restored as Cert3_Sales, you need to first drop the existing certificate.

Listing 4-24. *Restoring a Backedup Certificate*

```
DROP CERTIFICATE Cert3_Sales;
GO

CREATE CERTIFICATE Cert3_Sales
FROM FILE = N'c:\Cert3_Sales.cer'
WITH PRIVATE KEY
(
  FILE = N'c:\Cert3_Sales.pvk',
  DECRYPTION BY PASSWORD = N'@oo$k3-9!'
);
```

Digital Signatures

One of the challenges of storing digital data is validating its authenticity. How can you be certain that the data hasn't been tampered with? SQL Server provides two functions to digitally sign your data. The SignByCert function accepts a certificate ID and varbinary data to be signed. The function returns a varbinary signature. Listing 4-25 uses the previously created Cert1_Sales certificate to sign the product descriptions stored in the SalesLT.ProductDescription table. The Cert1_Sales certificate used in this example was created in Chapter 3.

Listing 4-25. *Signing Data in the Database with a Certificate*

```
CREATE TABLE SalesLT.ProductDecriptionSigs
(
  ProductDescriptionID int not null primary key,
  Signature varbinary(256)
);
GO

INSERT INTO SalesLT.ProductDecriptionSigs
(
  ProductDescriptionID,
  Signature
)
SELECT
  ProductDescriptionID,
  SignByCert(Cert_ID(N'Cert1_Sales'), Description)
FROM SalesLT.ProductDescription;
GO
```

The sample code first creates a table to hold the generated signatures for each product description entry. Then the INSERT statement uses the SignByCert function to sign the product descriptions and store the signatures in the table. The example uses the simplest form of the SignByCert function, which requires the certificate ID and the plaintext to sign. You can also specify a third parameter, *password*, which is the password used to protect the certificate's private key. Only use the *password* parameter if your certificate's private key is protected by password as opposed to protection by the DMK.

The SignByCert function will sign up to 8,000 bytes of data. If you pass a larger LOB data type value to the function, everything after the first 8,000 bytes will be ignored during the signing process. Anything altered after the first 8,000 bytes of data will not be detected by this function. Listing 4-26 queries the product descriptions and their associated signatures, with partial results shown in Figure 4-7.

Listing 4-26. *Querying the Product Descriptions and Their Signatures*

```
SELECT
  pd.ProductDescriptionID,
  pd.Description,
  s.Signature
FROM SalesLT.ProductDescription pd
INNER JOIN SalesLT.ProductDecriptionSigs s
ON pd.ProductDescriptionID = s.ProductDescriptionID;
```

	ProductDescriptionID	Description	Signature
1	3	Chromoly steel.	0xBBDB5EA03B1BA5DCA173A487E74F5F7422D3ED7F9B60DD...
2	4	Aluminum alloy cups; large diameter spindle.	0x17170DE7C1F758E2AC0EA698D32C0F3ED2796C1E1595EEB...
3	5	Aluminum alloy cups and a hollow axle.	0xE20D9EE9B1C7FC19C8A64BD6B84AD6A6EA7D1571A8DC5E...
4	8	Suitable for any type of riding, on or off-road. Fits any bud...	0xEBA8602778E38AC15CAEED49DF47B6C9C4EFC9E2C295F6A...
5	64	This bike delivers a high-level of performance on a budget...	0x9245582299A35B8428CDBD10A10FAB470D2474C034A57261...
6	88	For true trail addicts. An extremely durable bike that will g...	0x159266EDA6F0113F332EC36797E3C21EA5EB7FB3EB137921...
7	128	Serious back-country riding. Perfect for all levels of compe...	0x97B7F61D78E06B6BE473359A3FDFEB751E22E9F892182A60...
8	168	Top-of-the-line competition mountain bike. Performance-e...	0x189B5887AB013788AD276D0A0B9A601DCAD194F8EC1EAB5...
9	170	Suitable for any type of off-road trip. Fits any budget.	0x5104F1B5218B12B64CECC45F9580454C126128129DA35003...
10	209	Entry level adult bike; offers a comfortable ride cross-coun...	0x7C709B7B16884A346FD2B631126C9A1FEE2D68DE8AF05610...
11	249	Value-priced bike with many features of our top-of-the-line...	0x302F0717E8EB98EF10F9DB1CD34E4370F838F1F3308AD1DE...
12	320	Same technology as all of our Road series bikes, but the f...	0xDBAC9E7F01F2E46E55CEF1BAB8598D3F3CDEA760600E267...
13	321	Same technology as all of our Road series bikes. Perfect ...	0x53CDC609531E6E43B11772A636F36046DED56503F374A626...
14	337	A true multi-sport bike that offers streamlined riding and a ...	0xD04ED36417C8859441E341403C87F4BCDDB2D283F86AAB9...
15	375	Cross-train, race, or just socialize on a sleek, aerodynami...	0x38639CF6DDFD022B52067B89F72670023C40EEB93C455678...

Figure 4-7. *Product descriptions and their signatures*

To verify that your data hasn't been tampered with, simply pass in the certificate ID, the previously signed data, and the previously generated signature. The VerifySignedByCert function generates a new signature for the current data and compares it to the existing signature to determine if it's been tampered with. The function returns 1 if no tampering has occurred and 0 if the data does not match the existing signature. Listing 4-27 verifies that the signatures match the signed data. Partial results are shown in Figure 4-8.

Listing 4-27. Verifying the Certificate Signatures on Product Descriptions

```
SELECT
  pd.ProductDescriptionID,
  pd.Description,
  s.Signature,
  VerifySignedByCert
  (
    Cert_ID(N'Cert1_Sales'), pd.Description, s.Signature
  ) AS Verified
FROM SalesLT.ProductDescription pd
INNER JOIN SalesLT.ProductDecriptionSigs s
ON pd.ProductDescriptionID = s.ProductDescriptionID;
```

	ProductDescriptionID	Description	Signature	Verified
1	3	Chromoly steel.	0xBBDB5EA03B1BA5DCA173A467E74F5F7422D3ED7F9B60...	1
2	4	Aluminum alloy cups; large diameter spindle.	0x17170DE7C1F758E2AC0EA698D32C0F3ED2796C1E1595...	1
3	5	Aluminum alloy cups and a hollow axle.	0xE20D9EE9B1C7FC19C6A64BD6B84AD6A6EA7D1571A8D...	1
4	8	Suitable for any type of riding, on or off-road. ...	0xEBA8602778E38AC15CAEED49DF47B6C9C4EFC9E2C295...	1
5	64	This bike delivers a high-level of performance ...	0x9245582299A35B8426CDBD10A10FAB470D2474C034A57...	1
6	88	For true trail addicts. An extremely durable bik...	0x159266EDA6F0113F332EC36797E3C21EA5EB7FB3EB137...	1
7	128	Serious back-country riding. Perfect for all lev...	0x97B7F61D78E06B6BE473359A3FDFEB751E22E9F892182...	1
8	168	Top-of-the-line competition mountain bike. Per...	0x189B5887AB013788AD276D0A0B9A601DCAD194F8EC1E...	1
9	170	Suitable for any type of off-road trip. Fits any b...	0x5104F1B5218B12B64CECC45F9580454C126128129DA35...	1
10	209	Entry level adult bike; offers a comfortable ride...	0x7C709B7B16884A346FD2B631126C9A1FEE2D68DE8AF05...	1
11	249	Value-priced bike with many features of our to...	0x302F0717E8EB98EF10F9DB1CD34E4370F838F1F3308AD...	1
12	320	Same technology as all of our Road series bik...	0xDBAC9E7F01F2E46E55CEF1BAB8598D3F3CDEA760600E...	1
13	321	Same technology as all of our Road series bik...	0x53CDC609531E8E43B11772A836F36046DED56503F374A...	1
14	337	A true multi-sport bike that offers streamlined r...	0xD04ED36417CB859441E341403C87F4BCDDB2D263F86A...	1
15	375	Cross-train. race. or just socialize on a sleek. ...	0x38639CF6DDFD022B52067B89F72670023C40EEB93C455...	1

Figure 4-8. Results of signature verification

In addition to signing data with certificates and verifying certificate-signed data, SQL Server provides the SignByAsymKey and VerifySignedByAsymKey functions. These functions operate similarly to the SignByCert and VerifySignedByCert functions, but using asymmetric keys.

Signing Modules

You can use certificates to sign code modules, including stored procedures and user-defined functions. This is a feature that's useful for assigning permissions to stored procedures and functions without explicitly granting your users those rights.

Database-Level Permissions

You can create database users for certificates and sign procedures to propagate permissions. For the example of stored procedure signing, I'll build on previous examples to force users to call a stored procedure to decrypt the previously encrypted credit card data. I'll also generate a log entry every time a user calls the stored procedure to decrypt the data. Listing 4-11 performs the initial setup by creating a logging table and populating the source table with encrypted credit card data (see Listing 4-28).

Listing 4-28. Create a Logging Table and Encrypt Credit Card Data

```
-- Create a logging table
CREATE TABLE SalesLT.DecryptCreditCardInfoLog
(
  LogID int not null identity(1, 1) primary key,
  SalesOrderID int,
  LogDate datetime,
  LogUser sysname
);
GO
-- Wipe out the sample data in the table
TRUNCATE TABLE SalesLT.EncryptedCreditCardInfo;
GO

OPEN SYMMETRIC KEY SymKey7_Sales
DECRYPTION BY CERTIFICATE Cert2_Sales;

-- Encrypt sample random credit card data
INSERT INTO SalesLT.EncryptedCreditCardInfo
(
  SalesOrderID,
  CreditCardNumber,
  CreditCardExpirationDate,
  TotalCharge
)
SELECT
  SalesOrderID,
  EncryptByKey(Key_GUID(N'SymKey7_Sales'), CreditCardNumber),
  EncryptByKey(Key_GUID(N'SymKey7_Sales'), CAST
    (
      CreditCardExpirationDate AS varbinary(10)
    )
  ),
  EncryptByKey(Key_GUID(N'SymKey7_Sales'), CAST
```

```
  (
    TotalCharge AS varbinary(10)
  )
 )
FROM SalesLT.CreditCardInfo;

CLOSE SYMMETRIC KEY SymKey7_Sales;
GO
```

The next step is to create a stored procedure that accesses the encrypted data. The
SalesLT.GetOrderSummary procedure will accept a sales order ID number and return summary
information about the order with the decrypted credit card information for that order. Listing 4-29
creates this procedure.

Listing 4-29. Sample Procedure to Decrypt Credit Card Information

```
CREATE PROCEDURE SalesLT.GetOrderSummary @SalesOrderID int
AS
BEGIN
  OPEN SYMMETRIC KEY SymKey7_Sales
  DECRYPTION BY CERTIFICATE Cert2_Sales;

  SELECT
    soh.SalesOrderID,
    soh.OrderDate,
    soh.ShipDate,
    soh.Status,
    soh.TotalDue,
    sod.ProductID,
    p.Name AS ProductName,
    CAST
    (
      DecryptByKey (ecc.CreditCardNumber) AS nvarchar(100)
    ) AS CreditCardNumber,
    CAST
    (
      DecryptByKey (ecc.CreditCardExpirationDate) AS datetime
  ) AS CreditCardExp
FROM SalesLT.SalesOrderHeader soh
INNER JOIN SalesLT.SalesOrderDetail sod
  ON soh.SalesOrderID = sod.SalesOrderID
INNER JOIN SalesLT.Product p
  ON sod.ProductID = p.ProductID
INNER JOIN SalesLT.EncryptedCreditCardInfo ecc
  ON soh.SalesOrderID = ecc.SalesOrderID
WHERE soh.SalesOrderID = @SalesOrderID;
```

```
INSERT INTO SalesLT.DecryptCreditCardInfoLog
(
   SalesOrderID,
   LogUser,
   LogDate
)
VALUES
(
   @SalesOrderID,
   USER_NAME(),
   GETDATE()
);

CLOSE SYMMETRIC KEY SymKey7_Sales;
END;
GO
```

Next we'll create a certificate named Cert_SignModules and a database user named CCDecryptor based on this certificate. Listing 4-30 creates the certificate and the database user based on it.

Listing 4-30. Create a Certificate and User Based on the Certificate

```
CREATE CERTIFICATE Cert_SignModules
WITH SUBJECT = N'Certificate to sign modules',
START_DATE = '20090101',
EXPIRY_DATE = '20201231';
GO

CREATE USER CCDecryptor
FOR CERTIFICATE Cert_SignModules;
GO
```

Now that I've created a user based on a certificate, it's time to grant that user some rights. Specifically, I'm going to grant this user rights to execute the stored procedure and to open and utilizethe symmetric key and the certificate protecting the symmetric key. Listing 4-31 grants these permissions to the CCDecryptor user.

Listing 4-31. Granting Permissions to the CCDecryptor User

```
GRANT CONTROL ON SYMMETRIC KEY::SymKey7_Sales
TO CCDecryptor;
GO

GRANT CONTROL ON CERTIFICATE::Cert2_Sales
TO CCDecryptor;
GO
```

These are the permissions that are necessary to access the keys used to encrypt the credit card data in the SalesLT.EncryptedCreditCardInfo table. Next, we'll create a database user named Bob and assign him rights to execute the SalesLT.GetOrderSummary procedure. The WITHOUT LOGIN clause of the CREATE USER statement indicates that Bob's user account should not be mapped to a server login account (see Listing 4-32).

Listing 4-32. Giving User Bob Permissions to Execute the Procedure

```
CREATE USER Bob
WITHOUT LOGIN;
GO

GRANT EXECUTE ON SalesLT.GetOrderSummary
TO Bob;
GO
```

Bob won't have direct access to the SalesLT.EncryptedCreditCardInfo table and he doesn't yet have the ability to decrypt the data in this table, even when executing the stored procedure, as demonstrated in Listing 4-33. This code sample uses the EXECUTE AS USER statement to change the context to the Bob user.

Listing 4-33. Bob Tries to Query the Source Table and Execute the Procedure

```
EXECUTE AS USER = N'Bob';
SELECT *
FROM SalesLT.EncryptedCreditCardInfo;
REVERT;
GO

EXECUTE AS USER = N'Bob';
EXEC SalesLT.GetOrderSummary 71774;
REVERT;
GO
```

The SELECT query in Listing 4-33 results in the following error message.

```
Msg 229, Level 14, State 5, Line 2

The SELECT permission was denied on the object 'EncryptedCreditCardInfo',

database 'AdventureWorksLT2008', schema 'SalesLT'.
```

The EXEC statement returns some order information, but the credit card information is not decrypted. The credit card number and expiration date are returned as NULL, as shown in Figure 4-9.

	SalesOrderID	OrderDate	ShipDate	Status	TotalDue	ProductID	ProductName	CreditCardNumber	CreditCardExp
1	71774	2004-06-01 ...	2004-06-08 ...	5	972.785	838	ML Road Frame-W - Yellow, 48	NULL	NULL
2	71774	2004-06-01 ...	2004-06-08 ...	5	972.785	822	ML Road Frame-W - Yellow, 38	NULL	NULL

Figure 4-9. Executing the SalesLT.GetOrderSummary procedure

You can see why the decryption didn't work by taking a look at the error message displayed on the Management Studio Messages tab, as shown in the following code.

```
Msg 15151, Level 16, State 1, Procedure GetOrderSummary, Line 4

Cannot find the symmetric key 'SymKey7_Sales', because it does not exist or

you do not have permission.


(2 row(s) affected)


(1 row(s) affected)

Msg 15315, Level 16, State 1, Procedure GetOrderSummary, Line 45

The key 'SymKey7_Sales' is not open. Please open the key before using it.


Msg 15151, Level 16, State 1, Procedure GetOrderSummary, Line 4

Cannot find the symmetric key 'SymKey7_Sales', because it does not exist

or you do not have permission.
```

As you can see, even though Bob has permissions to execute the SalesLT.GetOrderSummary he doesn't yet have permission to access the symmetric key and the certificate protecting it. Rather than granting Bob explicit permissions to control the symmetric key and its certificate, we can propagate the permissions that are already assigned to CCDecryptor to Bob through the certificate used to sign the stored procedure. The concept of propagating user permissions through certificates was introduced in SQL Server 2005, and it might be new to many DBAs and developers. Figure 4-10 shows how the permissions propagate from users through a signed procedure.

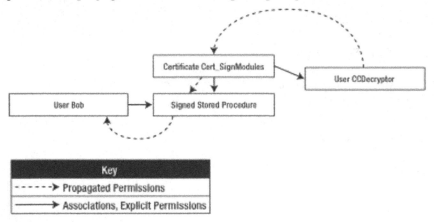

Figure 4-10. Propagation of permissions through a signed procedure

As you can see in Figure 4-10, the permissions of the CCDecryptor user, which was created from the Cert_SignModules certificate, flow through the certificate and certificate-signed procedure and to users like Bob, who have permissions to execute the signed procedure.

The way I implement this permission propagation is by signing the stored procedure with thesame Cert_SignModules certificate that I used to create the CCDecryptor user. Listing 4-34 signs the procedure with this certificate.

Listing 4-34. Signing a Stored Procedure with a Certificate

```
ADD SIGNATURE TO SalesLT.GetOrderSummary
BY CERTIFICATE Cert_SignModules;
GO
```

Now when Bob executes the stored procedure, as shown in Listing 4-35, the CCDecryptor user permissions are propagated back through the certificate and to the other users with permissions to execute it, like Bob. The results, including properly decrypted credit card information, are shown in Figure 4-11.

Listing 4-35. Executing the Stored Procedure As Bob

```
EXECUTE AS USER = N'Bob';
EXEC SalesLT.GetOrderSummary 71774;
REVERT;
GO
```

	SalesOrderID	OrderDate	ShipDate	Status	TotalDue	ProductID	ProductName	CreditCardNumber	CreditCardExp
1	71774	2004-06-01...	2004-06-08 ...	5	972.785	836	ML Road Frame-W - Yellow, 48	0999-8034-9070-1442	2005-07-25 ...
2	71774	2004-06-01...	2004-06-08 ...	5	972.785	822	ML Road Frame-W - Yellow, 38	0999-8034-9070-1442	2005-07-25 ...

Figure 4-11. Results after signing the procedure with a certificate

You can see that the stored procedure run was logged in the `SalesLT.DecryptCreditCardInfoLog` table by running the query shown in Listing 4-36. Results are shown in Figure 4-12.

Listing 4-36. Querying the Log Table

```
SELECT
  LogID,
  SalesOrderID,
  LogDate,
  LogUser
FROM SalesLT.DecryptCreditCardInfoLog;
```

	LogID	SalesOrderID	LogDate	LogUser
1	1	71774	2009-03-28 17:31:04.937	Bob

Figure 4-12. Contents of the log table

Ownership Chaining and the Execute As Clause

Ownership chaining can be a complex subject, and the details are outside the scope of this book. I mention it here because signing procedures with certificates provides an alternative method of giving users access to stored procedures, access, and other permissions within the database. Ownership chaining has been written about extensively, and there are many good treatments of the subject available. One of my favorite introductions to the topic is MVP Erland Sommarskog's whitepaper, "Giving Permissions Through Stored Procedures," available at `www.sommarskog.se/grantperm.html`.

The `EXECUTE AS` clause in the `CREATE PROCEDURE` statement allows you to execute a stored procedure using the context of a different user, and with it you can accomplish a result that is similar to what I've demonstrated in this section with certificates and signed procedures. However, because it changes the security context during execution, the `EXECUTE AS` clause would change the user name being logged into the table in these examples. It's very important to understand these, and other, subtle differences when deciding which methods fit best into your overall security strategy.

A side effect of signing a procedure with a certificate is that the signature is dropped if you alter or drop and recreate the procedure. This means if you issue an ALTER PROCEDURE statement against the SalesLT.GetOrderSummary procedure, the CCDecryptor user will no longer be able to propagate its permissions to Bob. In terms of this example, Bob won't be able to access the symmetric key used to encrypt the credit card data. To reestablish the link between Bob and the CCDecryptor user's permissions, you'll need to sign the procedure again with the ADD SIGNATURE statement.

Server-Level Permissions

You can also assign server-level permissions by creating a login from a certificate created in the master database. To grant both server and database-level permissions through a certificate, you need to install the same certificate in both the master database and in the user database. For example, you can use server-level permissions to grant users bulk insert permissions. Finally, you can sign a procedure with more than one certificate if the users of the procedure need rights assigned to users created with different certificates.

Erland Sommarskog provides one of the best examples of this I've encountered in his white paper "Giving Permissions Through Stored Procedures," available at http://www.sommarskog.se/grantperm.html. The code sample in this section is derived from his example in that paper. The code in Listing 4-37 builds a simple table called State, which will contain information about US states.

Listing 4-37. Building the State Table

```
USE AdventureWorksLT2008;
GO

CREATE TABLE dbo.State
(
    abbreviation nvarchar(2) not null primary key,
    name nvarchar(100) not null,
    capital nvarchar(100) not null,
    flag_graphic nvarchar(20) not null,
    entry_date date not null,
    fact nvarchar(2000) not null,
    capital_address nvarchar(50) not null,
    zip_code nvarchar(5) not null,
    longitude float not null,
    latitude float not null
);
GO
```

This table will be populated from an XML file called State-List.xml. This XML file is located in the sample download file in the Source code section of the Apress web site at http://www.apress.com. The file looks like the snippet shown in Listing 4-38, with one entry for each of the 50 states.

Listing 4-38. State-List.xml File Snippet

```
<capitals>
   <state name = "Alabama"
          Abbreviation = "AL"
          capital = "Montgomery"
          flag = "AL.gif"
          date = "December 14, 1819"
          fact = "Rosa Parks refused to give up her seat ..."
          address = "600 Dexter Ave"
          zip = "36130"
          long = "-86.301963"
          lat = "32.377189" />
   . . .
</capitals>
```

To assign server-level permissions through a certificate, you need to first create a certificate in the master database. Then you need to create a login for the certificate and assign server-level permissions to the login. In this case, I've assigned Administer Bulk Operations permissions, the permissions required for bulk insert. Finally, you need to backup the certificate with the BACKUP CERTIFICATE statement. Listing 4-39 performs all of these steps.

Listing 4-39. Creating a Certificate and Login in the Master Database

```
-- Create certificate in master database
USE master;
GO

CREATE CERTIFICATE LoadStates_Cert
   ENCRYPTION BY PASSWORD = N'1oa8p3rm$'
   WITH SUBJECT = N'Load states permissions',
   START_DATE = '20090101',
   EXPIRY_DATE = '20160101'
GO

-- Create a login for the certificate
CREATE LOGIN LoadStates_Login
FROM CERTIFICATE LoadStates_Cert;
GO

-- Assign "Administer Bulk Operations" permissions to the login
GRANT ADMINISTER BULK OPERATIONS
TO LoadStates_Login;
GO
```

```
-- Backup the certificate to a file
BACKUP CERTIFICATE LoadStates_Cert
TO FILE = N'C:\Windows\Temp\LoadStates_Cert.cer'
WITH PRIVATE KEY
(
  FILE = N'C:\Windows\Temp\LoadStates_Cert.pvk' ,
  ENCRYPTION BY PASSWORD = N'f!133nc#',
  DECRYPTION BY PASSWORD = N'l0a8p3rm$'
);
GO
```

In order for this assignment of server-level permissions through a certificate to work, you have to recreate the certificate in the target database. In this case, I've used the backup of the certificate, created in Listing 4-39, to create the exact same certificate in the AdventureWorksLT2008 database. Listing 4-40 re-creates the certificate in the target database.

■ **Caution** Be sure to delete the certificate backup files from the local storage when you are done. Don't leave them lying around unsecured on your hard drive.

Listing 4-40. Re-create Certificate in Target Database

```
-- Recreate the certificate in AdventureWorksLT 2008 database
-- from the backup.  Be sure to delete the backup files from
-- the local hard drive after you recreate the certificate!
USE AdventureWorksLT2008;
GO

CREATE CERTIFICATE LoadStates_Cert
FROM FILE = N'C:\Windows\Temp\LoadStates_Cert.cer'
WITH PRIVATE KEY
(
  FILE = N'C:\Windows\Temp\LoadStates_Cert.pvk',
  DECRYPTION BY PASSWORD = N'f!133nc#',
  ENCRYPTION BY PASSWORD = N'l0a8p3rm$'
)
GO
```

Listing 4-41 creates the stored procedure that uses SQL Server's OPENROWSET with BULK option to load the XML file into an xml variable and populates the target table. This code listing also signs the stored procedure with the LoadStates_Cert certificate.

Listing 4-41. Create and Sign the LoadStates Stored Procedure

```
-- Now create the LoadStates procedure to bulk load an XML file
-- and shred into a relational table
CREATE PROCEDURE dbo.LoadStates
AS
BEGIN
  DECLARE @x xml;

  EXEC dbo.sp_executesql N'SELECT @x = BulkColumn
    FROM OPENROWSET
    (
      BULK N''c:\state-list.xml'', SINGLE_BLOB
    ) AS x;',
    N'@x xml OUTPUT',
    @x = @x OUTPUT;

  INSERT INTO dbo.State
  (
    abbreviation,
    name,
    capital,
    flag_graphic,
    entry_date,
    fact,
    capital_address,
    zip_code,
    longitude,
    latitude
  )
  SELECT c.value(N'@abbreviation[1]', N'nvarchar(2)'),
    c.value(N'@name[1]', N'nvarchar(100)'),
    c.value(N'@capital[1]', N'nvarchar(100)'),
    c.value(N'@flag[1]', N'nvarchar(20)'),
    c.value(N'@date[1]', N'date'),
    c.value(N'@fact[1]', N'nvarchar(2000)'),
    c.value(N'@address[1]', N'nvarchar(50)'),
    c.value(N'@zip[1]', N'nvarchar(5)'),
    c.value(N'@long[1]', N'float'),
    c.value(N'@lat[1]', N'float')
  FROM @x.nodes(N'//state') t(c);
END;
GO

-- Sign the test procedure with the certificate
ADD SIGNATURE TO LoadStates
BY CERTIFICATE LoadStates_Cert
WITH PASSWORD = N'l0a8p3rm$';
GO
```

107

After the procedure is signed, you can create logins and users and assign them permissions to execute the signed stored procedure. In Listing 4-42, I create a login and an associated database user, both named Joe. Permissions are granted to Joe the user to execute the LoadStates procedure.

Listing 4-42. Creating a Login and User to Execute the Procedure

```
CREATE LOGIN Joe
WITH PASSWORD = 'p@$$w0rd';
GO

CREATE USER Joe
FOR LOGIN Joe;
GO

GRANT EXECUTE ON dbo.LoadStates
TO Joe;
GO
```

You've now created two server logins and one database user. Here's how they interact with one another:

- LoadStates_Login is a login based on the certificate. This login has been assigned Administer Bulk Operations permissions.

- The Joe login is a login that is not assigned any permissions.

- The Joe database user is based on the Joe login, and is assigned permissions to execute the LoadStates stored procedure.

Since the LoadStates_Login was created for a certificate, its server-level permissions are passed through to any login that is signed with the certificate, but only in the context of the signed procedure. In this case, the Administer Bulk Operations permissions are passed to any login that has execute permission on the LoadStates procedure, but only when executing the procedure. So the Joe login gets the Administer Bulk Operations permissions, but only when running the procedure. The Joe user provides database access for the Joe login. Listing 4-43 uses the Joe login to execute the procedure.

Listing 4-43. Executing the Procedure Using the Joe Login

```
-- Execute as Joe
EXECUTE AS LOGIN = N'Joe';
GO

EXEC dbo.LoadStates;
GO

REVERT;
GO
```

Notice that when executing the procedure in Listing 4-43, I used EXECUTE AS LOGIN, not EXECUTE AS USER. This is because server-level permissions are available through the certificate at thelogin level. If you try to execute as Joe the user, the statement will fail with an error message like the following:

```
Msg 4834, Level 16, State 1, Line 5

You do not have permission to use the bulk load statement.
```

You can verify the results of running the stored procedure with a SELECT query, like the one shown in Listing 4-44. Partial results are shown in Figure 4-13.

Listing 4-44. *Verifying the Results of the LoadStates Procedure*

```sql
SELECT abbreviation,
  name,
  capital,
  flag_graphic,
  entry_date,
  fact,
  capital_address,
  zip_code,
  longitude,
  latitude
FROM dbo.State;
```

	abbreviation	name	capital	flag_graphic	entry_date	fact	capital_address	zip_code	longitude	latitude
1	AK	Alaska	Juneau	AK.gif	1959-01-03	In 1867 United States Secretary of State William H. Seward ...	120 4th Street	99801	-134.410699	58.301072
2	AL	Alabama	Montgomery	AL.gif	1819-12-14	Rosa Parks refused to give up her seat on a Montgomery bu...	600 Dexter Ave	36130	-86.301963	32.377189
3	AR	Arkansas	Little Rock	AR.gif	1836-06-15	The state has 6 national parks, 2.5 million acres of national f...	Woodlane St and W Capitol Ave	72201	-92.28785	34.746292
4	AZ	Arizona	Phoenix	AZ.gif	1912-02-14	Arizona is home of the Grand Canyon National Park.	1700 West Washington St	85007	-112.095704	33.448543
5	CA	California	Sacramento	CA.gif	1850-09-09	The state motto is Eureka!, a Greek word meaning 'I have fo...	1501 Capitol Ave	95814	-121.488066	38.575105
6	CO	Colorado	Denver	CO.gif	1876-08-01	Colorado became the only state to turn down the Olympics w...	E Colfax Ave and Lincoln St	80202	-104.986236	39.740086
7	CT	Connecticut	Hartford	CT.gif	1788-01-09	The oldest U.S. newspaper still being published is The Hartfo...	210 Capitol Ave	06106	-72.68227	41.762664
8	DE	Delaware	Dover	DE.gif	1787-12-07	Delaware was the first state to ratify the U.S. Constitution on ...	166 William Penn St	19901	-75.520208	39.156598
9	FL	Florida	Tallahassee	FL.gif	1845-03-03	Prior to becoming a territory (and later a state), Florida had tw...	400 S Monroe St	32301	-84.280499	30.439
10	GA	Georgia	Atlanta	GA.gif	1788-01-02	Coca-Cola was invented in May 1886 by Dr. John S. Pember...	206 Washington St SE	30303	-84.387887	33.750597
11	HI	Hawaii	Honolulu	HI.gif	1959-08-21	More than a third of the world's commercial supply of pineapp...	415 S Beretania St	96813	-157.859171	21.310671

Figure 4-13. *Results of executing LoadStates procedure*

Summary

Asymmetric encryption within the database was first introduced in SQL Server 2005 and continued in SQL Server 2008. SQL Server provides several options for creating and managing asymmetric keys and certificates on the server. While asymmetric encryption is designed specifically to protect symmetric keys that encrypt data through the encryption hierarchy, SQL Server also exposes functions to encrypt data with certificates and asymmetric keys.

In addition to protecting symmetric keys and data, asymmetric keys and certificates can be used to digitally sign data and verify previously generated signatures. This can be useful in protecting against unauthorized data tampering.

Finally, you can use asymmetric keys and certificates to sign procedures and propagate database-level and server-level permissions to users of the procedure. This can prove a very powerful alternative to classic ownership chaining methods of assigning implicit permissions.

In the next chapter, I'll discuss how you can take advantage of one of the exciting new encryption features available in SQL Server 2008, Extensible Key Management (EKM).

CHAPTER 5

■ ■ ■

Extensible Key Management

In very high security situations laws, regulations and IT policies impose very strict prohibitions againststoring encryption keys in the same database (or even on the same physical device) as the datawhich it protects. To address this need, SQL Server 2008 provides an option known as extensible keymanagement (EKM). EKM allows you to create, store, manage, and access encryption keys on dedicated encryption appliances separate from your SQL Server databases. In this chapter, I will use theLuna SA hardware security module (HSM) provided by SafeNet to demonstrate EKM, although theconcepts and tools apply to all SQL Server-enabled HSMs. SQL Server 2008 introduces new T-SQL statements, and new options for existing statements, designed to take advantage of EKM functionality. I'll discuss these T-SQL language extensions in this chapter.

What Is EKM?

EKM is an interface that Microsoft has defined for third-party vendors to extend the capabilities of SQL Server 2008 encryption through dedicated hardware and T-SQL language extensions. The EKM vendor must supply two things in order for EKM to work: a dedicated encryption appliance, known as a hardware security module (HSM), and a dynamic link library (DLL) file that conforms to the Microsoft-defined EKM provider interface. Figure 5-1 shows how these EKM components logically fit within the SQL Server 2008 EKM framework.

Figure 5-1. Relationship between SQL Server and EKM components

The role of the HSM appliance is to create, store, and manage encryption keys, and to perform encryption and decryption of data. The EKM provider's DLL file allows SQL Server to communicate with the HSM. Figure 5-2 shows the SafeNet Luna SA HSM that I used to test the examples in this chapter.

Figure 5-2. SafeNet Luna SA HSM appliance

■ **Note** You can find out more about the SafeNet Luna SA at the SafeNet website, http://www.safenet-inc.com.

Why would you want to use EKM and an HSM appliance? There are two key benefits:

- The HSM manages its own encryption keys, so you can store encryption keys away from the data it protects. In some cases, this is a mandatory requirement.

- The HSM is dedicated encryption hardware, so SQL Server can offload the tasks of encryption and decryption to the appliance. This can result in a significant performance boost and free up resources on your SQL Server instance.

Either one of these benefits could be justification enough to move toward an off-server encryption appliance, but with the SQL Server EKM implementation you get both. You can use EKM toeffectively replace the default encryption hierarchy key management functionality in SQL Server, or you can use it to supplement existing functionality.

In this chapter, I'll discuss how to configure and use your EKM-enabled HSM with SQL Server 2008. Because HSM setup is vendor-specific I assume in this chapter that your HSM appliance is already configured. In Appendix C, I'll walk you through setup and configuration of the SafeNet Luna SA HSM that I use throughout this chapter.

Configuring EKM

The first step to take advantage of SQL Server 2008's EKM functionality is to turn it on in SQL Server via the sp_configure system stored procedure. Listing 5-1 enables EKM provider functionality in SQL Server.

Listing 5-1. Enabling EKM Functionality in SQL Server

```
EXEC sp_configure 'show advanced options', 1;
GO

RECONFIGURE;
GO

EXEC sp_configure 'EKM provider enabled', 1;
GO

RECONFIGURE;
GO
```

The next steps assume that you've already set up and configured you HSM. I won't go into the details here, since the individual steps will be different for every HSM vendor. I do document the process of setting up the SafeNet Luna SA HSM in Appendix C, including the necessary steps to set up and configure the encryption appliance.

After you've enabled SQL Server 2008 EKM functionality with sp_configure and your HSM has been set up and configured, you need to register a vendor-supplied DLL with SQL Server. This is done through the CREATE CRYPTOGRAPHIC PROVIDER statement. Simply take the vendor's DLL and place it where your SQL Server instance can access it. Then specify the full path to the file in the CREATE CRYPTOGRAPHIC PROVIDER statement. In Listing 5-2, I've placed the SafeNet-provided LunaEKM.DLL file in a local folder named c:\LunaSA\EKM.

Listing 5-2. Registering the Luna SA Cryptographic Provider with SQL Server

```
CREATE CRYPTOGRAPHIC PROVIDER LunaEKMProvider
FROM FILE = N'c:\LunaSA\EKM\LunaEKM.dll';
```

■ **Note** SQL Server verifies the cryptographic signature on the vendor's DLL. You may have to install the necessary certificates from the DLL on the local server during the HSM setup. I describe this in Appendix C.

The next step is to create a credential for the cryptographic provider. The credential you create is used by SQL Server to authenticate with the HSM. You can create this credential with the CREATE CREDENTIAL statement, as shown in Listing 5-3.

Listing 5-3. Creating an EKM Credential

```
CREATE CREDENTIAL LunaEKMCredential
WITH IDENTITY = 'SQL2008\Michael',
SECRET = 'x9SP-PH9C-L/FK-q/TW'
FOR CRYPTOGRAPHIC PROVIDER LunaEKMProvider;
GO
```

```
ALTER LOGIN [SQL2008\Michael]
ADD CREDENTIAL LunaEKMCredential;
GO
```

When you create a credential using the code in Listing 5-3, you'll want to replace my Windows login in the WITH IDENTITY clause (*SQL2008\Michael*) with your own. You'll also want to replace the login secret in the SECRET clause (*x9SP-PH9C-L/FK-q/TW*) with your own. This secret authentication value is assigned by your HSM appliance during the hardware setup process. The ALTER LOGIN statement adds the newly created credential to a login. If you don't execute this statement the EKM provider won't recognize your ability to access the HSM appliance.

After you've registered your HSM with SQL Server, you can verify that everything went smoothly by looking under Security in the Management Studio's Object Explorer, as shown in Figure 5-3.

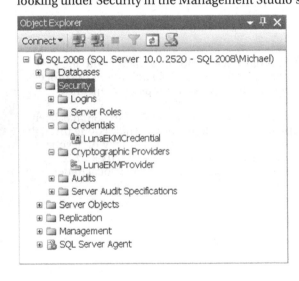

Figure 5-3. Viewing cryptographic providers and credentials in Management Studio

You can also query the sys.cryptographic_providers, sys.credentials, and sys.dm_cryptographic_provider_properties cryptographic system views to validate your EKM registration. Listing 5-4 demonstrates querying these views with results shown in Figure 5-4.

Listing 5-4. Querying Catalog Views and DMVs to Validate EKM Registration

```
SELECT provider_id,
  name,
  guid,
  version,
  dll_path,
  is_enabled
FROM sys.cryptographic_providers;
```

```
SELECT
  credential_id,
  name,
  credential_identity,
  create_date,
  target_type,
  target_id
FROM sys.credentials;

SELECT
  provider_id,
  guid,
  provider_version,
  sqlcrypt_version,
  friendly_name,
  authentication_type,
  symmetric_key_support,
  asymmetric_key_support
FROM sys.dm_cryptographic_provider_properties;
```

Results							
	provider_id	name	guid		version	dll_path	is_enabled
1	65535	LunaEKMProvider	3E16C4F9-1B3F-46FE-B740-F19C75670347		1.0.0.1	c:\LunaSA\EKM\LunaEKM.dll	1

	credential_id	name	credential_identity	create_date	target_type	target_id
1	65543	LunaEKMCredential	SQL2008\Michael	2009-03-28 21:40:28.733	CRYPTOGRAPHIC PROVIDER	65535

	provider_id	guid	provider_ver...	sqlcrypt_ver...	friendly_name	authe...	symmetric_key...	asymmetric_key...
1	65535	3E16C4F9-1B3F-46FE-B740-F19C756...	1.00.0000.01	1.01.0000.00	SafeNet EKM Provider	BASIC	1	1

Figure 5-4. Using system views to validate EKM registration

Creating Asymmetric Keys

You can create asymmetric keys on HSMs that support asymmetric key creation and management, likethe Luna SA. Unlike T-SQL on SQL Server 2008, EKM providers generally support asymmetric key backup and other management functions through built-in HSM support. You won't be able to access thebackup and restore functionality directly through T-SQL statements, however.

When you create an asymmetric key through EKM, you have to use a slight variation on the CREATE ASYMMETRIC KEY syntax. This different form of the statement indicates a provider and has some options specific to EKM. Listing 5-5 generates an asymmetric encryption key on the HSM.

Listing 5-5. Creating an Asymmetric Key on the HSM

```
CREATE ASYMMETRIC KEY Luna_RSA2048_Key
FROM PROVIDER LunaEKMProvider
WITH ALGORITHM = RSA_2048,
PROVIDER_KEY_NAME = 'Luna_RSA2048_Key',
CREATION_DISPOSITION = CREATE_NEW;
```

This CREATE ASYMMETRIC KEY statement creates an RSA key with a 2048-bit private key on the HSM. This variation of the statement requires you to specify the EKM provider name in the FROM PROVIDER clause. You also need to specify the key name on the provider (which can be different from the SQL Server identifier) with the PROVIDER_KEY_NAME option. The CREATION_DISPOSITION canbe set to CREATE_NEW if you are creating a new asymmetric key on the HSM, or OPEN_EXISTING if the asymmetric key already exists on the HSM. You can verify that the asymmetric key creation succeeded by querying the sys.asymmetric_keys system view, as shown in Listing 5-6. Results are shown in Figure 5-5.

Listing 5-6. *Verifying Asymmetric Key Creation Success*

```
SELECT
  name,
  asymmetric_key_id,
  pvt_key_encryption_type_desc,
  algorithm_desc,
  key_length,
  provider_type
FROM sys.asymmetric_keys
WHERE pvt_key_encryption_type = N'CP';
```

	name	asymmetric_key_id	pvt_key_encryption_type_desc	algorithm_desc	key_length	provider_type
1	Luna_RSA2048_Key	263	ENCRYPTED_BY_CRYPTOGRAPHIC_PROVIDER	RSA_2048	2048	CRYPTOGRAPHIC PROVIDER

Figure 5-5. *Contents of sys.asymmetric_keys system view after key creation*

Protecting Symmetric Keys

Asymmetric keys that are created on the HSM are not protected by the SQL Server service master key. The HSM itself provides security for the asymmetric keys it contains. You can, however, use asymmetric keys on the HSM to protect symmetric keys you create on the server. Listing 5-7 creates a new symmetric key on the SQL Server instance and protects it using the asymmetric key I previously created on the HSM.

Listing 5-7. *Creating a Symmetric Key Protected by an HSM Asymmetric Key*

```
CREATE SYMMETRIC KEY SymKey_ProtectedByLunaKey
WITH ALGORITHM = AES_256
ENCRYPTION BY ASYMMETRIC KEY Luna_RSA2048_Key;
```

This statement uses the HSM-managed asymmetric Luna_RSA2048_Key to protect a SQL Server-managed 256-bit AES symmetric encryption key, SymKey_ProtectedByLunaKey. Notice that even though it's protected by an asymmetric key on the Luna SA HSM, the newly created symmetric key is created in the database and is itself managed by SQL Server. You can verify that this key was created and that it's protected by an asymmetric key stored on the cryptographic provider by joining the sys.symmetric_keys, sys.key_encryptions and sys.asymmetric_keys system views as shown in Listing 5-8 with results shown in Figure 5-6.

Listing 5-8. Verifying Symmetric Key Protection by an HSM Asymmetric Key

```
SELECT
  sk.name AS sym_name,
  sk.symmetric_key_id AS sym_id,
  sk.key_length AS sym_len,
  sk.algorithm_desc AS sym_algo,
  ke.crypt_type_desc AS sym_crypt_type,
  ak.name AS asym_key_name,
  ak.algorithm_desc As asym_algo,
  ak.key_length AS asym_len,
  ak.provider_type AS asym_key_provider
FROM sys.symmetric_keys sk
INNER JOIN sys.key_encryptions ke
  ON sk.symmetric_key_id = ke.key_id
INNER JOIN sys.asymmetric_keys ak
  ON ke.thumbprint = ak.thumbprint
WHERE ak.pvt_key_encryption_type = N'CP';
```

	sym_name	sym_id	sym_len	sym_algo	sym_crypt_type	asym_key_name	asym_algo	asym_len	asym_key_provider
1	SymKey_ProtectedByLunaKey	278	256	AES_256	ENCRYPTION BY ASYMMETRIC KEY	Luna_RSA2048_Key	RSA_2048	2048	CRYPTOGRAPHIC PROVIDER

Figure 5-6. List of symmetric keys protected by asymmetric key

This query simply determines which symmetric keys are encrypted by asymmetric keys and then narrows the results to the asymmetric keys that are protected by an EKM cryptographic provider (asindicated by the WHERE ak.pvt_key_encryption_type = N'CP' clause).

An asymmetric key created and managed by an HSM through an EKM provider can be used just like other asymmetric keys on SQL Server. You can use it to protect SQL Server-managed symmetric keys in the encryption key hierarchy or you can use it to encrypt data directly.

Encrypting Data Directly

EKM providers offload the encryption and decryption responsibilities to the dedicated HSM hardware. Encryption and decryption by dedicated hardware is significantly faster than it is in the local SQL Server instance's CryptoAPI-based software implementations. In some simple performance testing, I found theLuna SA hardware implementation was able to decrypt data that was previously encrypted with a 2048-bit RSA key over 200 times faster than the CryptoAPI software implementation in SQL Server. This performance enhancement makes direct asymmetric encryption of data much more palatable when using EKM than it is when using a SQL Server-managed asymmetric key.

■ **Note** The performance results I achieved are specific to my hardware and network configuration. Your performance may vary, but in general you can expect dedicated encryption hardware will outperform software implementations like the CryptoAPI in almost every case.

117

Listing 5-9 creates a table, SalesLT.EncryptedSalesOrderDetail, to hold data encrypted with the previously created HSM-based asymmetric key.

Listing 5-9. Create a Table to Hold Encrypted Sales Order Detail Information

```
CREATE TABLE SalesLT.EncryptedSalesOrderDetail
(
  SalesOrderID int not null,
  SalesOrderDetailID int not null,
  OrderQty varbinary(256) not null,
  ProductID varbinary(256) not null,
  UnitPrice varbinary(256) not null,
  UnitPriceDiscount varbinary(256) not null,
  PRIMARY KEY (SalesOrderID, SalesOrderDetailID)
);
GO
```

In Listing 5-10, I use the previously created HSM-managed RSA key to encrypt selected sales order to detail data from the SalesLT.SalesOrderDetail table.

Listing 5-10. Encrypting Data with an HSM Asymmetric Key

```
INSERT INTO SalesLT.EncryptedSalesOrderDetail
(
  SalesOrderID,
  SalesOrderDetailID,
  OrderQty,
  ProductID,
  UnitPrice,
  UnitPriceDiscount
)
SELECT
  SalesOrderID,
  SalesOrderDetailID,
  EncryptByAsymKey(AsymKey_ID(N'Luna_RSA2048_Key'), CAST
    (
      OrderQty AS varbinary(10)
    )
  ),
  EncryptByAsymKey(AsymKey_ID(N'Luna_RSA2048_Key'), CAST
    (
          ProductID AS varbinary(10)
      )
  ),
  EncryptByAsymKey(AsymKey_ID(N'Luna_RSA2048_Key'), CAST
    (
      UnitPrice AS varbinary(40)
    )
  ),
  EncryptByAsymKey(AsymKey_ID(N'Luna_RSA2048_Key'), CAST
```

```
    (
        UnitPriceDiscount AS varbinary(40)
    )
)
FROM SalesLT.SalesOrderDetail;
GO
```

You can verify the encryption succeeded with a simple query like the one in Listing 5-11. Partial results are shown in Figure 5-7.

Listing 5-11. Querying the Encrypted Sales Order Detail Data

```
SELECT
    SalesOrderID,
    SalesOrderDetailID,
    OrderQty,
    ProductID,
    UnitPrice,
    UnitPriceDiscount
FROM SalesLT.EncryptedSalesOrderDetail;
```

	SalesOrderID	SalesOrderDetai...	OrderQty	ProductID	UnitPrice	UnitPriceDiscount
1	71774	110562	0x773C863BFFB381...	0x92A3691C32BE493F...	0x1F84893331921D72F...	0x09DEE7FAFC53A3...
2	71774	110583	0x3B09F97A3EBE52...	0x9409B27FA45F3036...	0x6393236472DECD57...	0x8BFDFB9AD07096...
3	71776	110567	0x9A109A92EA047C...	0xC5700A36F74BCE9...	0xB6870CEC0871EA32...	0x5A755F44BF9126...
4	71780	110616	0x95F4A1769E08F1...	0x0EF16496F2231DE0...	0x3867D3FB64E75934...	0x59990785BCA665...
5	71780	110617	0x0B54954F2B9844...	0x1288F42F4075F371...	0x80F671FBC0A5D10C...	0x4AD79477DA5522...
6	71780	110618	0x59B8A6B3A4342E...	0x65200403E137BFAF...	0x5FCF8A0CA5EAD397...	0x9814133C3C7266...
7	71780	110619	0x55DDE5E3B73A4...	0xA2C0F1EE51C6E8A...	0x57D234B406BB38F1...	0x1797E55D2FCB9E...
8	71780	110620	0xA9F74C1E23FEC...	0x4D9D9B13F2C6E46...	0x5D393CBC961E7F5A...	0x50ACC1009E2AB7...
9	71780	110621	0x9DD76F13C943B...	0x00357C475EF0882E...	0x8CEC6F5530FDA45D...	0x85987E15B54A65...
10	71780	110622	0x08AC8686361C3A...	0x75CFF522FE20CD9...	0x8D7724820B758C9A...	0x453582DCBCDBD...
11	71780	110623	0x8E83CC410E87B...	0xC0D38CA6348BC5B...	0x0E00EA7A211B721F...	0x2E0219A0488A84...
12	71780	110624	0x508DE377D52EE...	0xAD55B1CDFC97999...	0xB5E3F4DA3343673F...	0x4B695678D6C92D...

Figure 5-7. Encrypted sales order detail data

Decrypting the encrypted data is simply a matter of calling the DecryptByAsymKey function with the HSM-enabled asymmetric encryption key, as shown in Listing 5-12. Partial results are shown in Figure 5-8.

Listing 5-12. Decrypting Data with an HSM-enabled Asymmetric Key

```
SELECT
    SalesOrderID,
    SalesOrderDetailID,
    CAST
```

```
    (
        DecryptByAsymKey(AsymKey_ID(N'Luna_RSA2048_Key'),
            OrderQty) AS smallint
    ) AS OrderQty,
    CAST
    (
        DecryptByAsymKey(AsymKey_ID(N'Luna_RSA2048_Key'),
            ProductID) AS int
    ) AS ProductID,
    CAST
    (
        DecryptByAsymKey(AsymKey_ID(N'Luna_RSA2048_Key'),
            UnitPrice) AS money
    ) AS UnitPrice,
    CAST
    (
        DecryptByAsymKey(AsymKey_ID(N'Luna_RSA2048_Key'),
            UnitPriceDiscount) AS money
    ) AS UnitPriceDiscount
FROM SalesLT.EncryptedSalesOrderDetail;
```

	SalesOrderID	SalesOrderDetailID	OrderQty	ProductID	UnitPrice	UnitPriceDiscount
1	71774	110562	1	836	356.898	0.00
2	71774	110563	1	822	356.898	0.00
3	71776	110567	1	907	63.90	0.00
4	71780	110616	4	905	218.454	0.00
5	71780	110617	2	983	461.694	0.00
6	71780	110618	6	988	112.998	0.40
7	71780	110619	2	748	818.70	0.00
8	71780	110620	1	990	323.994	0.00
9	71780	110621	1	926	149.874	0.00
10	71780	110622	1	743	809.76	0.00
11	71780	110623	4	782	1376.994	0.00
12	71780	110624	2	918	158.43	0.00

Figure 5-8. Result of HSM-enabled asymmetric decryption

Creating Symmetric Keys

In addition to creation and management of asymmetric keys, EKM providers can also create and manage symmetric keys on HSMs that support it. When you create a symmetric key on an HSM it's protected and managed by the HSM. This means you don't need to specify that the symmetric key will be encrypted by certificate, asymmetric key, or password. Listing 5-13 creates a symmetric key directly on the HSM appliance.

Listing 5-13. *Creating a Symmetric Key on the HSM*

```
CREATE SYMMETRIC KEY Luna_AES256_Key
FROM PROVIDER LunaEKMProvider
WITH PROVIDER_KEY_NAME='Luna_AES256_Key',
CREATION_DISPOSITION = CREATE_NEW,
ALGORITHM = AES_256;
```

You can verify that the 256-bit AES key was successfully created by querying the sys.symmetric_keys system view as shown in Listing 5-14. The result is shown in Figure 5-9.

Listing 5-14. *Querying sys.symmetric_keys to Verify Key Creation*

```
SELECT
  name,
  symmetric_key_id,
  key_length,
  algorithm_desc,
  provider_type
FROM sys.symmetric_keys
WHERE provider_type = N'CRYPTOGRAPHIC PROVIDER';
```

▦ Results

	name	symmetric_key_id	key_length	algorithm_desc	provider_type
1	Luna_AES256_Key	279	256	AES_256	CRYPTOGRAPHIC PROVIDER

Figure 5-9. *Verification the encryption key was created on the HSM*

As I mentioned previously, because the symmetric encryption key was created on the HSM, you don't need to specify an asymmetric key, password, or certificate to protect it. The HSM handles the details of securing the symmetric key. Another nice feature of HSM-protected symmetric keys is that you don't have to explicitly open and close the symmetric key when you want to use it. Listing 5-15 creates a table called SalesLT.EncryptedProduct that will hold encrypted product pricing information from the SalesLT.ProductTable.

Listing 5-15. Creating Table to Hold Encrypted Product Price Information

```
CREATE TABLE SalesLT.EncryptedProduct
(
  ProductID int not null primary key,
  Name nvarchar(50),
  StandardCost varbinary(80),
  ListPrice varbinary(80)
);
GO
```

The next step is to populate the table with encrypted data. For this task, I'll use the 256-bit AES key I previously created on the HSM appliance. Listing 5-16 performs the encryption and queries the result to demonstrate the data is encrypted. Partial results are shown in Figure 5-10.

Listing 5-16. Encrypting Data with an HSM Symmetric Key

```
INSERT INTO SalesLT.EncryptedProduct
(
  ProductID,
  Name,
  StandardCost,
  ListPrice
)
SELECT
  ProductID,
  Name,
  EncryptByKey(Key_GUID(N'Luna_AES256_Key'),
    CAST
    (
      StandardCost AS varbinary(40)
    )
  ),
  EncryptByKey(Key_GUID(N'Luna_AES256_Key'),
    CAST
    (
      ListPrice AS varbinary(40)
    )
  )
FROM SalesLT.Product;
GO
```

```
SELECT
  ProductID,
  Name,
  StandardCost,
  ListPrice
FROM SalesLT.EncryptedProduct;
```

	ProductID	Name	StandardCost	ListPrice
1	680	HL Road Frame - Black, 58	0x00CC3FA82848EC479FF31E77BA1E0F7...	0x00CC3FA82848EC479FF31E77BA1E0F7A01000...
2	706	HL Road Frame - Red, 58	0x00CC3FA82848EC479FF31E77BA1E0F7...	0x00CC3FA82848EC479FF31E77BA1E0F7A01000...
3	707	Sport-100 Helmet, Red	0x00CC3FA82848EC479FF31E77BA1E0F7...	0x00CC3FA82848EC479FF31E77BA1E0F7A01000...
4	708	Sport-100 Helmet, Black	0x00CC3FA82848EC479FF31E77BA1E0F7...	0x00CC3FA82848EC479FF31E77BA1E0F7A01000...
5	709	Mountain Bike Socks, M	0x00CC3FA82848EC479FF31E77BA1E0F7...	0x00CC3FA82848EC479FF31E77BA1E0F7A01000...
6	710	Mountain Bike Socks, L	0x00CC3FA82848EC479FF31E77BA1E0F7...	0x00CC3FA82848EC479FF31E77BA1E0F7A01000...
7	711	Sport-100 Helmet, Blue	0x00CC3FA82848EC479FF31E77BA1E0F7...	0x00CC3FA82848EC479FF31E77BA1E0F7A01000...
8	712	AWC Logo Cap	0x00CC3FA82848EC479FF31E77BA1E0F7...	0x00CC3FA82848EC479FF31E77BA1E0F7A01000...
9	713	Long-Sleeve Logo Jersey, S	0x00CC3FA82848EC479FF31E77BA1E0F7...	0x00CC3FA82848EC479FF31E77BA1E0F7A01000...
10	714	Long-Sleeve Logo Jersey, M	0x00CC3FA82848EC479FF31E77BA1E0F7...	0x00CC3FA82848EC479FF31E77BA1E0F7A01000...
11	715	Long-Sleeve Logo Jersey, L	0x00CC3FA82848EC479FF31E77BA1E0F7...	0x00CC3FA82848EC479FF31E77BA1E0F7A01000...
12	716	Long-Sleeve Logo Jersey, XL	0x00CC3FA82848EC479FF31E77BA1E0F7...	0x00CC3FA82848EC479FF31E77BA1E0F7A01000...
13	717	HL Road Frame - Red, 62	0x00CC3FA82848EC479FF31E77BA1E0F7...	0x00CC3FA82848EC479FF31E77BA1E0F7A01000...
14	718	HL Road Frame - Red, 44	0x00CC3FA82848EC479FF31E77BA1E0F7...	0x00CC3FA82848EC479FF31E77BA1E0F7A01000...
15	719	HL Road Frame - Red, 48	0x00CC3FA82848EC479FF31E77BA1E0F7...	0x00CC3FA82848EC479FF31E77BA1E0F7A01000...

Figure 5-10. Encrypted product pricing data

Notice that you don't need to use the OPEN SYMMETRIC KEY and CLOSE SYMMETRIC KEY statements to open and close the symmetric key for use. The HSM handles key opening and closing of keys for you automatically. You also don't need to open or close symmetric keys when decrypting data, as shown in Listing 5-17.

Listing 5-17. Decrypting Data with an HSM Symmetric Key

```
SELECT
  ProductID,
  Name,
  CAST(DecryptByKey(StandardCost) AS money) AS StandardCost,
  CAST(DecryptByKey(ListPrice) AS money) AS ListPrice
FROM SalesLT.EncryptedProduct;
```

EKM Limitations

EKM inherits some limitations from the SQL Server-defined interface. For instance, even though an HSM is a dedicated hardware encryption appliance, EKM limits the amount of data that can be encrypted at once. Specifically, the result of your encryption can't be larger than 8,000 bytes in length.

EKM may also have other limitations created by a combination of adherence to the EKM interface standards and the implementation of the HSM hardware and firmware. As an example, when testing the Luna SA I was unable to create an HSM-based encryption key hierarchy in which HSM-based symmetric keys could be used to encrypt other symmetric keys. The fact of the matter is that this is not a particularly problematic limitation since the HSM provides adequate security for your symmetric keys.

Basically, the encryption key hierarchy is unnecessary to secure your keys when you have an HSM to protect them.

The T-SQL extensions for EKM do not support HSM-based certificates. While you can use asymmetric keys on HSMs that support them, you cannot create or utilize certificates stored on the HSMfrom within T-SQL. Additionally, you can't use EKM provider-generated asymmetric keys to sign procedures or database objects with the ADD SIGNATURE statement. You also can't use EKM asymmetric keys to generate digital signatures for data with the SignByAsymKey function.

Finally, you are limited in whatever the HSM hardware and firmware supports for encryption key management and encryption/decryption functionality. Only algorithms supported by the HSM can be used through the EKM provider. If your HSM supports algorithms that the SQL Server EKM interface doesn't recognize, you won't be able to utilize them. As an example, the Luna SA appliance supports algorithms like CAST-128 and Elliptical Curve Cryptography (ECC) that the SQL Server T-SQL language extensions can't access.

While the Luna SA HSM I'm using implements all of the encryption algorithms and key lengths currently supported by SQL Server 2008, other EKM providers may not provide support for some algorithms or options. You can query the sys.dm_cryptographic_provider_algorithms DMF to get a list of algorithms that your EKM provider supports, as shown in Listing 5-18. Results for the Luna SA HSM are shown in Figure 5-11.

Listing 5-18. Querying the List of Cryptographic Provider Algorithms

```
SELECT
  algorithm_id,
  algorithm_tag,
  key_type,
  key_length
FROM sys.dm_cryptographic_provider_algorithms (65535);
```

	algorithm_id	algorithm_tag	key_type	key_length
1	1	RSA_512	ASYMMETRIC KEY	512
2	2	RSA_1024	ASYMMETRIC KEY	1024
3	3	RSA_2048	ASYMMETRIC KEY	2048
4	4	RC2	SYMMETRIC KEY	128
5	5	RC4	SYMMETRIC KEY	40
6	6	RC4_128	SYMMETRIC KEY	128
7	7	DES	SYMMETRIC KEY	64
8	8	Triple_DES	SYMMETRIC KEY	128
9	9	TRIPLE_DES_3KEY	SYMMETRIC KEY	192
10	10	AES_128	SYMMETRIC KEY	128
11	11	AES_192	SYMMETRIC KEY	192
12	12	AES_256	SYMMETRIC KEY	256

Figure 5-11. List of Luna SA-supported algorithms

You can also query the sys.dm_cryptographic_provider_properties DMV to determine if your EKM provider supports symmetric encryption, asymmetric encryption, and additional related options. Idiscussed the sys.dm_cryptographic_provider_properties DMV in Chapter 2. Additionally, you can get a list of keys being stored on the HSM by querying the sys.dm_cryptographic_provider_keys DMF.

Summary

The SQL Server 2008 EKM implementation includes new T-SQL language extensions that provide access to third-party dedicated encryption hardware, like the SafeNet Luna SA. In this chapter, I discussed the advantages of EKM, which include the ability to physically separate your encryption keys from the data they protect. You can also gain performance advantages in hardware implementations of cryptographic algorithms.

The Microsoft-defined EKM interface allows you to access key management and encryption functionality exposed by dedicated HSMs. Although the features provided by a given HSM is vendor-specific, EKM supports creation, management, storage, and security of asymmetric keys and symmetric keys through HSMs. EKM also supports HSM-enabled data encryption and decryption, allowing you to offload these responsibilities to dedicated encryption hardware.

In this chapter, I've reviewed the functionality available through third party EKM providers that you register with SQL Server with code samples demonstrating the use of these features. In the next chapter, I'll look at another new SQL Server

2008 encryption feature—Transparent Data Encryption (TDE).

CHAPTER 6

■■■

Transparent Data Encryption

Up to this point, I've focused on cell-level encryption, which represents a significant portion of SQL Server's encryption functionality. Cell-level encryption can be an extremely useful tool for targeted data encryption, but it does have some drawbacks. For one thing, a proper strategy involving cell-level encryption requires careful planning to balance the needs of security and performance. Cell-level encryption can be difficult, or impossible in some cases, to implement when you already have a database in production. The cost of refactoring a complex database (and its dependent applications) can be a significant deterrent to implementing cell-level encryption.

SQL Server 2008 provides a new option to handle these situations—Transparent Data Encryption (TDE). TDE allows you to encrypt an entire database at once, significantly improving the feasibility of adding encryption to legacy databases. In this chapter, I'll discuss the features and functionality of TDE.

What Is TDE?

TDE is a new feature of SQL Server 2008 that allows you to transparently encrypt your databases. It is available only on the Enterprise and Developer editions of SQL Server. TDE operates at SQL Server's I/O level, essentially sitting between your physical storage devices and the transient storage (RAM, virtual memory) that SQL Server uses. Figure 6-1 shows a simplified logical representation of TDE.

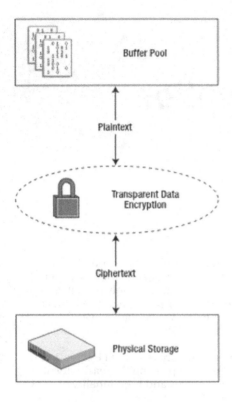

Figure 6-1. Logical representation of TDE

As you can see in the figure, TDE encrypts data before committing it to physical storage and decrypts it after fetching it for the buffer pool. The buffer pool is the transient memory that SQL Server uses to store data in 8 KB blocks of the virtual address space. This has two big implications worth considering when implementing TDE:

1. TDE allows the SQL Server query optimizer to take advantage of the entire class of efficient query operators, including index seeks, that it can't use on encrypted cell-level data.

2. As data is pulled from physical storage, it's stored in memory in unencrypted form. Cell-level encryption has a similar implication, except that with TDE entire 8 KB pages of data are stored in memory unencrypted, including physically adjacent data that might not be part of your query's result set.

As the figure also shows, plaintext in the buffer pool moves through TDE and is encrypted before it is committed to physical storage. When SQL Server requests encrypted data pages from physical storage, they're passed back through TDE and decrypted before being delivered to the buffer pool. It is TDE's positioning between physical storage and the SQL Server buffer pool that allows it to operate with seeming invisibility to clients.

What Is Encrypted

In addition to encrypting the designated database in physical storage, TDE also automatically encrypts the tempdb system database. This means that data stored in tempdb must be encrypted when written and decrypted when read, for every database on the same SQL Server instance. For this reason, TDE can affect performance of non-encrypted databases residing on the same SQL Server instance as an encrypted database, especially those that make heavy use of tempdb.

Unencrypted Data on the Wire

TDE, like cell-level encryption, is designed to encrypt your data at rest on your physical storage devices. However, it does not protect your data in transit or "over-the-wire." To protect data being transmitted over your network you need to secure your SQL Server communications channels by enabling Secure Sockets Layer (SSL) connections on your SQL Server instance. Keep in mind that, like cell-level encryption, TDE is designed strictly to encrypt your data "at rest."

TDE encrypts all of a database's data pages in physical storage, and as I mentioned it also automatically encrypts the tempdb database that SQL Server uses for temporary storage of result sets. In addition, TDE prevents data leakage by encrypting the log files associated with a database. Database snapshots, backups, and memory dumps for a TDE-encrypted database are also automatically encrypted by TDE.

■ **Note** TDE does not go back and encrypt log file data that was already written in unencrypted plaintext. TDE does force the log writer to cycle back to the beginning of the log file, and overwrites existing entries over time. Your log files may contain unencrypted artifacts until they are overwritten.

What Isn't Encrypted

There are some things that TDE does not automatically protect, however. For instance, SQL Server also does not encrypt data in the server's transient storage—the buffer pool I referenced earlier—even when TDE is turned on. This means that your data will be unencrypted in memory and portions may even spill over to disk when SQL Server pages out memory. TDE also does not encrypt header information, such as cyclic redundancy check (CRC) data corruption checksums, database version, and other status information. All other data in each data page is fully encrypted by TDE in physical storage.

Because TDE operates between the buffer pool and physical storage, only data that's written through the buffer pool is encrypted. SQL Server features that bypass the buffer pool and interact directly with physical storage, like the new filestream feature, do not encrypt their data. If you are using TDE on a database used for mirroring or log shipping, both databases are encrypted and the log transactions transferred between databases is encrypted over the wire.

■ **Caution** As pointed out, data stored with the filestream feature is not encrypted by TDE. Data stored in full-text indexed columns will be stored on disk temporarily as unencrypted plaintext during full-text index scans. Replicated data is not encrypted by default.

Advantages of TDE

TDE has some definite advantages over cell-level encryption, a couple of which I've already visited. The advantages of TDE include the following:

- *Ease of implementation:* TDE is essentially a "flip-the-switch" solution that allows you to encrypt your entire database at once, without any database rework.

- *Transparency:* TDE has the advantage of being transparent. You can turn it on with no refactoring of client applications. It represents the ultimate in convenience in that regard.

- *Additional security:* TDE automatically encrypts tempdb and the database transaction log to prevent data leakage.

- *Use any data type:* TDE allows you to store data using any native data type, including large object data types. Cell-level encryption operates on the varbinary data type, and limits the amount of data that can be encrypted at once to 8,000 bytes or less.

- *Speed:* Because it decrypts data in the buffer pool, TDE allows SQL Server to take advantage of indexes to improve query performance. Cell-level encryption requires a performance tradeoff, which can be very hard to overcome in some instances, to protect your data. Implementing any encryption option will add overhead above and beyond storing and accessing non-encrypted data.

Of course, TDE also has some limitations when compared to cell-level encryption. There are some instances when cell-level encryption might make a better choice for your encryption needs, including the following:

- *When you only need to encrypt a small amount of data:* When you encrypt the entire database using TDE you add an estimated 3 to 5 percent overhead. This overhead can be lower for mostly memory access, but possibly much higher if you already have a heavy load on the server's CPU. If you are only encrypting a few columns in a large database, it might make sense to target your encryption efforts to avoid a performance penalty for the entire database.

- *When you need to maintain fine-grained control over access:* TDE is designed to provide transparent encryption of your entire database, so it does not provide options to limit access to sensitive data to particular users. Cell-level encryption can be limited by allowing or denying access to the keys that encrypt data on a very granular column, row, or cell level.

- *When you need to protect data against potential intruders on your servers:* TDE protects your data from physical theft—a malicious thief who steals a database backup, MDF database files, or LDF log files won't be able to restore or attach them to their SQL Server installation and access the data within. Cell-level encryption provides another level of protection, making encrypted data inaccessible to any intruder who gains access to your servers without permissions to access the encryption keys.

TDE is not necessarily a replacement for cell-level encryption. TDE provides very broad protection through encryption, and it can act as a complement to cell-level encryption in order to boost your overall security.

TDE protects you from wholesale database theft, including scenarios in which MDF or LDF database and log files or database backup files are lost or stolen. Cell-level encryption protects your data at the individual element level, protecting your data from attackers who gain access to your servers.

Enabling TDE

The TDE model uses a new specialized symmetric key called the database encryption key (DEK) to encrypt your database. The DEK is protected by a *server certificate*—a certificate created in the master database. The server certificate is protected by the master database DMK, which must be protected in turn by the SMK.

The first step to enabling TDE is to create a DMK in the master database (if one doesn't already exist), as shown in Listing 6-1.

Listing 6-1. Create DMK in the Master Database

```
USE master;
GO

CREATE MASTER KEY
ENCRYPTION BY PASSWORD = N'm*1u~pOa92+';
GO
```

After you've created the master database DMK you need to create a server certificate in the master database, as shown in Listing 6-2. This is the certificate that will protect the DEK that you'll create in subsequent steps.

Listing 6-2. Create a Server Certificate

```
USE master;
GO

CREATE CERTIFICATE TDE_Certificate
WITH SUBJECT = N'TDE Encryption Server Certificate';
GO
```

After you create your server certificate, you should immediately back it up using the BACKUP CERTIFICATE statement, as demonstrated in Listing 6-3. Immediately store the certificate backup in a secure facility. You'll need the server certificate if you want to restore the encrypted database from a backup or attach the database files to a different server in the future.

Listing 6-3. Backing Up the Server Certificate

```
USE master;
GO

BACKUP CERTIFICATE TDE_Certificate
TO FILE = N'c:\Server_Certificate.cer'
WITH PRIVATE KEY
(
  FILE = N'c:\Server_Certificate.pvk',
  ENCRYPTION BY PASSWORD = N'$$um)3loq:'
);
GO
```

Now that you have a server certificate you can switch back to your user database and create a DEK with the CREATE DATABASE ENCRYPTION KEY statement. You can only create one DEK per user database. Listing 6-4 creates an AES 256 bit DEK in the AdventureWorksLT2008 database I've been using throughout the book.

Listing 6-4. Create a Database Encryption Key

```
USE AdventureWorksLT2008;
GO

CREATE DATABASE ENCRYPTION KEY
WITH ALGORITHM = AES_256
ENCRYPTION BY SERVER CERTIFICATE TDE_Certificate;
GO
```

You can specify any of the following encryption algorithms in the CREATE DATABASE ENCRYPTION KEY statement's ALGORITHM clause:

- AES_256 = AES with a 256-bit key

- AES_192 = AES with a 192-bit key

- AES_128 = AES with a 128-bit key

- TRIPLE_DES_3KEY = Triple DES (3 Key)

You can use the ALTER DATABASE ENCRYPTION KEY statement to regenerate the DEK using the same or different algorithm. You can also use the DROP DATABASE ENCRYPTION KEY statement to drop the DEK. If you decide to drop the DEK, you'll need to turn database encryption off first and wait until the database is completely decrypted.

The final step is to enable TDE in the target database with the ALTER DATABASE statement, as shown in Listing 6-5.

Listing 6-5. Turning on TDE

```
USE AdventureWorksLT2008;
GO

ALTER DATABASE AdventureWorksLT2008
SET ENCRYPTION ON;
GO
```

You can turn TDE off at any time with the ALTER DATABASE statement's SET ENCRYPTION OFF clause.

Using TDE with EKM

You can use TDE in conjunction with EKM by creating an asymmetric key in the master database through your EKM provider's HSM. A *server asymmetric key* on an HSM, as opposed to a server certificate stored on the local server, can be used to secure your database encryption key. Listing 6-6 begins by creating a server asymmetric key in the master database.

■ **Note** You'll have to remove the existing DEK and turn off TDE in the AdventureWorksLT2008 database to run the following code samples.

Listing 6-6. Using DEK with EKM

```
USE master;
GO

CREATE ASYMMETRIC KEY TDE_Luna_AsymKey
FROM PROVIDER LunaEKMProvider
WITH ALGORITHM = RSA_2048,
PROVIDER_KEY_NAME = N'TDE_Luna_AsymKey',
CREATION_DISPOSITION = CREATE_NEW;
GO
```

To use EKM with TDE, you need to create a credential and a login for the asymmetric key. You then have to assign the credential to the login you created, as demonstrated in Listing 6-7.

Listing 6-7. Creating a Credential and a Login for the EKM

```
CREATE CREDENTIAL TDE_Luna_Credential
WITH IDENTITY = 'SQL2008\Michael',
SECRET = 'x9SP-PH9C-L/FK-q/TW'
FOR CRYPTOGRAPHIC PROVIDER LunaEKMProvider;
GO

CREATE LOGIN TDE_Luna_Login
FROM ASYMMETRIC KEY TDE_Luna_AsymKey;
GO

ALTER LOGIN TDE_Luna_Login
ADD CREDENTIAL TDE_Luna_Credential;
GO
```

You must then create a DEK in the AdventureWorksLT2008 database and turn TDE back on, as shown in Listing 6-8.

Listing 6-8. Creating a DEK and Turning on TDE

```
USE AdventureWorksLT2008;
GO

CREATE DATABASE ENCRYPTION KEY
WITH ALGORITHM = AES_256
ENCRYPTION BY SERVER ASYMMETRIC KEY TDE_Luna_AsymKey;
GO

ALTER DATABASE AdventureWorksLT2008
SET ENCRYPTION ON;
```

Using TDE with an EKM-managed server asymmetric key provides an elegant and secure solution for full-database encryption.

Checking Status

At any point, you can use the sys.dm_database_encryption_keys DMV to determine which databases are currently encrypted (or in the process of being encrypted) on your server. This DMV also gives you the status of the encryption process on newly encrypted databases. Listing 6-9 queries sys.dm_database_encryption_keys on my local server instance. Results are shown in Figure 6-2.

Listing 6-9. Listing Encrypted Databases

```
SELECT
  DB_NAME(database_id) AS database_name,
  database_id,
  CASE encryption_state
    WHEN 0 THEN N'No database encryption key present, no encryption'
    WHEN 1 THEN N'Unencrypted'
    WHEN 2 THEN N'Encryption in progress'
    WHEN 3 THEN N'Encrypted'
    WHEN 4 THEN N'Key change in progress'
    WHEN 5 THEN N'Decryption in progress'
  END AS encryption_state,
  key_algorithm,
  key_length,
  percent_complete
FROM sys.dm_database_encryption_keys;
```

	database_name	database_id	encryption_state	key_algorithm	key_length	percent_complete
1	tempdb	2	Encrypted	AES	256	0
2	AdventureWorksLT2008	8	Encrypted	AES	256	0

Figure 6-2. Encrypted databases and statuses

Backups and Compression

When you encrypt an entire database with TDE activated, database backups are also encrypted. This ensures that your backups are protected from nefarious hackers who could otherwise steal them and restore them to their own SQL Server instances to browse your confidential data at will.

To restore a TDE-encrypted database to a SQL Server instance, the server certificate or server asymmetric key used to protect the DEK must be installed on the instance. This means that before you restore a TDE-protected database backup to a different SQL Server instance you need to first install the server certificate or server asymmetric key used to protect the DEK.

■ **Tip** As I mentioned earlier in this chapter in the "Enabling TDE" section, once you create a server certificate you should immediately take a backup.

In addition, if you set up log shipping or replication between encrypted databases you need to have the same server certificate or server asymmetric key installed on both SQL Server instances.

As discussed in Chapter 1, a goal of any good encryption algorithm is to remove recognizable patterns from the encrypted ciphertext. This is completely at odds with the needs of a good compression algorithm—namely to identify patterns in uncompressed data. The simplest compression algorithms try to identify patterns of duplicated data and replace those patterns with considerably smaller tokens. Consider the very simple example in Figure 6-3.

Uncompressed Text:	I would not like them here or there I would not like them anywhere
Tokens:	1 = "I would not like them" 2 = "here"
Compressed Text:	1 2 or t2 1 anyw2

Figure 6-3. Very simple compression example

In this simple example, with uncompressed text courtesy of Dr. Seuss, the compression algorithm has determined a pattern consisting of two repetitive strings of characters that can be replaced with much smaller tokens. The character strings are replaced with the tokens "1" and "2" resulting in highly compressed text.

The point is that encrypted ciphertext removes these patterns, considerably diminishing the ability to compress the data after encryption. As you can see in Figure 6-4, which represents the sizes of backups of the AdventureWorksLT 2008 database on my local machine, a compressed backup of a database with no TDE can result in a significant reduction in backup file size. A backup of the same database with TDE turned on does not compress well.

Backup File	Size
AdventureWorksLT2008-Uncompressed-Unencrypted.bak	14,425 KB
AdventureWorksLT2008-Compressed-Unencrypted.bak	7,843 KB
AdventureWorksLT2008-Compressed-Encrypted.bak	14,300 KB

Figure 6-4. Effects of encryption on backup compression

You might want to take the effect that encryption has on compression before you turn on TDE, particularly if your databases are very large.

Windows-Based Encryption Options

In addition to SQL Server's TDE option, Windows provides file system-level encryption built into the operating system. The two main options available to secure your data through Windows are the Encrypting File System (EFS) and BitLocker. I'll discuss both of these options in the following sections.

Encrypting File System

Since Windows 2000 Microsoft's flagship operating system has included the EFS option to encrypt files or folders at the filesystem level on NTFS. This feature has seen some improvements since then, like the addition of file sharing for encrypted files and support for more encryption algorithms. This feature is available in Windows XP, Windows 2003, Windows Vista, Windows Server 2008, and Windows 7.

EFS operates at the OS level, encrypting and decrypting data as it is read from and written to physical storage. Like TDE, EFS does not encrypt your data in memory and it does not encrypt data as it's transmitted across the network.

EFS as an option is similar in functionality to TDE, except that EFS does not automatically encompass the many database-specific files that SQL Server might use. If you use EFS to encrypt a single database MDF file, for instance, it won't automatically encrypt tempdb, log files, backups, etc. EFS can be used in conjunction with TDE, to encrypt filestream data, for instance. TDE is also only available in the enterprise and developer editions of SQL Server 2008. If you're using a different edition of SQL Server TDE might not be an option, but EFS is available through the OS.

EFS require exclusive access to files to encrypt them. What this means in SQL Server terms is that you first have to detach a database or take it offline to encrypt it with EFS. You can take a database offline via the ALTER DATABASE statement or from within Management Studio, as shown in Figure 6-5. If you don't first detach the database or take it offline, EFS won't be able to encrypt the file since SQL Server is using it.

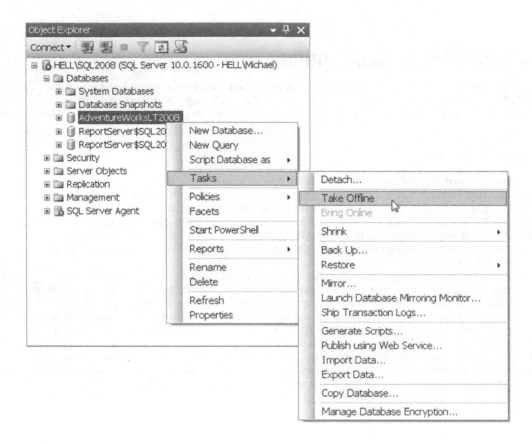

Figure 6-5. *Taking a database offline*

Once detached or offline, you can encrypt a database file or a folder containing a database file by right-clicking on the object in Windows Explorer and clicking the *Advanced* button on the *Attributes* tab. Then check the *Encrypt contents to secure data* checkbox, as shown in Figure 6-6.

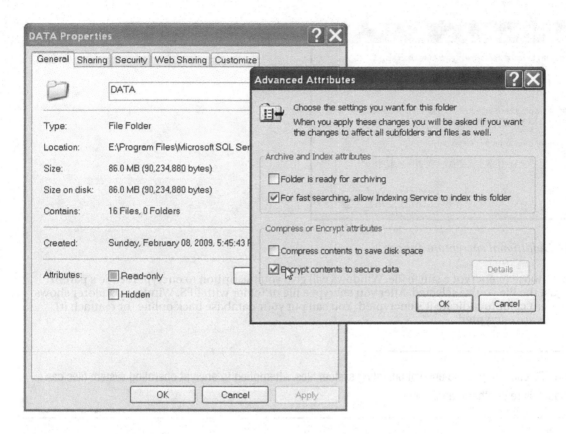

Figure 6-6. Enabling EFS on a folder

Once you select *OK*, Windows gives you additional options. For a folder, the OS will ask if you want to encrypt only the current folder or the folder, subfolders and files, as shown in Figure 6-7.

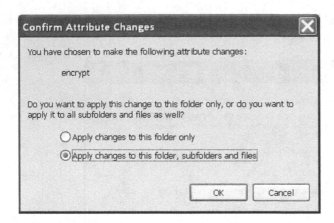

Figure 6-7. *Additional encryption options*

If you choose to encrypt a single file, Windows will give you the option to encrypt the file's parent folder or just the file you've selected. After you encrypt a file or folder with EFS, Windows Explorer shows it in a different color to indicate it's encrypted. You can put your database back online (or reattach it) once the files are encrypted.

■ **Caution** EFS can't be used to encrypt operating system files. Attempting to encrypt operating system files can result in boot failure or other malfunctions.

EFS supports the Triple DES, DESX, and AES algorithms as provided through the Windows CryptoAPI and Data Protection API (DPAPI). Some operating systems may require you to install service packs or additional high encryption upgrades in order to take advantage of all of these algorithms. Using a different algorithm from the default may also require you to edit registry settings.

To encrypt your files EFS generates a file encryption key (FEK) for each file you wish to encrypt. The FEK is protected by a certificate that's tied to the currently logged in user's login credentials. When you use EFS, Windows attempts to obtain a certificate from a certificate authority (CA). If you're not in an enterprise CA or Public Key Infrastructure (PKI) environment, Windows will issue a self-signed EFS certificate. Although an in-depth discussion of the inner workings of EFS are beyond the scope of this book, here are some general hints and tips for a good EFS implementation:

- Ensure that you back up your EFS certificates immediately. If you obtain your certificates from a trusted third-party CA, they should be able to supply you with replacement certificates in the event something happens.

- Trusted third-party CA certificates are considered more secure than self-signed certificates. You should use CA-issues certificates when possible, particularly in a domain.

- Because the certificates are tied to a user's login credentials ensure that you don't delete a domain user without first recovering all of that user's EFS encrypted data.

- EFS can use a domain recovery agent certificate to recover encrypted data in the event something happens to a domain user account.

- You can use the Microsoft Management Console (MMC) Certificates add-in to export your EFS certificates and private keys to back them up.

- During the initial file encryption process EFS might store the plaintext in temporary files. The temporary files are automatically deleted, but there's no guarantee that artifacts of the plaintext might remain on the hard drive in unallocated space until they are overwritten.

■ **Tip** More information about implementing EFS file encryption solutions in general can be found by searching for "EFS" on Microsoft TechNet at `http://technet.microsoft.com` and on MSDN at `http://msdn.microsoft.com`

BitLocker

With the introduction of Windows Vista, Microsoft introduced complete volume encryption via the BitLocker Drive Encryption option. The name is a bit misleading, since BitLocker actually operates on logical volumes, which may be defined as a portion of a physical drive or even span multiple drives. BitLocker is available in Windows Vista Enterprise, Windows Vista Ultimate, Windows Server 2008, and in prerelease versions of Windows 7 Ultimate.

Currently, BitLocker is only available in a limited number of Windows OS editions. If you're running an edition of Windows that doesn't include BitLocker support, you'll have to go with another encryption option like EFS. BitLocker is particularly useful for protecting entire laptop volumes that carry sensitive information, which may include SQL Server databases on any edition of SQL Server. BitLocker also includes Trusted Platform Module support, described later in this section, which ensures the integrity of your computer's boot path. As with other encryption options, BitLocker adds additional overhead to file access.

While EFS protects files and folders from unauthorized access by people who can access other resources on the computer, BitLocker protects entire volumes against thieves who gain physical control of a computer or its hard drives. Also unlike EFS, BitLocker encrypts operating system files, including the system swap file. In fact, BitLocker and EFS complement each other well.

When used with a computer that has a Trusted Platform Module (TPM) version 1.2 chip installed, BitLocker ensures the integrity of the trusted boot path. The TPM 1.2 is a chip installed in a computer that holds boot-time information about the system. It accomplishes this via Static Root of Trust for Measurement (SRTM). In SRTM, each component required to boot is brought online in a predetermined order, and each component measures the next component in the chain. The TPM 1.2 chip is brought up and measures the BIOS, for instance. Then the BIOS measures the MBR, and so on.

■ **Note** When these components "measure" one another, they calculate hash values for each component to determine if the component has been altered since BitLocker was activated. As each component is measured, the hash value returned is used to "extend" the TPM chip's platform configuration registers (PCRs). The extension process involves appending the new hash value to a PCR's existing hash value and generating a new hash from the combined contents of the PCR.

As the components measure one another in the chain, they extend one of the TPM module's platform configuration registers (PCRs). If the PCRs do not match the values calculated when BitLocker was activated, the TPM know that something has been altered (such as a hacker swapping out a BIOS chip) and the system cannot be trusted. If BitLocker determines that the system can't be trusted it boots to recovery mode and requires an authorized user to enter a recovery password.

When used with or without a TPM 1.2 chip, BitLocker encrypts all data on a logical volume. BitLocker can be configured to require authorized users to supply a USB key or PIN to gain access to the system and the encrypted volume. To install BitLocker on Windows Vista, you should install the BitLocker and EFS enhancements from Windows Update, as shown in Figure 6-8. These enhancements include the BitLocker Drive Preparation Tool to prepare your computer for BitLocker activation.

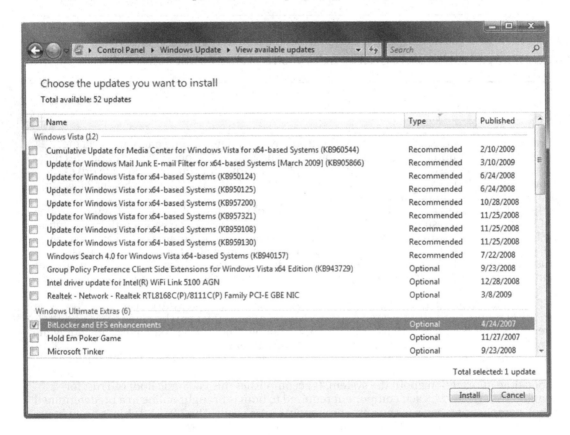

Figure 6-8. *Installing the BitLocker and EFS enhancements from Windows Update*

Once you've installed the BitLocker and EFS enhancements for Windows Vista, you can run the BitLocker Drive Preparation Tool from the start menu. This utility prepares your computer for BitLocker activation by creating a 1.5 GB partition for a *split-load configuration*. The split-load configuration separates the primary operating system partition from the active system partition. The drive preparation tool shrinks the primary partition if necessary, creates a new active partition, and copies the boot files to the new partition. Figure 6-9 shows the BitLocker Drive Preparation Tool in action.

■ **Caution** The new partition created for BitLocker use is not encrypted. You should not store anything on this partition, as it will not be protected by BitLocker.

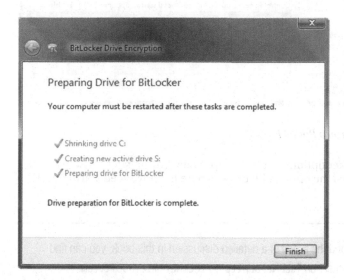

Figure 6-9. Preparing a drive for BitLocker

The changes made by the drive preparation tool require a reboot to take effect. After the reboot, you can change the default BitLocker settings in the Group Policy Editor. To access the Group Policy Editor, go to the start menu and enter gpedit.msc, as shown in Figure 6-10.

Figure 6-10. Accessing the Group Policy Editor

Once in the Group Policy Editor, you can access the BitLocker options by navigating to Computer Configuration ➤ Administrative Templates ➤ Windows Components ➤ BitLocker Drive Encryption menu, as shown in Figure 6-11.

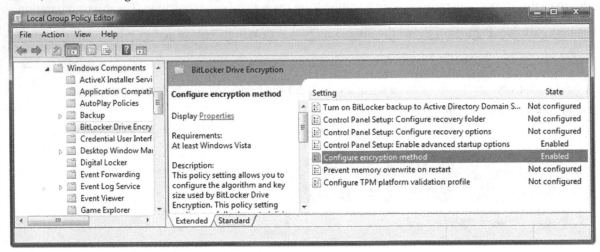

Figure 6-11. Viewing BitLocker options in the Group Policy Editor

Although you can configure several BitLocker options in the Group Policy Editor, such as Active Directory Domain support and recovery options, the options I'll discuss here are advanced startup and encryption method.

■ **Tip** Although many of the BitLocker options are beyond the scope of a detailed discussion in this book, you can find detailed information about them by searching for "BitLocker" on TechNet at http://technet.microsoft.com.

The advanced startup options allow you to install BitLocker on "unsupported" hardware—computers without a TPM chip. To install BitLocker on a computer without a TPM chip, simply double-click *Control Panel Setup: Enable advanced startup options* in the Group Policy Editor and check the *Allow BitLocker without a compatible TPM* option, as shown in Figure 6-12.

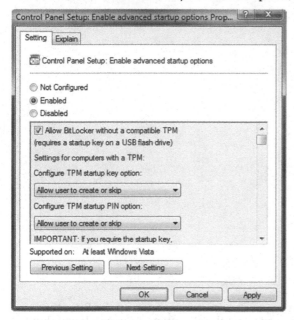

Figure 6-12. Configuring BitLocker to run on a computer with no TPM chip

The second option, *Configure encryption method*, allows you to choose the type of encryption BitLocker will use. The default is AES encryption with a 128-bit key and a diffuser. The diffuser option mixes up the bits of a sector prior to encryption, further obfuscating your data, and providing additional protection against attacks on the data. As shown in Figure 6-13, you can choose from four different options for BitLocker encryption.

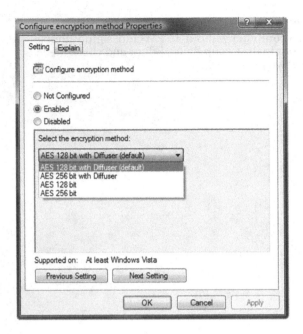

Figure 6-13. *Selecting a BitLocker encryption method*

After you've configured BitLocker options to fit your requirements, simply open up the *BitLocker Drive Encryption* item in your Control Panel. You'll then need to set the startup preferences. If you don't have a TPM chip, your only option is to require a USB key at startup, as shown in Figure 6-14.

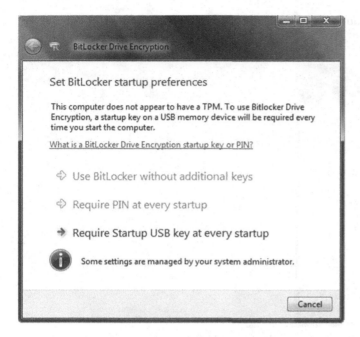

***Figure 6-14.** Setting BitLocker startup preferences*

You'll be prompted to insert a USB device to save your startup key, as Figure 6-15 illustrates.

***Figure 6-15.** Saving a startup key on a USB memory device*

If for some reason you need to recover your system, you'll need a copy of the recovery password. BitLocker will prompt you to save or print a recovery password during the setup process, as Figure 6-16 shows.

Figure 6-16. Save a recovery password

Once you've completed the setup, BitLocker encrypts the volume. As you can see in Figure 6-17, the BitLocker drive encryption process displays a status box indicating the percent of the encryption process completed.

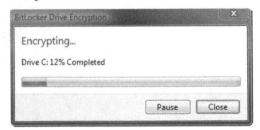

Figure 6-17. BitLocker encrypting a volume

Working While Encrypting

The encryption process can take a considerable amount of time—several hours, in fact. Your computer is accessible and usable during the encryption process. You can run other programs while the encryption is taking place, but your computer may be less responsive than usual. In addition to the CPU usage and the constant physical disk read and write activity during encryption, BitLocker consumes almost your entire hard drive leaving very little free space to perform other activities.

Rather than trying to locate all free space on the volume and encrypting it, BitLocker passes this task on to the underlying OS by creating a single file that takes up most of the free space on the drive. Because of this, you may encounter an out of disk space error while running other applications during the encryption process. For this reason, I would advise against running other applications, particularly those that are resource intensive, during the encryption process.

BitLocker will inform you with a message once the encryption is complete. Once BitLocker has been enabled, you'll need to supply the key storage media or enter the access PIN (depending on the options you chose at configuration) every time you turn your computer on. Figure 6-18 shows the boot screen requesting the key storage media for my laptop with BitLocker enabled.

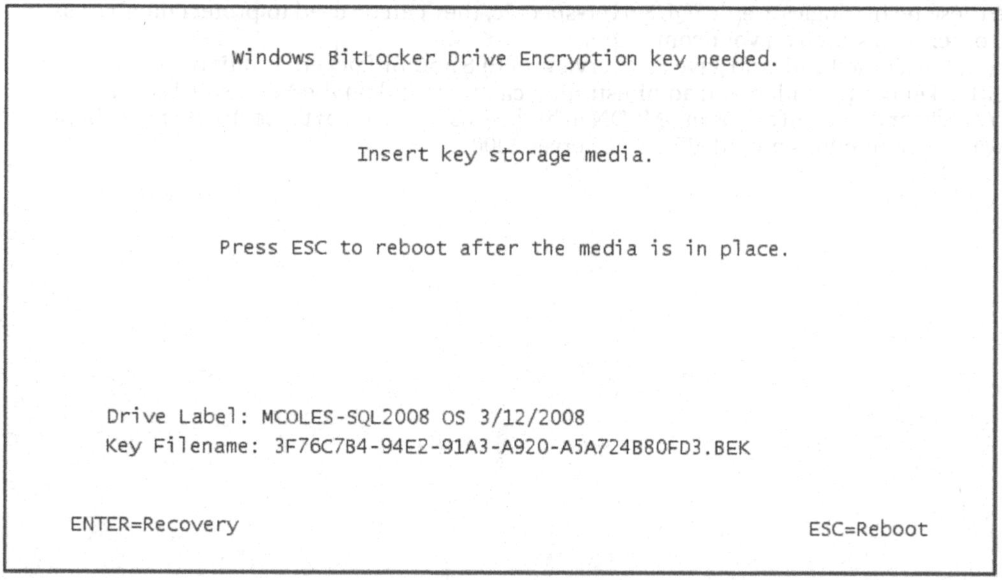

```
          Windows BitLocker Drive Encryption key needed.


                    Insert key storage media.


         Press ESC to reboot after the media is in place.




      Drive Label: MCOLES-SQL2008 OS 3/12/2008
      Key Filename: 3F76C7B4-94E2-91A3-A920-A5A724B80FD3.BEK


   ENTER=Recovery                              ESC=Reboot
```

Figure 6-18. *Boot screen requesting drive encryption key*

If you lose the key storage media or encounter other access problems, you may have to enter recovery mode, in which case you'll need the recovery password. As with other encryption technologies, make sure you keep your BitLocker key storage media, PIN numbers, and recovery keys secure.

Summary

As laptop computers become more powerful, they are increasingly used to store and process sensitive data with powerful applications like SQL Server. This makes these computers a prime target for data thieves who would otherwise have difficulty penetrating a secure corporate network to steal data. Encrypting data at rest is particularly important on laptop computers and on other computers that process sensitive data. This is particularly true for computers that aren't physically secured, such as desktop computers in open work areas.

SQL Server 2008 provides the new TDE feature to encrypt entire databases at once. This feature provides encryption security to SQL Server at the I/O level. TDE complements the functionality of SQL Server's extensive cell-level encryption and protects against theft of database files, log files, and backups.

In addition to SQL Server's new TDE functionality, Windows provides built-in encryption functionality that can be used to protect your data at rest. Windows's EFS option allows you to encrypt individual files and folders on a computer, while BitLocker encrypts an entire volume at once. BitLocker, when used with TPM 1.2 chips, can also ensure the integrity of critical components of your computer at boot time. While these technologies aren't SQL Server-specific, they can be used to protect databases, system files, and other data stored on your computers.

In this chapter, I discussed TDE and gave an overview of EFS and BitLocker. Additional information about EFS and BitLocker configuration and administration can be found on the Microsoft TechNet website at http://technet.microsoft.com and MSDN at http://msdn.microsoft.com. In the next chapter, I'll discuss one-way hash functions provided by SQL Server 2008.

CHAPTER 7

■ ■ ■

Hashing

In addition to the extensive cell-level encryption and TDE functionality that I discussed in previous chapters, SQL Server provides the ability to "fingerprint" your data via collision-free, one-way cryptographic hash functions. Cryptographic hash functions are also used to securely store login passwords, so you can avoid sending plaintext passwords over the wire. In this chapter, I'll explain cryptographic hash functions in general and discuss the hashing functionality available in SQL Server 2008.

Cryptographic Hash Functions

A cryptographic hash function is a well-defined procedure that accepts a block of data and generates a fixed-length bit string known as the *hash value* or *digest*. A good cryptographic hash function is defined by its properties, including the following:

- A cryptographic hash function is *deterministic*, so that a given block of input data will generate the same hash value no matter how many times it is run through the same hash function.

- A hash function is *one-way*, meaning the hash function procedure is irreversible. There is no function to derive the plain source data from the hash value.

- A small change in the source data should generate a substantial change in the hash value. This is known as a *cascading effect*.

- A hash function should be *collision-free*, so that the odds of two different blocks of source data generating the same hash value should be extremely unlikely. When two different source data blocks generate the same hash value it's known as a *collision*.

Cryptographic hash functions are used in a variety of applications, including secure password authentication procedures and change detection processes.

Hash Collisions

One of the main goals of a good cryptographic hash function is to eliminate hash collisions, or two different blocks of data generating the same hash value. A general hash collision can be generated by totally random data.

As an example, a general hash collision might be generated by a random block of data with no inherent meaning or structure. This is often the type of hash collision hackers look for when they are trying to access secure systems where hashes of the login passwords are stored, instead of the actual passwords themselves.

A more specific type of hash collision is known as a *meaningful hash collision*. A meaningful hash collision can be generated by a block of data that appears to have some structure and inherent meaning. Consider a situation in which Alice generates an asymmetric encryption certificate and she generates a hash value for the certificate. Now imagine that Eve acquires Alice's hash value and generates a modified certificate of her own. Eve's certificate would have the same structure as Alice's, but would contain different data. Eve then generates the same hash value for this certificate that Alice generated for hers. A system relying on the hash value of the certificate as a verification of authenticity will be fooled, possibly with disastrous results. The fact that Eve generated the same hash value as Alice, and both hash values were generated based on different data contained in structurally similar certificates, results in a meaningful hash collision.

Table 7-1 provides a quick comparison of the hash algorithms available through SQL Server 2008's HashBytes function.

Table 7-1. HashBytes-Supported Hash Functions

Algorithm	Name	Digest Length
SHA-1	SHA, SHA1	160 bits
MD5	MD5	128 bits
MD4	MD4	128 bits
MD2	MD2	128 bits

SHA Hash Function

The Secure Hash Algorithm (SHA) hash functions come in several varieties. The SHA-1 algorithm, the only SHA-family algorithm supported natively by SQL Server, operates on 32-bit words at a time. Figure 7-1 illustrates a single round of SHA-1 hashing.

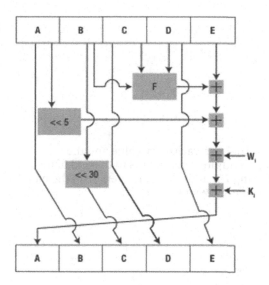

Figure 7-1. One iteration of the SHA-1 hash algorithm

As you can see from the figure, hashing is a convoluted enterprise that involves a lot of logical operations and shifting bits to generate a hash value from your plaintext. The boxes marked A through E represent 32-bit words in the SHA-1 internal state. The box marked F represents a varying nonlinear function. The "<< 5" and "<< 30" boxes represent left bit rotations of 5 bits and 30 bits, respectively. W_i and K_i represent the expanded message word and round constant of round *i*. Finally, the ⊞ symbol represents addition modulo 2^{32}. Fortunately, all of this calculation is abstracted away and performed under the covers, so all we have to worry about is passing the plaintext to the algorithm.

SHA-1 represents an improvement over the SHA-0 algorithm (often referred to simply as SHA) that it was designed to supersede. SHA-1 returns a 160-bit (20 byte) digest from a message with a maximum length of $2^{64} - 1$ bits (approximately $2^{61} - 1$ bytes). By comparison, SQL Server's LOB data types hold a maximum of 2^{31}, or approximately 2.1 billion, bytes of data. Although the SHA-1 algorithm can generate hashes of extremely large messages, the SQL Server implementation can hash only up to 8,000 bytes (slightly less than 2^{13} bytes) at a time.

Using HashBytes SHA-1

The SQL Server HashBytes function accepts two parameters: an algorithm name and a varbinary block of data to hash. The block of data to hash can be other data types, such as varchar or nvarchar, but it must be either implicitly convertible to varbinary or you must explicitly convert it. Listing 7-1 uses the HashBytes function to generate an SHA-1 hash of a name with results shown in Figure 7-2.

Listing 7-1. Generating an SHA-1 Hash of a Name in SQL Server

```
SELECT HashBytes('SHA1', 'Galileo Galilei');
```

Figure 7-2. *SHA-1 hash value of Galileo Galilei*

In this example, the string *Galileo Galilei* is implicitly converted to a varbinary value and then hashed using the SHA-1 algorithm. A slight change, like adding a couple of characters to the end of the string to hash, results in a significantly different hash value. Listing 7-2 adds the characters *IV* to the end of Galileo Galilei's name, with the significantly different hash value shown in Figure 7-3.

Listing 7-2. *SHA-1 Hash of a Slightly Modified Name*

```
SELECT HashBytes('SHA1', 'Galileo Galilei IV');
```

	(No column name)
1	0xD02F56405EE2E715ADFDC2A66D35E054BEB13D93

Figure 7-3. *SHA-1 hash value of Galileo Galilei IV*

Because the string data is implicitly converted to varbinary before the hash value is generated, the same string represented as nvarchar will produce a different result from its varchar representation. Listing 7-3 demonstrates the different hash values produced by the same string represented using the varchar and nvarchar data types. Results are shown in Figure 7-4.

Listing 7-3. *Hashing the Same String As varchar and nvarchar*

```
SELECT
    'varchar' AS Type,
    HashBytes('SHA1', 'Albert Einstein') AS HashValue

UNION ALL

SELECT
    'nvarchar',
    HashBytes('SHA1', N'Albert Einstein');
```

Results

	Type	HashValue
1	varchar	0x7303D2C9C8D914BA6BC4E91AB6A8DDD36ACCF5CC
2	nvarchar	0x647165187DE6D58C81C83D65657E4A8D860858F1

Figure 7-4. Differences between varchar and nvarchar hash values

HashBytes SHA-1 Limitations

One thing you may notice about the HashBytes function is that the only SHA-family hash function it supports is the SHA-1 function. You can use the hash function name SHA or SHA1 to generate an SHA-1 hash value with HashBytes.

Also important is that the HashBytes function supports only 8,000 bytes of input plaintext data. If you use a large object (LOB) data type, like varchar(max), and it contains a string of more than 8,000 bytes of data the HashBytes function truncates the data to 8,000 bytes before hashing it. Listing 7-4 demonstrates by hashing two strings, one of them greater than 8,000 bytes. The result is shown in Figure7-5.

Listing 7-4. Comparing SHA-1 Hashes of an 8,000 Byte String and a 9,000 Byte String

```
DECLARE
  @string8000 varchar(max) = REPLICATE('A', 8000),
  @string9000 varchar(max) = REPLICATE('A', 8000) + REPLICATE('Z', 1000);

SELECT
  '8,000 bytes' AS Length,
  HashBytes('SHA1', @string8000) AS HashValue
UNION ALL
SELECT
  '9,000 bytes',
  HashBytes('SHA1', @string9000);
```

Results

	Length	HashValue
1	8,000 bytes	0xD2967D6425E56C18BA979EEFB4E0DBD1269D9BC9
2	9,000 bytes	0xD2967D6425E56C18BA979EEFB4E0DBD1269D9BC9

Figure 7-5. Comparison of SHA-1 hashes of 8,000 and 9,000 byte input strings

The input data to the HashBytes function calls in Listing 7-4 consists of an input string consisting of 8,000 letter A's and an input string consisting of 8,000 letter A's concatenated with 1,000 letter Z's. Obviously the two strings are different, but they produce the same hash value, as you can see in Figure 7-5. The reason they produce the same hash values is simple: the HashBytes function truncates the 9,000 character input string to a mere 8,000 bytes. Since the first 8,000 bytes of both strings are equivalent (8,000 letter A's), the hash values generated are identical.

Hash Function Extension

You can circumvent the SQL Server 8,000-byte limit on the HashBytes function input data with a user-defined function to implement SHA-1 hash function *extension*. The idea behind hash function extension is relatively simple: You simply break your LOB data up into chunks and hash each chunk. You then calculate the SHA-1 hash value for the chunks one at a time and concatenate the hash values together. After generating hash values for two chunks of data, you generate the hash value of the concatenated hash values. Figure 7-6 shows a simplified representation of the process of calculating an extended hash value.

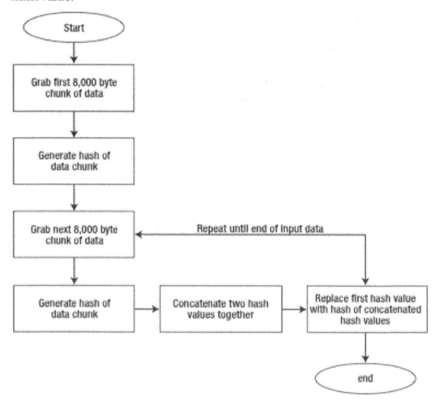

Figure 7-6. Calculating an extended hash for LOB data

They key to this figure is that, after the hash is generated for an 8,000 byte chunk of data, the hash value generated is concatenated with the previous hash value. Then a new hash is generated for the concatenated hash values and the process repeats until you run out of 8,000-byte chunks of plaintext. Listing 7-5 is an implementation of the SHA-1 hash extension shown in Figure 7-6. This implementation is a simple user-defined function named Sha1ExtendedHash.

Listing 7-5. User-Defined Function to Generate an Extended SHA-1 Hash

```
CREATE FUNCTION dbo.Sha1ExtendedHash (@input varchar(max))
RETURNS varbinary(20)
AS
BEGIN
  DECLARE
    @hashRegister1 varbinary(20) = NULL,
    @hashRegister2 varbinary(40) = NULL,
    @i int = 1;

  SELECT @hashRegister1 = HashBytes('SHA1', SUBSTRING(@input, @i, 8000));
  SET @i = @i + 8000;

  WHILE @i < DATALENGTH(@input)
  BEGIN
    SET @hashRegister2 = @hashRegister1 +
      HashBytes ('SHA1', SUBSTRING(@input, @i, 8000));
    SET @hashRegister1 = HashBytes('SHA1', @hashRegister2);
    SET @i = @i + 8000;
  END;

  RETURN @hashRegister1;
END;
GO
```

Listing 7-6 is a sample run of the Sha1ExtendedHash function with results shown in Figure 7-7. As you can see in the results, the Sha1ExtendedHash function accounts for the input data beyond the 8,000-byte HashBytes limit.

Listing 7-6. Testing the Extended Hash Function

```
DECLARE
  @string8000 varchar(max) = CAST(REPLICATE('A', 8000) AS varchar(max)),
  @string9000 varchar(max) = CAST(REPLICATE('A', 8000) AS varchar(max)) + REPLICATE('Z',
1000);

SELECT
  '8,000 bytes, normal' AS Length,
  HashBytes('SHA1', @string8000) AS HashValue

UNION ALL

SELECT
  '8,000 bytes, extended',
  dbo.Sha1ExtendedHash(@string8000)
```

```
UNION ALL

SELECT
  '9,000 bytes, extended',
  dbo.Sha1ExtendedHash(@string9000);
```

	Length	HashValue
1	8,000 bytes, normal	0xD2967D6425E56C18BA979EEFB4E0DBD1269D9BC9
2	8,000 bytes, extended	0xD2967D6425E56C18BA979EEFB4E0DBD1269D9BC9
3	9,000 bytes, extended	0x370E5BC985E28550BFA549EC31203887A088D8CD

Figure 7-7. Results of extended hash function

SHA-1 Security

A brute force attack requires time complexity of 2^{80}, meaning you would need over 10^{24} operations to find a collision. There has been a published theoretical attack on SHA-1 with time complexity 2^{63} (less than 10^{19} operations), which is significantly lower than a brute force attack on SHA-1. Currently, most cryptanalyst attacks on SHA-1 concern themselves with finding collisions in early rounds of computation, which is an important step in mounting successful attacks against the full algorithm. Because of the similarity of the algorithms, successful attacks on SHA-1's predecessor (SHA-0) have also raised concerns about the collision-resistance of SHA-1.

The end result of all this cryptanalysis is that the National Institute of Standards and Technology (NIST) has dictated that Federal agencies will use SHA-2 hash functions in place of SHA-1 after 2010. For now, however, SHA-1 is the most secure and collision-resistant hash algorithm available directly through the SQL Server HashBytes function.

Message Digest Family of Hash Functions

The Message Digest family of hash functions includes MD5, MD4, and MD2—all algorithms invented by Ron Rivest. These hash functions are available through the SQL Server HashBytes function. Like the SHA-1 hash functionality, HashBytes restricts the input data to hash to 8,000 bytes. I'll begin this section with a discussion of the once-popular MD5 hash function.

MD5 Hash Function

The MD5 hash function was designed as a replacement for Ron Rivest's MD4 hash function. This MD5 function uses a combination of nonlinear functions and rotation operations performed in rounds. Figure 7-8 illustrates a single round of MD5 hashing.

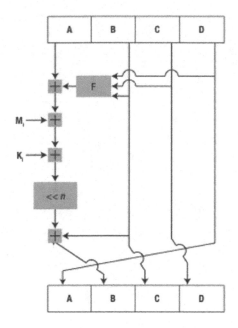

Figure 7-8. MD5 hashing round

As you can see in the figure, the Message Digest (MD) family of algorithms is somewhat convoluted, but still simpler than the SHA family of algorithms. The boxes marked A through D indicate the 32-bit words of the hash state. The box marked F is a nonlinear function that varies per round. The $<<_n$ box represents a left bit rotation operation, with the number of bits shifted varying per round. M_i and K_i represent a 32-bit block of the message and a round constant, respectively. The ⊞ symbol represents addition modulo 32. As with the SHA algorithms, the processing and calculations required to implement MD family algorithms is abstracted by the HashBytes function, so you don't have to deal with it directly.

The MD5 algorithm can accept an arbitrarily long block of input data, although SQL Server limits the input data to 8,000 bytes. The algorithm always returns a 128-bit (16-byte) hash value. Listing 7-7 generates MD5 hash values of rows stored in the SalesLT.Address table, storing them in a new table called SalesLT.AddressHash, with partial results shown in Figure 7-9. Notice the COALESCE function is used to eliminate NULL from the input source, since the string concatenation with NULL returns NULL.

Listing 7-7. MD5 Hashing of Rows in a Table

```
SELECT
  AddressID,
  AddressLine1,
  AddressLine2,
  City,
  StateProvince,
  CountryRegion,
  PostalCode,
  HashBytes
```

```
(
    'MD5',
    COALESCE(AddressLine1, 0x00) + '|' +
    COALESCE(AddressLine2, 0x00) + '|' +
    COALESCE(City, 0x00) + '|' +
    COALESCE(StateProvince, 0x00) + '|' +
    COALESCE(CountryRegion, 0x00) + '|' +
    COALESCE(PostalCode, 0x00) + '|'
  ) AS AddressHash
INTO SalesLT.AddressHash
FROM SalesLT.Address;
GO

SELECT
  AddressID,
  AddressLine1,
  AddressLine2,
  City,
  StateProvince,
  CountryRegion,
  PostalCode,
  AddressHash
FROM SalesLT.AddressHash;
GO
```

	AddressID	AddressLine1	AddressLin..	City	StateProvince	CountryRegi...	PostalCode	AddressHash
1	532	#500-75 O'Connor Street	NULL	Ottawa	Ontario	Canada	K4B 1S2	0x8FB9027E516774ABE549323445A70A70
2	497	#9900 2700 Production Way	NULL	Burnaby	British Columbia	Canada	V5A 4X1	0x7FB636AC565BE605F6F3EAD6983DCD55
3	859	1050 Oak Street	NULL	Seattle	Washington	United States	98104	0x91DF2AE475F04B01CD1D8D7EAE5A6384
4	604	1200 First Ave.	NULL	Joliet	Illinois	United States	60433	0xC44F35F53F19670920E1231E85F82CF4
5	1038	123 Camelia Avenue	NULL	Oxnard	California	United States	93030	0x8529C401BB2AE5C99D068499E4928238
6	594	123 W. Lake Ave.	NULL	Peoria	Illinois	United States	61606	0xBFA1A9D57115807F55574A704C9C02E4
7	559	12345 Sterling Avenue	NULL	Irving	Texas	United States	75061	0xEFA6AEB0E1C729B757B779E4A6F2EC16
8	11	1318 Lasalle Street	NULL	Bothell	Washington	United States	98011	0xF7161DE99B338A7BF111C85CBFF83FC9
9	855	15 East Main	NULL	Port Orchard	Washington	United States	98366	0x9B9781BD926A49D0904A5C706082F113
10	11380	165 North Main	NULL	Austin	Texas	United States	78701	0xCB74AD73ED5A6909DC7E0D7F0AD65301
11	11381	2000 300th Street	NULL	Denver	Colorado	United States	80203	0x230EC81F7F9A86B6B837C1D7EDD31F07
12	491	20225 Lansing Ave	NULL	Montreal	Quebec	Canada	H1Y 2H7	0xFB91FB590479C5E9FC407EC136501F7F
13	578	220 Mercy Drive	NULL	Garland	Texas	United States	75040	0x8669643B79988FE3F5DAD8865A797120
14	905	225 South 314th Street	NULL	Federal Way	Washington	United States	98003	0x2C3B827F7AC2C3DDF086ADB98BC3C443
15	832	2251 Elliot Avenue	NULL	Seattle	Washington	United States	98104	0x72D855800324FAE170955D1FB48F86F2

Figure 7-9. Address data with hash values for each row

As in the SHA sample code, the HashBytes function in this example accepts only two parameters—the algorithm name and the block of data to hash. The algorithm name for MD5 is, of course, MD5. The data block in this instance consists of the concatenated values of the columns in the table.

■ **Tip** When concatenating columns, use the COALESCE function to handle NULL since passing NULL to the HashBytes function results in a NULL hash value.

This particular example demonstrates a useful feature of hash values. You can use them to detect changes in data. You can recalculate hash values later to determine if any of the rows' content has changes. By comparing the previously generated hash values with the newly generated hash values for each row, you can easily detect even the slightest change without performing value comparisons across several columns. This can provide a nice performance benefit at comparison time for very large tables.

■ **Tip** Using hash values to detect changes is a particularly useful method for increasing efficiency of Extract, Transform and Load (ETL) applications that support enterprise data warehousing. This is particularly important for reducing network traffic by transmitting hash values over the network instead of raw data when resources like network bandwidth are at a premium.

MD5 Security

Although MD5 was one of the most widely used hash algorithms throughout the 1990s and into the early 2000s, it has recently fallen prey to ingenious attacks that have compromised its security. Cryptanalysts have been able to come up with methods to quickly generate MD5 hash collisions, and have even created high-quality meaningful collisions like fake certificates.

These exploits are widely known and MD5 is definitely not the hash algorithm of choice for high-security applications. If you are hashing passwords or using a hash function for other applications that require heightened levels of security, use an SHA-family algorithm instead of MD5.

Attacking the Hash

When we talk about cryptanalysts attacking an encryption algorithm the meaning is pretty clear. Basically, the attacker is trying to find a way to decrypt data without knowledge of the secret key used to encrypt the data. When we talk about attacking a hash algorithm the meaning is slightly different. The point of attacking a hash algorithm is to find one or more blocks of different source data that generate the same hash value—generating a hash collision.

The security of a hash algorithm is initially estimated by the number of bits in the resulting hash values. The SHA-1 algorithm, for instance, generates a 160-bit hash value. Finding a value that generates a specific hash value through brute force would be expected to have an estimated complexity of 2^{80} operations. To compromise the security of a hash algorithm cryptanalysts try to find a shortcut to generate hash collisions.

With SHA-1, this shortcut was discovered in 2005 when Chinese researchers discovered a way to lower the complexity to 2^{69} operations to find a collision. This was refined about six months later and a reduced complexity of 2^{63} operations to find a collision was determined. Collisions are the primary threat to cryptographic hash functions, since the security of a hash function relies on its ability to generate unique values for given input data blocks.

MD4 and MD2

The MD4 algorithm was invented by Ron Rivest in 1990. Flaws in its security were quickly discovered, and it was almost immediately replaced with the improved MD5 algorithm in 1991. MD4 has proven vulnerable to cryptanalysis attacks and should not be used for secure applications. The SQL Server HashBytes function exposes the MD4 algorithm with the algorithm name MD4.

The MD2 algorithm, invented by Rivest in 1989, is still in use today in various applications. Because it has been shown to vulnerability to specific types of attacks by cryptanalysts, MD2 is no longer considered viable for secure applications. MD2 is exposed with the algorithm name MD2 by the HashBytes function.

It's highly recommended that you avoid using MD2 and MD4 hash functions, particularly for secure applications.

CHECKSUM Functions

The HashBytes function was introduced in SQL Server 2005 and continued in SQL Server 2008, but SQL Server has long had the ability to generate hashes of data in tables through the CHECKSUM function (and other related functions). CHECKSUM takes a variable number of values as parameters and generates a 32-bit hash value (an int) of the data. Listing 7-8 generates CHECKSUM values for the rows in the SalesLT.Address table. Partial results are shown in Figure 7-10.

Listing 7-8. Generating Checksum Hash Values for a Table

```
SELECT
  AddressID,
  CHECKSUM
  (
    AddressLine1,
    AddressLine2,
    City,
    StateProvince,
    CountryRegion,
    PostalCode
  ) AS AddressChecksums
FROM SalesLT.Address;
```

Results

	AddressID	AddressChecksums
1	532	355091013
2	497	-728560029
3	859	-60691066
4	604	-1988604453
5	1038	55821441
6	594	1443356654
7	559	390604245
8	11	-160303215
9	855	-1620019904
10	11380	41931144
11	11381	52708546
12	491	-404643219
13	578	2009634143
14	905	-568948531
15	832	-905659990

Figure 7-10. *Checksum hash values on SalesLT.Address rows*

Unfortunately the `CHECKSUM` family of functions has a couple of serious shortcomings. First, they generate only 32-bit `int` hash values, meaning collisions are extremely likely. In fact, a brute force search for collisions requires only 2^{16} operations without a shortcut.

The other problem is that the algorithm used is extremely simple. The simplicity of the algorithm means that collisions are not only possible, they're extremely likely. For one thing, the `CHECKSUM` algorithm seems to cycle after every 16 characters as shown in Listing 7-9. The results are shown in Figure 7-11.

Listing 7-9. *CHECKSUM Function 16-Character Cycle*

```
SELECT
  'LE' AS String,
  CHECKSUM('LE') AS CheckSumHash

UNION ALL

SELECT
  'AAAAAAAAAAAAAAAALE',
  CHECKSUM('AAAAAAAAAAAAAAAALE');
```

Results

	String	CheckSumHash
1	LE	2306
2	AAAAAAAAAAAAAAAALE	2306

Figure 7-11. *Results of CHECKSUM 16-character cycle query*

The 16-character cyclic nature of the CHECKSUM algorithm isn't the only shortcoming in the algorithm. We can achieve the same result with two characters, as shown in Listing 7-10 and with results shown in Figure 7-12.

Listing 7-10. Two-Character Collisions with CHECKSUM

```
SELECT
  'LE' AS String,
  CHECKSUM('LE') AS CheckSumHash

UNION ALL

SELECT
  'MU',
  CHECKSUM('MU');
```

	String	CheckSumHash
1	LE	2306
2	MU	2306

Figure 7-12. Two-character CHECKSUM collisions

Some simple tests prove that simple collisions like this with CHECKSUM aren't the exception, but rather they are the rule. In fact, of the 676 possible two-letter combinations of the letters A–Z ("AA," "AB," etc.) the CHECKSUM function generates 244 collisions. By definition this is not even close to "collision-free."

A variant of CHECKSUM, the BINARY_CHECKSUM function, takes case-sensitivity into account. You would think that a case-sensitive hash function would provide greater collision-resistance than a case-insensitive version of the same function. But that's actually not the case. Listing 7-11 shows how to generate collisions with the case-sensitive BINARY_CHECKSUM function. Results are shown in Figure 7-13.

Listing 7-11. BINARY_CHECKSUM Collisions

```
SELECT
  'LE' AS String,
  BINARY_CHECKSUM('LE') AS CheckSumHash

UNION ALL

SELECT
  'MU',
  BINARY_CHECKSUM('MU')

UNION ALL

SELECT
  'Ne',
  BINARY_CHECKSUM('Ne')
```

```
UNION ALL

SELECT
  'Ou',
  BINARY_CHECKSUM('Ou');
```

	String	CheckSumHash
1	LE	1157
2	MU	1157
3	Ne	1157
4	Ou	1157

Figure 7-13. Two-character collisions with BINARY_CHECKSUM

While the CHECKSUM and BINARY_CHECKSUM functions generate 32-bit checksums across rows of data and individual values, SQL Server also provides the CHECKSUM_AGG function which can supposedly detect changes in integer columns of a table. The simplicity of the similar algorithm behind the CHECKSUM_AGG function means it's not all that useful either.

Books Online indicates that for these hash functions "there is a small chance the checksum will not change." Microsoft advises against using CHECKSUM and related functions to try to detect change in tables. I'll go one step further and advise against using them to detect any type of data change anywhere, because there is a very *high* probability that you will miss some changes to your data. The probability of missing data changes increases significantly as your data set grows. And when hash code security is an issue, such as hashing passwords, don't even think about using the CHECKSUM family of hash functions. I would advise everyone not to use the CHECKSUM family of functions for cryptographic hashing applications. CHECKSUM is, however, handy for generating "random" numbers when used with the NEWID function, as demonstrated in Chapter 4.

■ **Note** My warning against CHECKSUM is not just theoretical. I've seen it fail to detect changes in production database tables with as few as 10,000 rows in them. I've also tested it against data sources, such as the common names lists distributed by the US Census Bureau. In some instances, with real data, the collision rate was as high as 10 percent. That's a lot of potential data changes to miss.

As you can tell, I am thoroughly convinced that CHECKSUM and its related functions are nearly useless. The only useful purpose I've found for them at this point is for use in generating somewhat random numbers with the NEWID function (as demonstrated in the random credit card number generation code in Chapter 4).

Summary

Hash algorithms and the hash values they generate are a useful tool for fingerprinting your data and detecting change. Hashes can be used to detect both expected changes during the normal course of business and changes introduced for more nefarious purposes. Hashes also provide a means of storing passwords, so that the plaintext passwords do not have to be stored or transmitted across an open network.

Your choice of hash algorithm should depend on your security needs as well as your need to avoid hash collisions. SHA-1 is the most secure and collision-free hash function available with SQL Server's built-in hashing functionality. Other hash functions, such as MD5, MD4, and MD2, are less secure and should be avoided when security is a primary determining factor. The CHECKSUM family of built-in functions should be avoided for change detection or for secure applications.

In the next chapter, I'll discuss how to access additional encryption functionality via SQL CLR. This includes even more powerful and more secure hash algorithms exposed by the .NET Framework. In Chapter 9, I'll revisit hashing and talk about more secure methods of generating hash codes in a discussion of indexing your data encrypted at the cell level.

CHAPTER 8

∎ ∎ ∎

SQL CLR Cryptography

Until this point, I've discussed the wide assortment of cryptographic functionality built in to SQL Server. The tools I've talked about include symmetric and asymmetric encryption functions, encryption key management, hashing, EKM, and TDE. These tools provide an impressive level of cryptographic functionality that can help make SQL Server databases more secure than ever.

Even as I've discussed the power of these built-in SQL Server encryption functions, however, I've also discussed their limitations. The symmetric encryption and hash functions can encrypt only 8,000 bytes of data, for instance. In this chapter, I'll talk about how you can use the SQL Server Common Language Runtime (SQL CLR) to overcome some of these limitations by accessing functions in the .NET Framework's System.Security.Cryptography namespace from T-SQL.

Encrypting By Passphrase

As I explained in Chapter 3, SQL Server's built-in EncryptByPassphrase function accepts a passphrase and a block of data. This function uses the passphrase to generate an encryption key and then uses the key to encrypt the data with the Triple DES algorithm. There are two limitations with this method of encryption—you can't specify a different algorithm and you can't encrypt more than 8,000 bytes at one time.

Fortunately, SQL CLR allows you to work around these limitations, as I'll demonstrate in the code samples in this section. These C# code samples implement two new functions, EncryptAesByPassPhrase and DecryptAesByPassPhrase. These two functions mirror the functionality of SQL Server's built-in EncryptByPassPhrase and DecryptByPassPhrase functions. The signatures of the new SQL CLR functions are shown in the following:

```
EncryptAesByPassPhrase (PassPhrase, Plaintext, AddAuthenticator, Authenticator)
DecryptAesByPassPhrase (PassPhrase, Ciphertext, AddAuthenticator, Authenticator)
```

The functions share three parameters in common: *PassPhrase* is the password or passphrase used to internally generate an AES encryption key. *AddAuthenticator* is a bit value, which should be 1, if you want to use an authenticator to encrypt the text, or it can be 0 or NULL if you don't want to use an authenticator. The *Authenticator* parameter is an nvarchar string that can be used to further obfuscate your ciphertext (assuming you set AddAuthenticator to 1). The SHA-1 hash value of the *Authenticator* value is appended to your *PassPhrase* prior to encryption key generation.

EncryptAesByPassPhrase Function

The EncryptAesByPassPhrase function accepts a varbinary(max) value for its *Plaintext* parameter. This plaintext is encrypted with the AES algorithm with a 256-bit encryption key. The result is an encrypted varbinary(max). Listing 8-1 is the C# source code listing for the EncryptByPassPhrase function.

■ **Note** The result of EncryptAesByPassPhrase has a 16-byte random initialization vector (IV)/salt value prepended to the encrypted ciphertext. The ciphertext is encrypted in CBC mode, which I described in Chapter 3.

Listing 8-1. *EncryptByPassPhrase Source Code*

```
[Microsoft.SqlServer.Server.SqlFunction
(
  IsDeterministic = false,
  DataAccess = DataAccessKind.None
)]
[return: SqlFacet(MaxSize = -1)]
public static SqlBytes EncryptAesByPassPhrase
(
  SqlString PassPhrase,
  [SqlFacet(MaxSize = -1)] SqlBytes Plaintext,
  SqlBoolean AddAuthenticator,
  SqlString Authenticator
)
{
  try
  {
    // Automatically return NULL if passphrase or plaintext is NULL
    if (PassPhrase.IsNull || Plaintext.IsNull)
      return SqlBytes.Null;

    // Generate hash for authenticator
    SHA1Managed Sha1 = new SHA1Managed();
    string AuthHash = "";  // If authenticator not used, use empty string
    // Convert the authenticator hash to Base64 to avoid conversion problems
    if (AddAuthenticator.IsTrue && !Authenticator.IsNull)
      AuthHash = Convert.ToBase64String
      (
        Sha1.ComputeHash
        (
          Encoding.Unicode.GetBytes(Authenticator.Value)
        )
      );
    // Append authenticator to passphrase
    string AuthPass = PassPhrase.Value + AuthHash;
```

```
// Next derive a key from the passphrase + authenticator
// with random 16 byte Salt
Rfc2898DeriveBytes KeyGenerator = new Rfc2898DeriveBytes(AuthPass, 16);

// Create a Rijndael/AES encryption object
Rijndael Aes = Rijndael.Create();
Aes.KeySize = 256;
Aes.Mode = CipherMode.CBC;
Aes.IV = KeyGenerator.GetBytes(Aes.BlockSize >> 3);  // Assign the IV
Aes.Key = KeyGenerator.GetBytes(Aes.KeySize >> 3);   // Assign the Key

// Now get the raw plain text
byte[] rawData = Plaintext.Value;

// Use a MemoryStream wrapping a CryptoStream with a Rijndael encryptor
// to encrypt the data
using (MemoryStream memoryStream = new MemoryStream())
{
  using
  (
    CryptoStream cryptoStream = new CryptoStream
    (
      memoryStream,
      Aes.CreateEncryptor(),
      CryptoStreamMode.Write
    )
  )
  {
    // First write out the 16 byte salt so we can regenerate the same
    // key next time
    memoryStream.Write(KeyGenerator.Salt, 0, 16);
    // Now write out the encrypted data
    cryptoStream.Write(rawData, 0, rawData.Length);
    cryptoStream.Close();

    // Convert the encrypted data in memory to an array and return
    // as a SqlBytes object
    byte[] encrypted = memoryStream.ToArray();
    return new SqlBytes(encrypted);
  }
}
}
catch

{
  // Return NULL if an encryption error occurs
  return SqlBytes.Null;
}
}
```

The first part of this listing is the function declaration, as shown in the following code snippet.

```
[Microsoft.SqlServer.Server.SqlFunction
(
  IsDeterministic = false,
  DataAccess = DataAccessKind.None
)]
[return: SqlFacet(MaxSize = -1)]
public static SqlBytes EncryptAesByPassPhrase
(
  SqlString PassPhrase,
  [SqlFacet(MaxSize = -1)] SqlBytes Plaintext,
  SqlBoolean AddAuthenticator,
  SqlString Authenticator
)
```

The declaration begins with the Microsoft.SqlServer.Server.SqlFunction attribute. Since this function doesn't access data, the DataAccess property is set to DataAccessKind.None. Also, since the encryption algorithm generates a random Salt/IV internally the result is nondeterministic, which is reflected by setting the IsDeterministic property to false. Setting the SqlFacet attribute's MaxSize property to -1 allows the function to return a varbinary(max) result. The parameters are declared as described previously in this section.

As the following code shows, the main body of the function is surrounded by a try...catch block.

```
try
{
  ...
}
catch
{
  // Return NULL if an encryption error occurs
  return SqlBytes.Null;
}
```

The try...catch block ensures that if an exception is thrown during the encryption process the function returns a NULL result. This is important and ensures that if an error occurs the function will degrade gracefully.

___

Tip You should always use try...catch blocks in your SQL CLR code to gracefully handle exceptions in your code.

___

The main body of the function that performs the actual encryption is based in the try block. As the following code shows, the first step is to degrade gracefully if NULL is passed in as either the *PassPhrase* or the *Plaintext*.

```
// Automatically return NULL if passphrase or plaintext is NULL
if (PassPhrase.IsNull || Plaintext.IsNull)
  return SqlBytes.Null;
```

The next step generates an SHA-1 hash for the *Authenticator* value, if one was supplied, and appends the hash value to the *PassPhrase*. Because the *PassPhrase* is a string value the SHA-1 hash is converted to a Base64 string to avoid binary to string conversion issues. The hash generation and *PassPhrase*/*Authenticator* combination is shown in the following code snippet.

```
// Generate hash for authenticator
SHA1Managed Sha1 = new SHA1Managed();
string AuthHash = "";  // If authenticator not used, use empty string
// Convert the authenticator hash to Base64 to avoid conversion problems
if (AddAuthenticator.IsTrue && !Authenticator.IsNull)
  AuthHash = Convert.ToBase64String
  (
    Sha1.ComputeHash
    (
      Encoding.Unicode.GetBytes(Authenticator.Value)
    )
  );
// Append authenticator to passphrase
string AuthPass = PassPhrase.Value + AuthHash;
```

The *PassPhrase*/*Authenticator* hash combination string is used by a .NET class called Rfc2898DeriveBytes to generate an encryption key and IV with a 16-byte salt, as shown in the following.

```
// Next derive a key from the passphrase + authenticator
// with random 16-bit Salt
Rfc2898DeriveBytes KeyGenerator = new Rfc2898DeriveBytes(AuthPass, 16);
```

Deriving Encryption Keys

The Rfc2898DeriveBytes function uses the Password-Based Key Derivation Function (PBKDF2) to generate encryption keys. The PBKDF2 algorithm applies a cryptographic function, such as a hash or HMAC, and a salt value in a repetitive process, to generate a cryptographically secure encryption key. The Rfc2898DeriveBytes class replaces the older PasswordDeriveBytes class.

Once the function derives an encryption key, it creates a Rijndael encryption object. Rijndael is the encryption algorithm known as AES. In fact, Rijndael supports more key size options than the approved AES version of the algorithm. Thus, AES is a subset of Rijndael. The IV and Key properties for the encryption object are assigned from the Rfc2898DeriveBytes key generation object created previously. The encryption object exposes the IV and key lengths in terms of bits, so I have to divide by eight (equivalent to a shift of three bits right) to calculate the length in bytes. This is shown in the following code snippet.

```
// Create a Rijndael/AES encryption object
Rijndael Aes = Rijndael.Create();
Aes.KeySize = 256;
Aes.Mode = CipherMode.CBC;
Aes.IV = KeyGenerator.GetBytes(Aes.BlockSize >> 3);  // Assign the IV
Aes.Key = KeyGenerator.GetBytes(Aes.KeySize >> 3);   // Assign the Key
```

171

The next step is to assign the raw *Plaintext* to a byte array.

```
// Now get the raw plain text
byte[] rawData = Plaintext.Value;
```

Up to now, everything in the function has revolved around setup for the actual encryption process. At this point, all that's left to do is perform the actual encryption. The encryption process wraps a .NET MemoryStream around a CryptoStream, using the Rijndael encryption object created previously. This is the wrapper around the actual encryption process, as shown in the following code snippet.

```
// Use a MemoryStream wrapping a CryptoStream with a Rijndael encryptor
// to encrypt the data
using (MemoryStream memoryStream = new MemoryStream())
{
  using
  (
    CryptoStream cryptoStream = new CryptoStream
    (
      memoryStream,
      Aes.CreateEncryptor(),
      CryptoStreamMode.Write
    )
  )
  {
    ...
  }
}
```

Once the MemoryStream and CryptoStream are created, the first step to returning an encrypted result is to output the unencrypted salt value directly to the MemoryStream. The next step is to write the plain text of the raw data out to the CryptoStream, which automatically encrypts as it writes.

```
// First write out the 16-byte salt so we can regenerate the same
// key next time
memoryStream.Write(KeyGenerator.Salt, 0, 16);
// Now write out the encrypted data
cryptoStream.Write(rawData, 0, rawData.Length);
cryptoStream.Close();
```

The last step is to convert the MemoryStream to a byte array in memory, convert the byte array to a SqlBytes object, and finally return it to SQL Server.

```
// Convert the encrypted data in memory to an array and return
// as a SqlBytes object
byte[] encrypted = memoryStream.ToArray();
return new SqlBytes(encrypted);
```

DecryptAesByPassPhrase

The DecryptAesByPassPhrase function is the inverse of the EncryptAesByPassPhrase function. It accepts the varbinary(max) output of the EncryptAesByPassPhrase function as its *Ciphertext* parameter. You also need to supply the matching *PassPhrase*, *AddAuthenticator*, and *Authenticator* values you used with EncryptAesByPassPhrase at encryption time. If these values don't match, the decrypted result won't be correct—and will probably be NULL, in fact. Listing 8-2 is the complete C# listing for the DecryptAesByPassPhrase function.

Listing 8-2. DecryptAesByPassPhrase Source Code

```
[Microsoft.SqlServer.Server.SqlFunction
(
  IsDeterministic = true,
  DataAccess = DataAccessKind.None
)]
[return: SqlFacet(MaxSize = -1)]
public static SqlBytes DecryptAesByPassPhrase
(
  SqlString PassPhrase,
  [SqlFacet(MaxSize = -1)] SqlBytes Ciphertext,
  SqlBoolean AddAuthenticator,
  SqlString Authenticator
)
{
  try
  {
    // Automatically return NULL if passphrase or plaintext is NULL
    if (PassPhrase.IsNull || Ciphertext.IsNull)
      return SqlBytes.Null;

    // Get the ciphertext into a byte array
    byte[] rawData = Ciphertext.Value;

    // Get the 16-byte salt from the byte array
    byte[] Salt = new byte[16];
    for (int i = 0; i < 16; i++)
      Salt[i] = rawData[i];

    // Generate hash for authenticator
    SHA1Managed Sha1 = new SHA1Managed();
    string AuthHash = "";    // If no authenticator, use empty string
    // Convert the authenticator hash to Base64 to avoid conversion problems
    if (AddAuthenticator.IsTrue && !Authenticator.IsNull)
    AuthHash = Convert.ToBase64String
      (
        Sha1.ComputeHash(Encoding.Unicode.GetBytes(Authenticator.Value))
      );
    // Append authenticator to passphrase
    string AuthPass = PassPhrase.Value + AuthHash;
```

```
    // Next derive a key from the passphrase + authenticator, with 16-bit Salt
    Rfc2898DeriveBytes keyGenerator = new Rfc2898DeriveBytes(AuthPass, Salt);

    // Create a Rijndael/AES encryption object
    Rijndael Aes = Rijndael.Create();
    Aes.KeySize = 256;
    Aes.Mode = CipherMode.CBC;
    Aes.IV = keyGenerator.GetBytes(Aes.BlockSize >> 3); // Assign the IV
    Aes.Key = keyGenerator.GetBytes(Aes.KeySize >> 3);  // Assign the key

    // Wrap a CryptoStream in a MemoryStream to decrypt the data
    using (MemoryStream memoryStream = new MemoryStream())
    {
      using
      (
        CryptoStream cryptoStream = new CryptoStream
        (
          memoryStream,
          Aes.CreateDecryptor(),
          CryptoStreamMode.Write
        )
      )
      {
        // Decrypt and write out the decrypted data with the CryptoStream
        // ...ignore the leading 16 bytes, the Salt
        cryptoStream.Write(rawData, 16, rawData.Length - 16);
        cryptoStream.Close();

        // Put the decrypted MemoryStream in a byte array and return as SqlBytes
        byte[] decrypted = memoryStream.ToArray();
        return new SqlBytes(decrypted);
      }
    }
  }
  catch
  {
    // If there's an exception return NULL
    return SqlBytes.Null;
  }
}
```

The DecryptAesByPassPhrase function listing is similar to the EncryptAesByPassPhrase function in many regards. There are some differences, though. Consider the declaration, shown below, which defines the function as deterministic with no data access.

```
[Microsoft.SqlServer.Server.SqlFunction
(
  IsDeterministic = true,
  DataAccess = DataAccessKind.None
)]
[return: SqlFacet(MaxSize = -1)]
public static SqlBytes DecryptAesByPassPhrase
```

```
(
  SqlString PassPhrase,
  [SqlFacet(MaxSize = -1)] SqlBytes Ciphertext,
  SqlBoolean AddAuthenticator,
  SqlString Authenticator
)
```

The decryption function is deterministic because its output is always determined entirely by the input parameters, with no random elements introduced by the function. Like its sister function, the body of the DecryptAesByPassPhrase function is wrapped in a try...catch block. This is particularly important for decryption since passing in a bad *PassPhrase* or *Authenticator* can result in an exception during the decryption process. The try...catch block ensures the function degrades gracefully, returning NULL, if an exception occurs.

While the encryption function setup generates a random salt for encryption key generation, the decryption function needs to use the previously generated salt to generate the same encryption key. This is shown in the following code snippet.

```
// Get the 16-byte salt from the byte array
byte[] Salt = new byte[16];
for (int i = 0; i < 16; i++)
  Salt[i] = rawData[i];

...

// Next derive a key from the passphrase + authenticator, with 16-bit Salt
Rfc2898DeriveBytes keyGenerator = new Rfc2898DeriveBytes(AuthPass, Salt);
```

Also, like the encryption function, the decryption function has its main functionality in a MemoryStream wrapping a CryptoStream. The difference is that the decryption function CryptoStream creates a Rijndael decryptor instead of an encryptor, as shown in the following snippet.

```
using (MemoryStream memoryStream = new MemoryStream())
{
  using
  (
    CryptoStream cryptoStream = new CryptoStream
    (
      memoryStream,
      Aes.CreateDecryptor(),
      CryptoStreamMode.Write
    )
  )
  {
    ...
  }
}
```

To decrypt the function simply writes the encrypted ciphertext to the CryptoStream. The write ignores the first 16 bytes of the ciphertext since that's where the EncryptAesByPassPhrase function stores the random salt/IV generated at encryption time. The heart of the decryption code is shown in the following code.

```
// Decrypt and write out the decrypted data with the CryptoStream
// ...ignore the leading 16 bytes, the Salt
cryptoStream.Write(rawData, 16, rawData.Length - 16);
cryptoStream.Close();

// Put the decrypted MemoryStream in a byte array and return as SqlBytes
byte[] decrypted = memoryStream.ToArray();
return new SqlBytes(decrypted);
```

Testing the Functions

One of the advantages of the EncryptAesByPassPhrase and DecryptAesByPassPhrase functions are that they can encrypt and decrypt binary large object (BLOB) data, up to 2.1 GB in size. The standard EncryptByPassPhrase and DecryptByPassPhrase functions are limited to encrypting and decrypting less than 8,000 bytes of data. Listing 8-3 demonstrates how to encrypt and decrypt a 20,000 byte string using the new functions. The results are shown in Figure 8-1.

Listing 8-3. Encrypting and Decrypting BLOB Data

```
-- Generate a 20,000 byte (10 chars X 2000 = 20,000 chars) character string
DECLARE @plaintext varchar(max);
SET @plaintext = REPLICATE(CAST('ABCDEFGHIJ' AS varchar(max)), 2000);

-- Encrypt the BLOB
DECLARE @encrypted varbinary(max);
SET @encrypted = dbo.EncryptAesByPassPhrase
  (
    'This is my passphrase',
    CAST(@plaintext AS varbinary(max)),
    1,
    'This is my authenticator'
  );

-- Decrypt the BLOB
DECLARE @decrypted varbinary(max);
SET @decrypted = dbo.DecryptAesByPassPhrase
  (
    'This is my passphrase',
    @encrypted,
    1,
    'This is my authenticator'
  );

-- Compare decrypted string and plaintext lengths
SELECT
  DATALENGTH(@decrypted) AS decrypted_len,
  DATALENGTH(@plaintext) AS plaintext_len;
```

```
-- Compare decrypted string and plaintext contents
SELECT
  CASE WHEN @decrypted = @plaintext
       THEN 'Decrypted value is equal to plaintext'
       ELSE 'Decrypted value is not equal to plaintext'
       END AS equal;
```

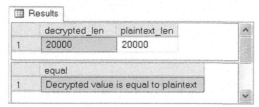

Figure 8-1. Comparison of results of encryption and decryption with SQL CLR functions

When using SQL CLR functions that act on LOB data, the SQL Server may not be able to take full advantage of parallelization in its query plan. Keep this in mind when performance is critical.

SQL CLR Hashing

SQL Server introduces another useful feature that I discussed in Chapter 7—cryptographic hashing. SQL Server exposes this data through the HashBytes function. HashBytes accepts the name of a hash algorithm and a varbinary value to hash. The HashBytes function has two limitations:

- The function can only hash using the SHA-1, MD2, MD4, or MD5 hash algorithms. The result is always 160 bits for SHA-1 or 128 bits for the other algorithms.

- The function can only hash up to 8,000 bytes of data. If you pass more than 8,000 bytes of data into the HashBytes function using an LOB data type the function will truncate the string. This can result in some unexpected results.

As I discussed in Chapter 7, the MD2, MD4, and MD5 hash algorithms are not recommended for cryptographically secure applications. The good news is that the .NET framework provides access to even more secure cryptographic hash functions from the SHA-2 series.

GetHash

Through the SQL CLR, you can access the SHA-256, SHA-384, and SHA-512 hash functions which return 256, 384, or 512 bit hash values, respectively. The improved SQL CLR GetHash function has the following signature:

GetHash (Algorithm, Plaintext)

Listing 8-4 is the C# source for the improved SQL CLR GetHash function.

Listing 8-4. *Improved GetHash Cryptographic Hash Function*

```
[Microsoft.SqlServer.Server.SqlFunction
(
  IsDeterministic = true,
  DataAccess = DataAccessKind.None
)]
public static SqlBytes GetHash
(
  SqlString Algorithm,
  [SqlFacet(MaxSize = -1)] SqlBytes Plaintext
)
{
  // Return NULL if Algorithm or Plaintext is NULL
  if (Algorithm.IsNull || Plaintext.IsNull)
    return SqlBytes.Null;

  bool HashDefined = true;
  HashAlgorithm Hash = null;
  switch (Algorithm.Value.ToUpper())
  {
    case "SHA256":
      Hash = new SHA256Managed();
      break;

    case "SHA384":
      Hash = new SHA384Managed();
      break;

    case "SHA512":
      Hash = new SHA512Managed();
      break;

    default:
      HashDefined = false;
      break;
  }
  if (!HashDefined)
    throw new Exception
      ("Unsupported hash algorithm - use SHA256, SHA384 or SHA512");

  // Generate the hash value
  byte[] HashBytes = Hash.ComputeHash(Plaintext.Value);
  // Convert result into a SqlBytes result
  return new SqlBytes(HashBytes);
}
```

The following function declaration defines the two parameters required to call the function and the return type. The GetHash function accepts the nvarchar name of an algorithm, one of SHA256, SHA384, or SHA512 and a varbinary(max) parameter named *Plaintext*.

```
[Microsoft.SqlServer.Server.SqlFunction
(
  IsDeterministic = true,
  DataAccess = DataAccessKind.None
)]
public static SqlBytes GetHash
(
  SqlString Algorithm,
  [SqlFacet(MaxSize = -1)] SqlBytes Plaintext
)
```

The first step in the main body of the function is to check for a NULL parameter value for either *Algorithm* or *Plaintext*. If either parameter is NULL, the result is automatically NULL as shown in the following code.

```
// Return NULL if Algorithm or Plaintext is NULL
if (Algorithm.IsNull || Plaintext.IsNull)
  return SqlBytes.Null;
```

The next step consists of a bit of setup code that determines which algorithm you specified in the function call. If you specify an unrecognized algorithm name, the function throws an exception as shown in the following code snippet.

```
bool HashDefined = true;
HashAlgorithm Hash = null;
switch (Algorithm.Value.ToUpper())
{
  case "SHA256":
    Hash = new SHA256Managed();
    break;

  case "SHA384":
    Hash = new SHA384Managed();
    break;

  case "SHA512":
    Hash = new SHA512Managed();
    break;

  default:
    HashDefined = false;
    break;
}
if (!HashDefined)
  throw new Exception
    ("Unsupported hash algorithm - use SHA256, SHA384 or SHA512");
```

Finally, the function generates a hash value using the algorithm you specified and returns the result as a SqlBytes value.

```
// Generate the hash value
byte[] HashBytes = Hash.ComputeHash(Plaintext.Value);
// Convert result into a SqlBytes result
return new SqlBytes(HashBytes);
```

You can test the GetHash function as shown in Listing 8-5, with results shown in Figure 8-2.

Listing 8-5. *Testing the GetHash Function*

```
-- Generate a 20,000 byte (10 chars X 2000) character string
DECLARE @plaintext varchar(max);
SET @plaintext = REPLICATE(CAST('ABCDEFGHIJ' AS varchar(max)), 2000);

-- Generate hash values using all three algorithms
DECLARE
  @sha256 varbinary(32),
  @sha384 varbinary(48),
  @sha512 varbinary(64);

SELECT
  @sha256 = dbo.GetHash('SHA256', CAST(@plaintext AS varbinary(max))),
  @sha384 = dbo.GetHash('SHA384', CAST(@plaintext AS varbinary(max))),
  @sha512 = dbo.GetHash('SHA512', CAST(@plaintext AS varbinary(max)));

-- Show results
SELECT
  'SHA-256' AS algorithm,
  @sha256 AS hash

UNION ALL

SELECT
  'SHA-384',
  @sha384

UNION ALL

SELECT
  'SHA-512',
  @sha512;
```

	algorithm	hash
1	SHA-256	0xE54F3D6AA2F19D738C8B5FA5A99CAA23180E810A7FA421ACC8CD3A266A6004FE
2	SHA-384	0x1EB8350810F60F4EB6954D4E94FD2654B9008D057A1CBA485277E879A05B4BE64988F861F90C3CD34CCC85EF784B3C37
3	SHA-512	0xA347451A19CC4BFBB3454C15477783711B8C151EBCB867783E252F8996731CC70E6C295B8A1200D11D5B0D3CC5DB5A964E1FCD2A35A7DF1030BAA53F8ADCDD9D

Figure 8-2. *Result of improved hash function test*

SaltedHash

Regardless of the hash algorithm you use, clever hackers have invented improved methods of attacking them. One tool that hackers use is a rainbow table, which is essentially a lookup table of hash values. Rainbow tables can provide hackers with a shortcut to attack hashed passwords, for instance.

The best defense against rainbow table attacks of your hash codes is to include a salt/IV value in your hashes. Salting your hash with a secret salt value renders the current generation of rainbow table attacks against your hashed data useless. The SaltedHash function presented in Listing 8-6 modifies the GetHash function to create salted hash values.

Listing 8-6. SaltedHash Cryptographic Hash Function

```
[Microsoft.SqlServer.Server.SqlFunction
(
  IsDeterministic = true,
  DataAccess = DataAccessKind.None
)]
public static SqlBytes SaltedHash
(
  SqlString Algorithm,
  [SqlFacet(MaxSize = -1)] SqlBytes PlainText,
  SqlBytes Salt
)
{
  // Return NULL if any of the parameters is NULL
  if (Algorithm.IsNull || PlainText.IsNull || Salt.IsNull)
    return SqlBytes.Null;

  // Determine which algorithm to use
  bool HashDefined = true;
  HashAlgorithm Hash = null;
  switch (Algorithm.Value.ToUpper())
  {
    case "SHA256":
      Hash = new SHA256Managed();
      break;

    case "SHA384":
      Hash = new SHA384Managed();
      break;

    case "SHA512":
      Hash = new SHA512Managed();
      break;

    default:
      HashDefined = false;
      break;
  }
```

```
if (!HashDefined)
  throw new Exception
    ("Unsupported hash algorithm - use SHA256, SHA384 or SHA512");

// Combine the plaintext with the salt
byte[] PlainTextWithSalt = new byte[PlainText.Length + Salt.Length];
for (long i = 0; i < Salt.Length; i++)
  PlainTextWithSalt[i] = Salt[i];
for (long i = Salt.Length; i < PlainText.Length; i++)
  PlainTextWithSalt[i] = PlainText.Value[i - Salt.Length];

// Generate the hash and return the result
byte[] HashBytes = Hash.ComputeHash(PlainTextWithSalt);
return new SqlBytes(HashBytes);
}
```

The SaltedHash function accepts three parameters—an *Algorithm*, a varbinary(max) *Plaintext*, and a *Salt*. The salted hash is created by combining the *Salt* with the *Plaintext* prior to generating the hash value. The code snippet below shows the modified function declaration.

```
public static SqlBytes SaltedHash
(
  SqlString Algorithm,
  [SqlFacet(MaxSize = -1)] SqlBytes PlainText,
  SqlBytes Salt
)
```

The majority of the function setup is just like the GetHash function. SaltedHash differs from GetHash by combining the salt with the plaintext just before it generates a hash value. The differing code is shown in the following.

```
...
// Combine the plaintext with the salt
byte[] PlainTextWithSalt = new byte[PlainText.Length + Salt.Length];
for (long i = 0; i < Salt.Length; i++)
  PlainTextWithSalt[i] = Salt[i];
for (long i = Salt.Length; i < PlainText.Length; i++)
  PlainTextWithSalt[i] = PlainText.Value[i - Salt.Length];

// Generate the hash and return the result
byte[] HashBytes = Hash.ComputeHash(PlainTextWithSalt);
return new SqlBytes(HashBytes);
```

You can test the SaltedHash function using queries like those shown in Listing 8-7. The results are shown in Figure 8-3.

Listing 8-7. Generating Salted Hashes

```
-- Generate a 20,000 byte (10 chars X 2000) character string
DECLARE @plaintext varchar(max);
SET @plaintext = REPLICATE(CAST('ABCDEFGHIJ' AS varchar(max)), 2000);
```

```
DECLARE @salt varbinary(16);
SET @salt = Crypt_Gen_Random(16);

DECLARE
  @sha256 varbinary(32),
  @sha384 varbinary(48),
  @sha512 varbinary(64);

SELECT
  @sha256 = dbo.SaltedHash('SHA256', CAST(@plaintext AS varbinary(max)), @salt),
  @sha384 = dbo.SaltedHash('SHA384', CAST(@plaintext AS varbinary(max)), @salt),
  @sha512 = dbo.SaltedHash('SHA512', CAST(@plaintext AS varbinary(max)), @salt);

SELECT
  'SHA-256' AS algorithm,
  @sha256 AS hash

UNION ALL

SELECT
  'SHA-384',
  @sha384

UNION ALL

SELECT
  'SHA-512',
  @sha512;
```

	algorithm	hash
1	SHA-256	0x6925703D34BABB51B0FC35459D12D3C4F110FCBD212BE057D23DE1786731AC14
2	SHA-384	0x49837E0BAC27346B9477C870F0DE1FC938CFB0C37C14BA75F23B4917C8A1FA37485E66AED9365 1E78512A8475905F899
3	SHA-512	0x0299CEC07C5EADC190F90E3CAAE0DC1303A80D8EA19EBD83309B365C593698EABACA5F8E98C07B12103AE630BB9798A2A6001CC406B0C99466BC0B9DA528AA8F

Figure 8-3. Result of salted hash function

Crypt_Gen_Random

In Listing 8-7, I introduced a new standard SQL Server 2008 cryptographic function, Crypt_Gen_Random. This function accepts up to two parameters—the number of bytes for the result and an optional random binary seed. The Crypt_Gen_Random function returns a random cryptographic binary string. In this example, I've used the binary string returned by this function as the salt value for the SaltedHash function. In a real-world application, you would need to store this salt value somewhere, possibly stored encrypted in a table, to regenerate the same salted hash value at a later time. To keep the code in this sample simple, I skipped the salt value storage here. I'll discuss this idea in greater detail in Chapter 9.

Additional SQL CLR Considerations

You may encounter a need to encrypt or hash data that is even larger than SQL Server's 2.1 GB large object (LOB) data type limit. For instance, you may store a 10 GB file with SQL Server using the filestream option. You can use SQL CLR to circumvent the 2.1 GB limitation in cases like this as well. In fact, when using SQL CLR for encryption, decryption, and hashing your only limitations are the limitations of the .NET framework.

One thing to keep in mind when using SQL CLR for encrypting, decrypting, and hashing LOB data the query optimizer cannot take advantage of parallel processing in a plan that uses the SQL CLR routine. Of course, this isn't an issue if you only have a single processor or don't rely on parallel processing. It should definitely be a consideration if you are heavily reliant on parallel processing for encryption and decryption functionality.

Summary

The hash functions that SQL Server exposes by default are useful for fingerprinting small quantities of data (8,000 bytes or less), but aren't as useful for LOB data. In this chapter, I described three enhancements to SQL Server cryptographic hash functionality that you can achieve through SQL CLR integration:

- You can use SQL CLR functions to get around the 8,000 byte limitation of the standard HashBytes function and hash up to 2.1 GB of LOB data at once.

- SQL CLR allows you to use additional hash algorithms like the SHA-2 hash family in the .NET framework.

- With SQL CLR you can implement more secure hashes, like the salted hashes demonstrated in this chapter.

Hackers have improved methods of attacking hashes with small hash values (like the 128-but MD5 hash algorithm) and better tools to attack hash algorithms in general, like rainbow tables. In many applications, it's important to use cryptographically secure algorithms and methods to hash your data.

In the next chapter, I'll discuss performance implications of encryption and how to maximize performance when searching encrypted data.

CHAPTER 9

■ ■ ■

Indexing Encrypted Data

Indexing, searching, and sorting data are related functions that all have requirements that contradict the needs of secure data encryption. Indexing, searching, and related functionality requires you to assign order to your data. Order, in turn, depends on recognizing patterns in your data. As I discussed in Chapter 1, the security of encryption algorithms depends on eliminating recognizable patterns from your data. This renders encrypted data essentially useless in terms of efficient search and sort.

In this chapter, I'll talk about the effects of encryption on database searches and queries, and discuss some methods for improving performance when searching encrypted data is unavoidable.

The Problem of Searching Encrypted Data

Normally, you'll want to avoid encrypting data on a cell-level when it needs to be searched. For instance, if you need to store encrypted social security numbers in a database you'll want to try to avoid allowing users to search or sort based on that data element. I'll discuss some of the problems you'll encounter when searching encrypted data in this section.

When you have a requirement to search confidential or sensitive encrypted data, one question to ask is whether or not searching for an entire encrypted data element is the "real" requirement. In many cases, the requirement might be able to be further refined. Let me give an example to explain what I mean.

Consider a requirement to search an encrypted credit card number data column. Consider Listing9-1, which combines listings from Chapters 2 and 3 to create the DMK, asymmetric key, symmetric key, and sample data. If you've already run the samples from Chapters 2 and 3, you'll already have these keys and sample tables created and populated in the database, and you won't need to run this listing.

Listing 9-1. Creating Encryption Keys and Sample Data

```
-- Create DMK, asymmetric key, symmetric key
CREATE MASTER KEY
ENCRYPTION BY PASSWORD = 'aO*Ui)4x-f';
GO
```

```
CREATE ASYMMETRIC KEY AsymKey1_Sales
FROM FILE = N'c:\AsymKey1_Sales.snk';
GO

CREATE SYMMETRIC KEY SymKey6_Sales
WITH ALGORITHM = AES_256
ENCRYPTION BY ASYMMETRIC KEY AsymKey1_Sales;
GO

-- Nonencrypted credit card info
CREATE TABLE SalesLT.CreditCardInfo
(
  SalesOrderID int not null primary key,
  CreditCardNumber nvarchar(50),
  CreditCardExpirationDate datetime,
  TotalCharge money
);

-- Encrypted credit card info
CREATE TABLE SalesLT.EncryptedCreditCardInfo
(
  SalesOrderID int not null primary key,
  CreditCardNumber varbinary(150),
  CreditCardExpirationDate varbinary(150),
  TotalCharge varbinary(150)
);
GO

-- Generate plaintext sample data
WITH Generate4Digits /* Generate 4 random digits */
AS
(
  SELECT SUBSTRING
  (
    CAST
      (
        ABS(CHECKSUM(NEWID())) % 10000 AS NVARCHAR(4)
      ) + N'0000', 1, 4
  ) AS Digits
),
CardNum /* Generate a 16 digit random credit card number */
AS
(
  SELECT N'0999-' +
  (
    SELECT Digits
    FROM Generate4Digits
  ) + N'-' +
  (
    SELECT Digits
    FROM Generate4Digits
  ) + N'-' +
```

```
  (
    SELECT Digits
    FROM Generate4Digits
  ) AS CardNumber
),
DaysToExpire /* Get a random amount of days to expiration */
AS
(
  SELECT ABS(CHECKSUM(NEWID()) % 700) AS Days
)
INSERT INTO SalesLT.CreditCardInfo
(
  SalesOrderID,
  CreditCardNumber,
  CreditCardExpirationDate,
  TotalCharge
)
SELECT
  SalesOrderID,
  CardNumber,
  DATEADD(DAY, Days, OrderDate),
  TotalDue
FROM SalesLT.SalesOrderHeader
CROSS APPLY CardNum
CROSS APPLY DaysToExpire;
GO

-- Wipe out the sample data in the table
TRUNCATE TABLE SalesLT.EncryptedCreditCardInfo;
GO

-- Open symmetric data encrypting key
OPEN SYMMETRIC KEY SymKey6_Sales
DECRYPTION BY ASYMMETRIC KEY AsymKey1_Sales;

-- Encrypt sample random credit card data
INSERT INTO SalesLT.EncryptedCreditCardInfo
(
  SalesOrderID,
  CreditCardNumber,
  CreditCardExpirationDate,
  TotalCharge
)
SELECT
  SalesOrderID,
  EncryptByKey(Key_Guid(N'SymKey6_Sales'), CreditCardNumber),
  EncryptByKey(Key_Guid(N'SymKey6_Sales'), CAST
    (
      CreditCardExpirationDate AS varbinary(10)
    )
  ),
  EncryptByKey(Key_Guid(N'SymKey6_Sales'), CAST
```

```
    (
      TotalCharge AS varbinary(10)
    )
  )
FROM SalesLT.CreditCardInfo;

-- Close data encrypting key
CLOSE SYMMETRIC KEY SymKey6_Sales;
GO
```

Once your sample encrypted data is ready, you can use it to test the performance of encrypted data search. Listing 9-2 performs a simple search of the encrypted credit card number column looking for matches. Figure 9-1 shows sample results from this query.

Listing 9-2. Simple Encrypted Data Search

```
-- First get a decrypted credit card number from the plaintext table
DECLARE @n nvarchar(50);

SELECT @n = CreditCardNumber
FROM SalesLT.CreditCardInfo
WHERE SalesOrderID = 71780;

-- Open the symmetric key
OPEN SYMMETRIC KEY SymKey6_Sales
DECRYPTION BY ASYMMETRIC KEY AsymKey1_Sales;

-- Perform the search and return the result
SELECT
  SalesOrderID,
  CAST(DecryptByKey(CreditCardNumber) AS nvarchar(50)) AS DecCreditCardNumber
FROM SalesLT.EncryptedCreditCardInfo
WHERE DecryptByKey(CreditCardNumber) = @n;

-- Close symmetric key
CLOSE SYMMETRIC KEY SymKey6_Sales;
```

Figure 9-1. Result of simple encrypted credit card search

> ■ **Note** Because the data is randomly generated, your results will vary from those shown in this chapter.

Figure 9-2 shows the query plan. You can see that the simple query from Listing 9-2 uses a *Clustered Index Scan* operator to locate the encrypted data. Essentially, SQL Server has to look at every single row in the table and decrypt every single `CreditCardNumber` value to fulfill the query predicate: `WHERE DecryptByKey(CreditCardNumber) = @n`. This business of decrypting each value can be a very expensive proposition if you have a large number of rows (think tens of thousands, hundreds of thousands, or even millions) in the table.

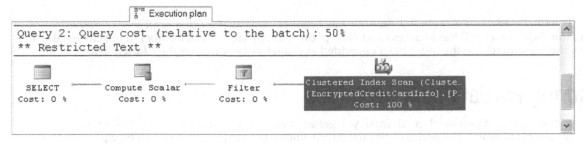

Figure 9-2. Query plan for simple encrypted credit card search

You might assume the fact that SQL Server has to look at every single row in the table can be attributed to poor indexing—there is no nonclustered index defined on the `CreditCardNumber` column of the table, after all. To test this theory, we can add a nonclustered index to the table on this column, as shown in Listing 9-3.

Listing 9-3. Create a Nonclustered Index on the CreditCardNumber Column

```
CREATE NONCLUSTERED INDEX IX_EncryptedCreditCardInfo
ON SalesLT.EncryptedCreditCardInfo
  (
    CreditCardNumber
  );
```

If you execute the query from Listing 9-2 again, with the new nonclustered index in place, you'll get the result in the query plan shown in Figure 9-3.

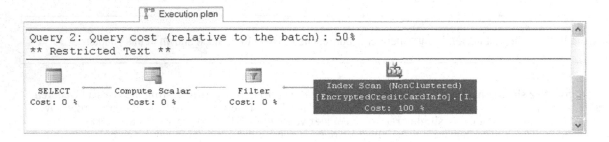

Figure 9-3. *Query plan for simple encrypted column search with nonclustered index in place*

The *Clustered Index Scan* in this example has been replaced by the *Index Scan (Nonclustered)* operator. SQL Server still has to access and decrypt every single credit card number in the entire table to see if there's a match, so the index hasn't provided any tangible benefit over the *Clustered Index Scan.*

Storing Partial Plaintext Values

One of the questions you need to ask when you get an encrypted column search is whether the requirement is to search the entire encrypted data element. In many cases, a search on a partial value (like the last four digits of a credit card number or social security number, for instance) might be adequate. If this is the case, you may be able to improve performance by simply adding a column to the table with the plaintext of the partial value. In this example, I'll add a column with the last four digits of the credit card number in it. Listing 9-4 begins by adding a CreditCardLast4 column to the SalesLT.EncryptedCreditCardInfo table and populates the column.

Listing 9-4. Adding a Column to Hold the Credit Card Number Last Four Digits

```
ALTER TABLE SalesLT.EncryptedCreditCardInfo
ADD CreditCardLast4 nvarchar(4);
GO

OPEN SYMMETRIC KEY SymKey6_Sales
DECRYPTION BY ASYMMETRIC KEY AsymKey1_Sales;

UPDATE SalesLT.EncryptedCreditCardInfo
SET CreditCardLast4 = RIGHT
  (
    CAST
      (
        DecryptByKey(CreditCardNumber) AS nvarchar(50)
      ), 4
  );

CLOSE SYMMETRIC KEY SymKey6_Sales;
GO
```

As shown in Listing 9-5, if you now query the table you'll see results similar to those shown in Figure 9-4.

Listing 9-5. Querying the Sample Data with the Last Four Credit Card Digits

```
SELECT
  SalesOrderID,
  CreditCardLast4,
  CreditCardNumber,
  CreditCardExpirationDate,
  TotalCharge
FROM SalesLT.EncryptedCreditCardInfo;
```

	SalesOrderID	CreditCardLast4	CreditCardNumber	CreditCardExpirationDate	TotalCharge
1	71774	6110	0x00BD551AC1492C49A1087960C73E2...	0x00BD551AC1492C49A1087960C73E2...	0x00BD551AC1492C49A1087960C73E2...
2	71776	2794	0x00BD551AC1492C49A1087960C73E2...	0x00BD551AC1492C49A1087960C73E2...	0x00BD551AC1492C49A1087960C73E2...
3	71780	5248	0x00BD551AC1492C49A1087960C73E2...	0x00BD551AC1492C49A1087960C73E2...	0x00BD551AC1492C49A1087960C73E2...
4	71782	6557	0x00BD551AC1492C49A1087960C73E2...	0x00BD551AC1492C49A1087960C73E2...	0x00BD551AC1492C49A1087960C73E2...
5	71783	3372	0x00BD551AC1492C49A1087960C73E2...	0x00BD551AC1492C49A1087960C73E2...	0x00BD551AC1492C49A1087960C73E2...
6	71784	4826	0x00BD551AC1492C49A1087960C73E2...	0x00BD551AC1492C49A1087960C73E2...	0x00BD551AC1492C49A1087960C73E2...
7	71796	8540	0x00BD551AC1492C49A1087960C73E2...	0x00BD551AC1492C49A1087960C73E2...	0x00BD551AC1492C49A1087960C73E2...
8	71797	8454	0x00BD551AC1492C49A1087960C73E2...	0x00BD551AC1492C49A1087960C73E2...	0x00BD551AC1492C49A1087960C73E2...
9	71815	1066	0x00BD551AC1492C49A1087960C73E2...	0x00BD551AC1492C49A1087960C73E2...	0x00BD551AC1492C49A1087960C73E2...
10	71816	9763	0x00BD551AC1492C49A1087960C73E2...	0x00BD551AC1492C49A1087960C73E2...	0x00BD551AC1492C49A1087960C73E2...
11	71831	1210	0x00BD551AC1492C49A1087960C73E2...	0x00BD551AC1492C49A1087960C73E2...	0x00BD551AC1492C49A1087960C73E2...
12	71832	5118	0x00BD551AC1492C49A1087960C73E2...	0x00BD551AC1492C49A1087960C73E2...	0x00BD551AC1492C49A1087960C73E2...
13	71845	2773	0x00BD551AC1492C49A1087960C73E2...	0x00BD551AC1492C49A1087960C73E2...	0x00BD551AC1492C49A1087960C73E2...
14	71846	2690	0x00BD551AC1492C49A1087960C73E2...	0x00BD551AC1492C49A1087960C73E2...	0x00BD551AC1492C49A1087960C73E2...
15	71856	6102	0x00BD551AC1492C49A1087960C73E2...	0x00BD551AC1492C49A1087960C73E2...	0x00BD551AC1492C49A1087960C73E2...
16	71858	3529	0x00BD551AC1492C49A1087960C73E2...	0x00BD551AC1492C49A1087960C73E2...	0x00BD551AC1492C49A1087960C73E2...
17	71863	5681	0x00BD551AC1492C49A1087960C73E2...	0x00BD551AC1492C49A1087960C73E2...	0x00BD551AC1492C49A1087960C73E2...

Figure 9-4. Encrypted credit card data with last 4 digits plain text column

Now that I've added the CreditCardLast4 column to the table, I'll recreate the nonclustered index on this column as shown in Listing 9-6.

Listing 9-6. Create Nonclustered Index on Last Four Digits of Credit Card Column

```
CREATE NONCLUSTERED INDEX IX_EncryptedCreditCardInfo
ON SalesLT.EncryptedCreditCardInfo
  (
    CreditCardLast4,
    CreditCardNumber
  )
WITH (DROP_EXISTING = ON);
```

The new nonclustered index is a covering index on the CreditCardLast4 and CreditCardNumber columns. Listing 9-7 shows the modified version of the query that uses the new CreditCardLast4 column to significantly narrow down the potential results before applying the DecryptByKey function.

Listing 9-7. Modified Query to Utilize the CreditCardLast4 Column

```
-- First get a decrypted credit card number from the plaintext table
DECLARE @n nvarchar(50);

SELECT @n = CreditCardNumber
FROM SalesLT.CreditCardInfo
WHERE SalesOrderID = 71780;

-- Open the symmetric key
OPEN SYMMETRIC KEY SymKey6_Sales
DECRYPTION BY ASYMMETRIC KEY AsymKey1_Sales;

-- Perform the search and return the result
SELECT
  SalesOrderID,
  CAST(DecryptByKey(CreditCardNumber) AS nvarchar(50)) AS DecCreditCardNumber
FROM SalesLT.EncryptedCreditCardInfo
WHERE CreditCardLast4 = RIGHT(@n, 4)
  AND DecryptByKey(CreditCardNumber) = @n;

-- Close symmetric key
CLOSE SYMMETRIC KEY SymKey6_Sales;
```

The results are the same as previously shown, but this time you'll notice an *Index Seek (Nonclustered)* in the query plan, as shown in Figure 9-5.

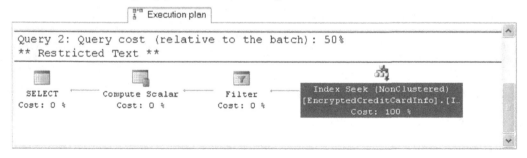

Figure 9-5. Revised query plan with index seek

The revised query plan is much more efficient because SQL Server can use the nonclustered index to quickly seek out the relatively few rows where the last four digits of the credit card numbers match the search criteria. Then it can decrypt those values and compare, instead of decrypting every single credit card number in the table.

The problem with this method, of course, is that you expose partial plaintext data in the database. While the complete data is protected, exposing even partial plaintext could present a security risk. Many cryptanalysis methods rely on the concept of a known-plaintext, and even a small amount of known-plaintext could provide a talented cryptanalyst with enough information to begin attacking your encrypted data.

Storing Hashed Values

In order to better protect your data while achieving the same performance as when storing partial plaintext, you can store hashes of your plaintext values. As described in Chapter 7, when you store a cryptographic hash of a value you are essentially fingerprinting your data. The advantage of cryptographic hashing is that the data is thoroughly obfuscated and can't be reverse-engineered. Listing 9-8 modifies the table created in the previous example to add an SHA-1 hash of the plaintext credit card number to the table.

Listing 9-8. Adding a Cryptographic Hash of the Plaintext Credit Card Number

```
-- Drop nonclustered index
DROP INDEX IX_EncryptedCreditCardInfo
ON SalesLT.EncryptedCreditCardInfo;
GO

-- Drop credit card last 4 digits column
ALTER TABLE SalesLT.EncryptedCreditCardInfo
DROP COLUMN CreditCardLast4;
GO

-- Add a credit card hash column
ALTER TABLE SalesLT.EncryptedCreditCardInfo
ADD CreditCardHash varbinary(64);
GO

-- Populate the credit card hash
OPEN SYMMETRIC KEY SymKey6_Sales
DECRYPTION BY ASYMMETRIC KEY AsymKey1_Sales;
```

```
UPDATE SalesLT.EncryptedCreditCardInfo
SET CreditCardHash = HashBytes
  (
    'SHA1',
    CAST(DecryptByKey(CreditCardNumber) AS nvarchar(50))
  );

CLOSE SYMMETRIC KEY SymKey6_Sales;
GO

-- Recreate nonclustered index
CREATE NONCLUSTERED INDEX IX_EncryptedCreditCardInfo
ON SalesLT.EncryptedCreditCardInfo
  (
    CreditCardHash,
    CreditCardNumber
  );
```

As shown in Listing 9-9, you can query this table to view the contents. An example of the contents is shown in Figure 9-6.

Listing 9-9. Querying the Encrypted Credit Card Info with Credit Card Hash

```
SELECT
  SalesOrderID,
  CreditCardHash,
  CreditCardNumber,
  CreditCardExpirationDate,
  TotalCharge
FROM SalesLT.EncryptedCreditCardInfo;
```

	SalesOrderID	CreditCardHash	CreditCardNumber	CreditCardExpirationDate	TotalCharge
1	71774	0x2B403D0B383B13BD68DDDF67932F1C5254508B6B	0x00BD551AC1492C49A10...	0x00BD551AC1492C49A10...	0x00BD551AC1492C49A10...
2	71776	0x7873FD373D08A53153FCB205710C23EDBE9D9683	0x00BD551AC1492C49A10...	0x00BD551AC1492C49A10...	0x00BD551AC1492C49A10...
3	71780	0x87353F9D6426B30A949DE4262932407F737C9E45	0x00BD551AC1492C49A10...	0x00BD551AC1492C49A10...	0x00BD551AC1492C49A10...
4	71782	0xF517534C987529098D0ACBBE0B287B475E595F4D	0x00BD551AC1492C49A10...	0x00BD551AC1492C49A10...	0x00BD551AC1492C49A10...
5	71783	0x9680A77F1A8DCBCE18F53E04831326F553802B9D	0x00BD551AC1492C49A10...	0x00BD551AC1492C49A10...	0x00BD551AC1492C49A10...
6	71784	0xA73FD05D9200BCF8EED2915BA8C6983E8A3C9064	0x00BD551AC1492C49A10...	0x00BD551AC1492C49A10...	0x00BD551AC1492C49A10...
7	71796	0x42069EE0AB518E6B937B0CF620D1B27908D2D296	0x00BD551AC1492C49A10...	0x00BD551AC1492C49A10...	0x00BD551AC1492C49A10...
8	71797	0xA5C99012D7F83195D624615F084A6C55221EFF9F	0x00BD551AC1492C49A10...	0x00BD551AC1492C49A10...	0x00BD551AC1492C49A10...
9	71815	0x55164C8B802699DB56A714E6D7EEB02741ED4DC4	0x00BD551AC1492C49A10...	0x00BD551AC1492C49A10...	0x00BD551AC1492C49A10...
10	71816	0x9D58803CF604FA401845FFEF95B703122E6D44E8	0x00BD551AC1492C49A10...	0x00BD551AC1492C49A10...	0x00BD551AC1492C49A10...
11	71831	0xB038E39097C04060F0F4082FA2DB825B72DF4CD1	0x00BD551AC1492C49A10...	0x00BD551AC1492C49A10...	0x00BD551AC1492C49A10...
12	71832	0x456676C922A0A30A8F953248FDF9EB1690BE60A1	0x00BD551AC1492C49A10...	0x00BD551AC1492C49A10...	0x00BD551AC1492C49A10...
13	71845	0xBAF5A837F194CBCEA31AE4791B12850B13E31413	0x00BD551AC1492C49A10...	0x00BD551AC1492C49A10...	0x00BD551AC1492C49A10...
14	71846	0x02A1B618944048657460DD81AEB941C4D31E9FEA	0x00BD551AC1492C49A10...	0x00BD551AC1492C49A10...	0x00BD551AC1492C49A10...
15	71856	0x25420D7C4DC3000335E48F997AE9A986515DF80C	0x00BD551AC1492C49A10...	0x00BD551AC1492C49A10...	0x00BD551AC1492C49A10...
16	71858	0x0EEBD18DE3F03E75BC338AB79CEA80F86CADB2...	0x00BD551AC1492C49A10...	0x00BD551AC1492C49A10...	0x00BD551AC1492C49A10...
17	71863	0xCE5313C34B459968DDFCE01A8B8ABE45C0DACC...	0x00BD551AC1492C49A10...	0x00BD551AC1492C49A10...	0x00BD551AC1492C49A10...
18	71867	0xECAA9E49E54451895D29D1E0392EED3C9E6B1BB0...	0x00BD551AC1492C49A10...	0x00BD551AC1492C49A10...	0x00BD551AC1492C49A10...

Figure 9-6. Sample data with CreditCardHash column included

The CreditCardHash column in this example is a cryptographic SHA-1 hash of the entire plaintext credit card number. You can query this column by looking for the SHA-1 hash of the credit card number you're seeking as shown in Listing 9-10. The query plan is shown in Figure 9-7.

Listing 9-10. Hash-Based Searching for Credit Card Numbers

```
-- First get a decrypted credit card number from the plaintext table
DECLARE @n nvarchar(50);

SELECT @n = CreditCardNumber
FROM SalesLT.CreditCardInfo
WHERE SalesOrderID = 71780;

-- Open the symmetric key
OPEN SYMMETRIC KEY SymKey6_Sales
DECRYPTION BY ASYMMETRIC KEY AsymKey1_Sales;

-- Perform the search and return the result
SELECT
  SalesOrderID,
  CAST(DecryptByKey(CreditCardNumber) AS nvarchar(50)) AS DecCreditCardNumber
FROM SalesLT.EncryptedCreditCardInfo
WHERE CreditCardHash = HashBytes('SHA1', @n)
  AND DecryptByKey(CreditCardNumber) = @n;

-- Close symmetric key
CLOSE SYMMETRIC KEY SymKey6_Sales;
```

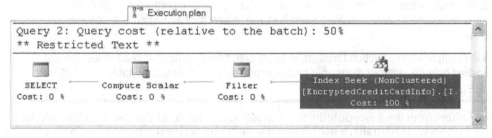

Figure 9-7. Query plan for search of hashed credit card number

As you can see from a review of the query plan, the hashed value method gives you the efficiency of the *Index Seek (NonClustered)* operator. Notice that in this example I hashed the entire credit card number, although you could also hash a portion of the data (like the last four digits) to make the example more comparable to the previous code sample.

Somewhere Over The Rainbow

I discussed rainbow table attacks in Chapter 8. For data that consists of a very specific static structure and contains a very limited set of characters (such as credit card numbers or social security numbers) the rainbow table attack is particularly effective.

Consider hashes of social security numbers, which would make a relatively easy target for rainbow table attacks. To begin with, social security numbers have a regular form, consisting of three groups of the numbers zero through nine, as listed in the following:

- The first group, or area number, is three digits in length.

- The second group, or group number, consists of two digits.

- The third group, or serial number, consists of four digits.

An example of a social security number is 987-65-4321. Don't worry—I wouldn't use a real social security number in an example. All social security numbers in the range 987-65-4320 to 987-65-4329 are reserved by the Social Security Administration for use in advertising and for other unofficial purposes.

The social security number essentially requires a rainbow table with one billion entries to provide a lookup for every possible combination of digits that can be hashed. This is not an infeasible task. But on top of that, a clever hacker who knows the rules of social security number assignment can easily narrow even that number down further. For instance, no social security number has ever been issued with an area number (first three digits) in the range 800–999. This means a hacker can automatically eliminate 200 million combinations of numbers from his rainbow table. With a little more work, a clever hacker can quickly pare this down to just a few hundred million possible combinations by incorporating additional social security number assignment rules. Attacking a few hundred million hashed values is a lot easier than attacking a billion.

Note that in the code example for this section I hashed an entire credit card number instead of just the last four digits. If you hashed only the last four digits your hacker would only need a rainbow table with 10,000 entries to recover the plaintext of your hashed values.

Plaintext hashing suffers from the susceptibility to rainbow table attacks, as discussed in the sidebar "Somewhere Over the Rainbow." Essentially, a hacker could potentially derive the plaintext of a data element through hash value lookup tables, particularly if the structure and content of the data elements are strictly constrained and well-defined as they are in the case of credit card numbers and social security numbers.

Storing Salted Hashed Values

While the idea of storing hashed plaintext values to increase search efficiency has some merit, it suffers from a couple of issues. One issue is that simple cryptographic hashing doesn't protect you from the rainbow table attacks described in the previous section.

Another issue is that it introduces a pattern from which outsiders can infer statistical information and open your data up to statistical attacks. Consider the SHA-1 hash for the money data type value $1,000,000.00, which is 0x8F1617F0536ACD0DDB1107A5CE504F8E72C3C6EA. Knowing this information a hacker can locate all $1,000,000.00 entries in a database. If a hacker is attacking a table with employee compensation information, she might be able to infer which employees are highly compensated and target those employees' records for further cryptanalysis.

As I described in Chapter 8, you can use salted hash values to protect against rainbow table attack and to make it even harder for intruders to infer significant information through statistical analysis. The built-in HashBytes function does not natively support salted hashes, so I'll use the SQL CLR function, SaltedHash, from Chapter 8 to generate salted hash values. Listing 9-11 demonstrates the use of the SaltedHash function to generate salted hash values of the last four digits of the credit card number.

Listing 9-11. Generating Salted Hashes of Credit Card Numbers

```
-- Populate the credit card hash
OPEN SYMMETRIC KEY SymKey6_Sales
DECRYPTION BY ASYMMETRIC KEY AsymKey1_Sales;

UPDATE SalesLT.EncryptedCreditCardInfo
SET CreditCardHash = dbo.SaltedHash
  (
    'SHA256',
    DecryptByKey(CreditCardNumber),
    0x359a82109cfe
  );

CLOSE SYMMETRIC KEY SymKey6_Sales;
GO
```

The SaltedHash function uses a salt value that you supply, in this case 0x359a82109cfe, to further obfuscate the hash value. A hash salted with a secret value is infeasible for a hacker to attack using current technology and methods, even rainbow tables.

The salted hash can still be used in combination with other data in the table to try to infer statistical information, but the secret hash value makes it nearly impossible to recover the plaintext data that was hashed. You can query the table using the salted hash using a query like the one shown in Listing 9-12. The query plan generated for this query is shown in Figure 9-8.

Listing 9-12. Salted Hash-Based Searching for Credit Card Numbers

```
-- First get a decrypted credit card number from the plaintext table
DECLARE @n nvarchar(50);

SELECT @n = CreditCardNumber
FROM SalesLT.CreditCardInfo
WHERE SalesOrderID = 71780;

-- Open the symmetric key
OPEN SYMMETRIC KEY SymKey6_Sales
DECRYPTION BY ASYMMETRIC KEY AsymKey1_Sales;

-- Perform the search and return the result
SELECT
  SalesOrderID,
  CAST(DecryptByKey(CreditCardNumber) AS nvarchar(50)) AS DecCreditCardNumber
FROM SalesLT.EncryptedCreditCardInfo
WHERE CreditCardHash = dbo.SaltedHash
```

```
(
  'SHA256',
  CAST(@n AS varbinary(100)),
  0x359a82109cfe
)
AND DecryptByKey(CreditCardNumber) = @n;

-- Close symmetric key
CLOSE SYMMETRIC KEY SymKey6_Sales;
```

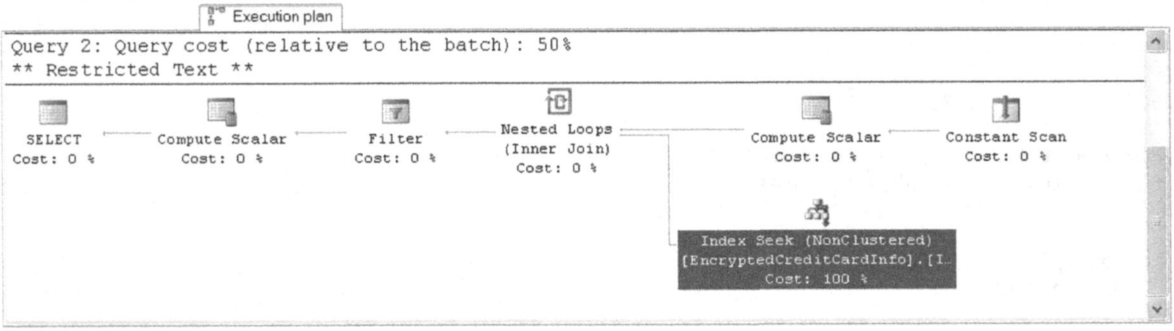

Figure 9-8. Query plan for salted hash search on encrypted data

Notice that the salted hash search query plan is highly optimized like the hash search, with an efficient *Index Seek (NonClustered)* operator. When you use a salted hash you can also safely use a smaller portion of the data, such as the last four digits of a social security number or credit card number. The secret salt value protects the hash values from rainbow table attacks and reverse lookups that would be devastating for short plaintext values.

Storing Hash-Based Message Authentication Codes

In Chapter 8, I explained how to create salted hash values using a trivial mechanism for combining a secret salt value with the plaintext prior to generating the hash. I implemented this mechanism in a SQL CLR user-defined function called SaltedHash.

The .NET Framework includes built-in functionality to generate hash-based message authentication codes (HMACs) using a more complex algorithm for combining a secret key value with your plaintext to generate keyed hash values. While the HMAC mechanism for generating keyed hash values uses a more complex mechanism than the simple salted hash I presented in Chapter 8, it serves the same function and returns a similar result.

The SQL CLR GetHmac function I introduce in this section uses the .NET Framework HMAC class to generate an HMAC using the specified hashing algorithm. The signature for this function is shown in the following:

```
GetHmac
(
  Algorithm nvarchar(4000),
  PlainText varbinary(max),
  Key varbinary(8000)
)
```

This function returns a varbinary hash value as its result. The valid algorithms you can specify in the first parameter include the following:

- SHA256 returns a 256-bit HMAC using the SHA-256 hash algorithm.
- SHA384 returns a 384-bit HMAC using the SHA-384 hash algorithm.
- SHA512 returns a 512-bit HMAC using the SHA-512 hash algorithm.
- RIPEMD160 returns a 160-bit HMAC using the RIPEMD-160 hash algorithm.

Listing 9-13 is the C# source for the SQL CLR GetHmac function that uses .NET Framework classes to generate an HMAC based on your input parameters.

Listing 9-13. SQL CLR GetHmac Function Source Listing

```
[Microsoft.SqlServer.Server.SqlFunction
(
  IsDeterministic = true,
  DataAccess = DataAccessKind.None
)]
public static SqlBytes GetHmac
(
  SqlString Algorithm,
  [SqlFacet(MaxSize = -1)] SqlBytes PlainText,
  SqlBytes Key
)
{
  if (Algorithm.IsNull || PlainText.IsNull || Key.IsNull)
    return SqlBytes.Null;
  bool HmacDefined = true;
  HMAC Hmac = null;
  switch (Algorithm.Value.ToUpper())
  {
    case "SHA256":
      Hmac = new HMACSHA256(Key.Value);
      break;

    case "SHA384":
      Hmac = new HMACSHA384(Key.Value);
      break;

    case "SHA512":
      Hmac = new HMACSHA512(Key.Value);
      break;

    case "RIPEMD160":
      Hmac = new HMACRIPEMD160(Key.Value);
      break;
```

```
      default:
        HmacDefined = false;
        break;
  }
  if (!HmacDefined)
    throw new Exception
      (
          "Unsupported hash algorithm - use SHA256, SHA384, SHA512 or RIPEMD160"
      );
  byte[] HmacBytes = Hmac.ComputeHash(PlainText.Value);
  return new SqlBytes(HmacBytes);
}
```

The code for this function is very similar to the source for the SaltedHash function presented in Chapter 8. The major differences are that the object being created is an HMAC object instead of a Hash object and the HMAC class combines the secret key value into the HMAC. When you use the HMAC class, you don't have to worry about combining the secret value as I did in the SaltedHash function.

Populating the sample table with HMACs using this function is relatively simple, as shown in Listing 9-14.

Listing 9-14. *Populating the Sample Table with HMACs*

```
-- Populate the credit card hash
OPEN SYMMETRIC KEY SymKey6_Sales
DECRYPTION BY ASYMMETRIC KEY AsymKey1_Sales;

UPDATE SalesLT.EncryptedCreditCardInfo
SET CreditCardHash = dbo.GetHmac
  (
    'SHA256',
    DecryptByKey(CreditCardNumber),
    0x359a82109cfe
  );

CLOSE SYMMETRIC KEY SymKey6_Sales;
GO
```

You can query with this function in the same way that you might use the SaltedHash function. Listing 9-15 queries the encrypted credit card data, using HMACs to efficiently retrieve the results. Figure 9-9 shows the query plan generated by Listing 9-15.

Listing 9-15. *Querying Encrypted Data with an HMAC Column*

```
-- First get a decrypted credit card number from the plaintext table
DECLARE @n nvarchar(50);

SELECT @n = CreditCardNumber
FROM SalesLT.CreditCardInfo
WHERE SalesOrderID = 71780;
```

```
-- Open the symmetric key
OPEN SYMMETRIC KEY SymKey6_Sales
DECRYPTION BY ASYMMETRIC KEY AsymKey1_Sales;

-- Perform the search and return the result
SELECT
  SalesOrderID,
  CAST(DecryptByKey(CreditCardNumber) AS nvarchar(50)) AS DecCreditCardNumber
FROM SalesLT.EncryptedCreditCardInfo
WHERE CreditCardHash = dbo.GetHmac
  (
    'SHA256',
    CAST(@n AS varbinary(100)),
    0x359a82109cfe
  )
  AND DecryptByKey(CreditCardNumber) = @n;

-- Close symmetric key
CLOSE SYMMETRIC KEY SymKey6_Sales;
```

Figure 9-9. Query plan produced by HMAC search of encrypted data

■ **Caution** When using the HMAC or salted hash mechanisms, you absolutely have to protect the secret IV or key value. Much like encryption keys used to encrypt your data, the security of your HMACs and salted hashes rests on protecting this secret value.

Range Queries

All of the examples in this chapter have been focused on optimizing the efficiency of exact match queries. This is because range queries and pattern match queries rely on certain well-established patterns in the data in order to efficiently return results.

■ **Tip** Range queries and pattern match queries are those that use >, <, >=, <=, BETWEEN, LIKE and related operators in the WHERE clause predicate. Exact match queries use = in the WHERE clause.

Consider a sample query like the one shown in the following code snippet:

```
SELECT *
FROM SalesLT.CreditCardInfo
WHERE CreditCardNum >= '5' AND CreditCardNumber <= '6';
```

This query takes advantage of well-established patterns in character data. In this case, the character digit for the numeral 5 comes before 6. When you encrypt your data these patterns are eliminated, making range searches extremely inefficient.

How can you encrypt your data and still obtain efficient queries of data using range and pattern matching predicates? Well, this brings us to a good news/bad news fork in the road. The bad news is that when you're talking about cell-level encryption there's no way to get around SQL Server looking at every single row of the table. The good news is that you can encrypt at the I/O level and get efficient queries on encrypted data.

You can encrypt at the I/O level by using TDE, BitLocker, or Windows EFS to encrypt an entire database at once, an entire volume at once, or individual files or folders in the file system, respectively.

When you encrypt at the I/O level the data encryption and decryption is handled by the SQL Server or Windows I/O subsystems. Because it is handled at such a low level, close to physical storage, SQL Server can still optimize queries on your encrypted data independent of the encryption. Note that you will still take a performance hit when you encrypt at the I/O level, but it is slight when compared to table scans of large tables encrypted at the cell level. In fact, the general rule is that encryption at the I/O level will impact performance by a small percentage—estimated at around 3 to 5 percent.

Summary

A common question that's often asked is, "How do I efficiently search encrypted data?" The answer, as with most things SQL Server, is "it depends." When you encrypt data, you remove the patterns from your data that efficient searching, indexing, and sorting all rely on.

When encrypting data at the cell level your first—and best—option is to avoid searching on your encrypted data. But there are circumstances where it becomes unavoidable, and you absolutely have to search on data encrypted at the cell level. In those cases, you will have to expose some information about your encrypted data in order to achieve efficient exact match searches on your encrypted data. There's no way around that. However, you can control and limit the type and amount of data you expose. Mechanisms like the SQL CLR HMAC generation function introduced in this chapter allow you to severely limit the type of information you expose to prevent hackers from retrieving useful information from your secure data.

When you have to perform range queries or pattern matching queries against data encrypted at the cell level there's no way to work around inefficient queries without exposing substantial patterns in your data, once again making it insecure. However, you do have the option of applying encryption at the I/O level via TDE, BitLocker, and Windows EFS. When data is encrypted at the I/O level, it's decrypted before it reaches the SQL Server query engine. What this means is SQL Server can optimize your queries without regard for encryption at the I/O level.

In the next chapter, I'll discuss additional encryption considerations, including configuring SQL Server SSL encryption to protect your data over the wire.

■ ■ ■

CHAPTER 10

Encrypting Connections to SQL Server 2008

As we have seen, encrypting sensitive data in SQL Server 2008 can be done at many different levels. Data can be encrypted on disk via an encrypted backup file. Data can also be encrypted where it is stored in a table or index via Transparent Data Encryption (TDE) that will be accessed via a stored procedure. You can even encrypt the stored procedure itself. These encryption techniques work primarily with data at rest. It goes without saying that this "resting" data will be accessed and the methods described thus far for encrypting and decrypting this data afford you a layer of protection at the instance level and on disk. It will not be easy for hackers to restore or otherwise interrogate an encrypted backup file, for example.

The questions we will address in this chapter do not deal with the secure storage of data, however. Here we are concerned with the full-flowing data across the ubiquitous wire where transmitting plain text would be tantamount to leaving the keys in your ignition. We will introduce some tools herein, such as network sniffers and certificate store management consoles that may be unorthodox to the DBA who is charged with configuring secure connections to the SQL Server infrastructure. However, these are tools that you must be familiar with to both set up and test secure communications to your SQL Server infrastructure.

Encryption Concepts

Before diving into the specifics of SQL Server-based network encryption and security, I'll introduce some of the key concepts that I'll cover in this chapter. Though some of these concepts were already introduced, particularily in reference to securing your data at rest, they are worth revisiting here in relation to their use for encrypting data over the wire.

- *Public Key Infrastructure (PKI)*: Provides a means of private and secure communication between computers and users via the use of digital certificates. In a PKI, public and private cryptographic keys issued by a Certificate Authority provide authentication, guarantee the certificate owner's identity, and are used to encrypt and decrypt messages between parties.

- *Certificate Authority (CA)*: Services that are part of a PKI that manage the distribution, allocation, and revocation of digital certificates that identify entities such as users and computers. The CA validates primarily via the public key certificates that it distributes that an entity is who it claims to be.

- *SSL/TLS-Secure Sockets Layer and Transport Layer Security*: These two security protocols are used to secure network data packets transmitted between client and server connections to application services such as Internet Information Services (IIS) and SQL Server. SSL is the precursor to TLS and both protocols are included in the Secure Channel (SChannel) security package and Cryptographic APIs for Windows operating systems. Windows will choose which protocol to be used in secure communications between applications based on compatibility between server and client systems, opting for the most secure protocol that both are capable of using. In this chapter when we refer to SSL or TSL, it is not always easy to determine which protocol is actually being used for communications for SQL Server as this responsibility is passed to Windows from SQL Server for determining the secure communications. Thus, we can say that SSL and TLS can both be used in secure communications with the certificate that is provisioned for SQL Server that we will demonstrate herein.

- *Packet sniffer (Network Monitor)*: A packet sniffer is a network administrator's tool that captures data packets on a network segment. In this chapter, we will use one such packet sniffer, Network Monitor, to capture and analyze packets sent to and from a SQL Server instance. Specifically, we will be looking to verify that the packets transmitted across the wire between SQL Server and client applications, such as SQL Server Management Studio, are encrypted and not sent across as plain text from which confidential information could be harvested.

Network Monitor

Network Monitor has been in existence for as long as I can remember, available either via a Windows Resource Kit or Systems Management Studio (SMS). There have been historically two releases of the application, the paired down version which captures packets to and from your local network interface and the other, more powerful sibling, which could be put in "promiscuous" mode to capture all traffic on the network segment. While I have used both versions in my career, the former version, updated over the years, will suffice for capturing and analyzing network packets for SQL Server encryption testing. Fortunately, there is an updated version of Network Monitor that we will use for this chapter, which incidentally does now support promiscuous mode, version 3.3, available from Microsoft at http://www.microsoft.com/downloads/details.aspx?displaylang=en&FamilyID=983b941d-06cb-4658-b7f6-3088333d062f.

Network Monitor is a fairly straightforward application, full of features for whittling down the potentially hundreds of thousands of packets to a handful that will aid you in your network investigations. All that you really need to do is select a network interface on which to capture packets, apply a capture filter (if required), and click on the start button. Since the version we are running here captures only packets on the local network interface, you will need to install and run Network Monitor on your SQL Server, the required disclaimer stating that you should build a test environment for this type of analysis and not run it directly in production unless absolutely essential.

While there are many other network monitoring applications out there in the world, such as Snort, Ethereal, and Wireshark, I chose Network Monitor for its simplicity, familiarity, and because it is a free Microsoft product.

Figure 10-1 shows a sample capture using Network Monitor on a wireless network (so much for data on the wire). We will use Network Monitor throughout this chapter to capture and analyze connections to SQL Server 2008.

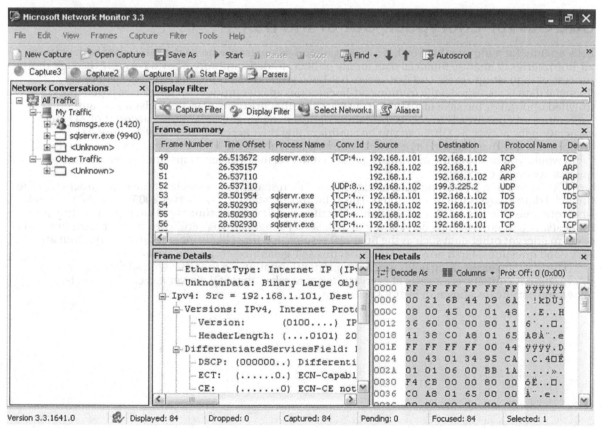

Figure 10-1. Sample capture using Network Monitor

There are three main tabs that are important to note while we are working with Network Monitor in this chapter: Capture Filter, Display Filter, and Select Networks. Within these tabs are four windows that will be of utmost importance to packet sleuthing DBAs. These windows are: Network Conversations, Frame Summary, Frame Details, and Hex Details.

It is within the Network Conversations that we will be able to determine what application the network traffic we are looking at is initiated from or destined for, such as sqlsever.exe. The Frame Summary window displays all of the captured packets on the network segment we are monitoring and the Frame Details and Hex Details allow us to further drill down into each packet to see not only packet-specific information, such as the packet header, source, and destination of the Frame Details window, but the actual hex payload of the packet, which could include plain text data, the kind we are ultimately concerned with. In this chapter, we will not configure a capture filter, which would allow us to only see packets sent from or received by SQL Server, for example, but will instead capture all packets. This is sometimes useful in analyzing packets that you really had no idea were received by your SQL Server, such as broadcast storms, which obviously could impact performance. After the capture is completed for each test, we will issue a display filter to limit the results, looking for SQL Server specific packets.

SQL Server Encryption Out of the Box

Let's assume for a minute that you have in your organization users who have been tasked with writing ad-hoc queries to analyze financial data for my publicly traded company. They have gone through the process of requesting access and that access has been granted to a reporting database where the financial data is refreshed daily (running ad-hoc queries against production databases is generally frowned upon). For the sake of argument, also assume that the users have been given SQL authenticated usernames and passwords to access the data as opposed to using their Windows account or AD group association for access. As DBA, can you be confident that their account credentials cannot be compromised with a tool such as Network Monitor? How about the financial data they are querying? What would you discover if you trained a packet sniffer on the SQL Server instance where the ad hoc queries are being executed?

If you are using SQL Server 2005 or higher, you can rest assured that at least the login process for the financial data analysts will be encrypted. This is because at startup, SQL Server 2005 and 2008 willcreate (if no other certificates exist) a self-generated certificate that it uses primarily to encrypt authentication requests. You might ask, how do I know that SQL Server generates this certificate, and furthermore, can I use it to encrypt other data such as the financial results, that most likely includes my salary? Both are very good questions. First, how do I know that this self-generated certificate exists?

The SQL Server Error log holds much pertinent information for the DBA. One such piece of information it contains is an entry at every startup that relays that SQL Server has created a self-generated certificate, shown in Figure 10-2.

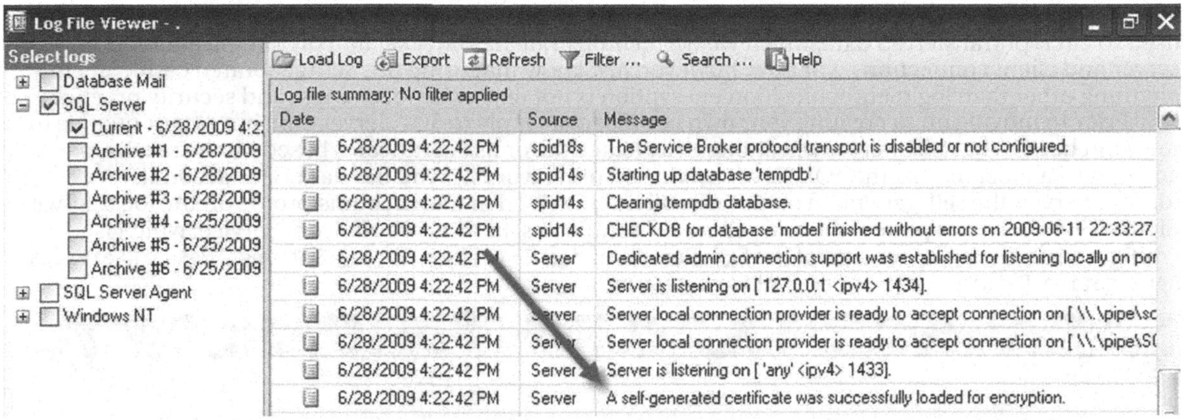

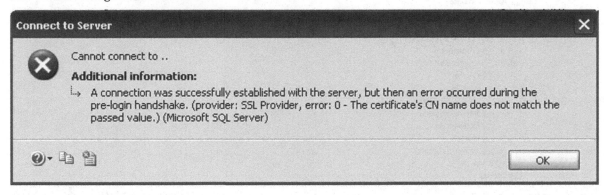

Figure 10-2. *Self generated certificate in SQL Server error logs*

There are a couple of caveats regarding this self-generated certificate. For one, since it is used primarily for login encryption, it is not intended for use to provide full channel encryption from server toclient. In other words, the public key is not exportable and therefore not available to clients to specifically request encryption because it cannot be trusted. If a client explicitly requests encryption from the SQL Server an error message will be generated like the one in Figure 10-3. You will notice the error is self-evident, "The certificate's CN does not match the passed value." You will receive this error anytime you try to connect to a SQL Server instance from a client that forces encryption when SQL Server has a self-generated certificate.

Figure 10-3. *Error connecting to SQL Server self-generated certificate from client*

It should be noted, though, that there is a circumstance where this self-generated certificate can be used to encrypt transferred data, which we will demonstrate in a later section on forcing encryption for server and client connections. For now, however, just know that using this self-generated certificate for anything other than login authentication encryption is not recommended as a sound security practice.

Prior to moving on to creating your own certificate to apply to SQL Server, one important nuance to mention here is that SQL Server will attempt to create and/or use certificates based on the service account that is set to start the SQL Server service. In other words, if you have a service account for SQL Server, the self-generated certificate will be generated in this accounts profile on the local server. Figure 10-4 shows the path of the self-generated certificates, in this case Network Service, which is configured as the logon account of the SQL Server service: `C:\Documents and Settings\NetworkService\ Application Data\Microsoft\Crypto\RSA\S-1-5-20`.

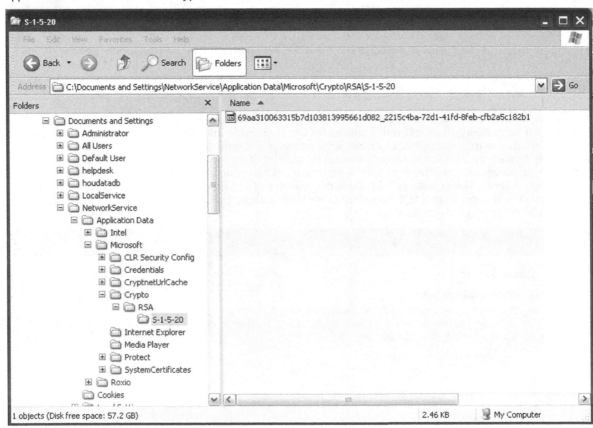

Figure 10-4. Default location of self-generated certificate

While there is not much you can do with the self-generated certificate, knowing its location could be important if for any reason access is revoked for this folder. If SQL Server cannot generate a certificate, then the SQL Server service will not be able to start successfully.

Applying a Self-Signed Certificate

We showed in the previous section how SQL Server creates a self-generated certificate if no other certificate exists that can be used. While this self-generated certificate will be used to encrypt sensitive information like login passwords otherwise passed as plain text, it is limited in scope on how a client can request encryption for other data transfers. What we really need is a certificate that can be used to encrypt all packets. There exists a chain of trust with certificates whereby the client application, such as a Web browser, trusts a certificate being used by a server. This can be most evident when applying a certificate to a Web server such as Internet Information Server (IIS). If the Web browser connects to a web site hosted by IIS with a certificate that does not follow the chain of trust back to a root certificate authority, you will receive a warning message stating that the certificate, though valid, cannot be verified as trusted. This will be the case for a self-signed certificate that we will use in this section for creating a self-signed certificate purely for the sake of testing secure connections to SQL Server 2008. Self-signed certificates differ from the self-generated certificate that SQL Server 2005 and beyond will use natively. First, you have the ability to create an exportable private key with the self-signed certificate we will create here. Secondly, you can specify the Fully Qualified Domain Name (FQDN) for the SQL Server where you will apply the self-signed certificate; this is a crucial requirement as otherwise you will not be able to assign the certificate to your SQL Server instance.

Self-signed certificates should be used for testing purposes only and not ever in a production environment because of the innate lack of trust of a valid root CA, such as those issued by a Windows Certificate Authority server for example, which we will cover in the next section. Without this chain of trust, the client has to trust that the SQL Server that is presenting the certificate is the server it claims to be and vice versa. With self-signed certificates, attacks like *Man in the Middle attacks* can be executed. In Man in the Middle attacks the public key of the SQL Server can be intercepted and used to impersonate the server and exploit the client.

There are several ways to create your own self-signed certificate for use in testing secure channel connections from client to server applications. Tools such as OpenSSL (http://www.openssl.org) and SelfSSL distributed with the IIS 6.0 Toolkit provide a fast and easy way to create a self-signed SSL certificate. Another tool that we will show here is the command makecert.exe. You can acquire makecert.exe from either the .Net Framework SDK or the Windows Server Platform SDK (http://msdn.microsoft.com/en-us/library/aa386968(VS.85).aspx). The version of makecert.exe used here is compatible with both Windows XP and Windows Server 2003. An example of makecert.exe that we will use to generate a self-signed certificate for use with a SQL Server 2008 instance is:

```
makecert -pe -n "CN=knrlt.apress.com" -ss my -sr Localmachine -a sha1
-eku 1.3.6.1.5.5.7.3.2,1.3.6.1.5.5.7.3.1 -r "sql_2008.cer"
```

Some important command-line options of note for the makecert.exe command are:

- -pe: Mark the private key as exportable.

- -n: Name of the certificate, which in this case will assign the CN (Common Name) as the fully qualified name of the SQL Server.

- -ss: Name of the certificate store.

- -sr: Registry location for the certificate store.

- -a: Hash algorithm to use, in this case, sha1. MD5; the default is the other valid choice.

- -eku: Specifies the insertion of enhanced key usage object identifiers (OID), such as 1.3.6.1.5.5.7.3.1, which sets the certificate as "server authentication," again a requirement for applying the certificate to be used by SQL Server.

- -r: Creates the certificate file as *certificatename*.cer.

Executing the makecert command in a Command Prompt window will create the certificate and deploy it to the certificate store specified. As you can see in Figure 10-5, though the output is minimal by way of a "Succeeded" message, at least we know it worked.

Figure 10-5. Creating a self-signed certificate with makecert.exe

Next we will want to verify the creation of the ticket in the certificate store. This can be accomplished in a number of ways, but the easiest way is to the use the Certificates snap-in for Microsoft Management Console (MMC). To view the certificate store via MMC, follow these steps:

1. Click Start ➤ Run and type MMC.

2. From the File menu on the Console select Add/Remove Snap-in.

3. Select the Add button in the Add/Remove Snap-In Dialogue box.

4. Next select the Certificates Snap-in and click Add. Choose Computer Account and click Next. (You have the option of selecting My user account. SQL Server can use certificates from either stores, a user account or a computer account.)

5. Select Local computer and then click Finish.

6. Finally, click Close on the Add Snap-in Dialogue and then click OK. You should now see the certificate store for the local computer. If we expand the Personal folder and click Certificates, we can see the deployed certificate from the makecert.exe command, as shown in Figure 10-6.

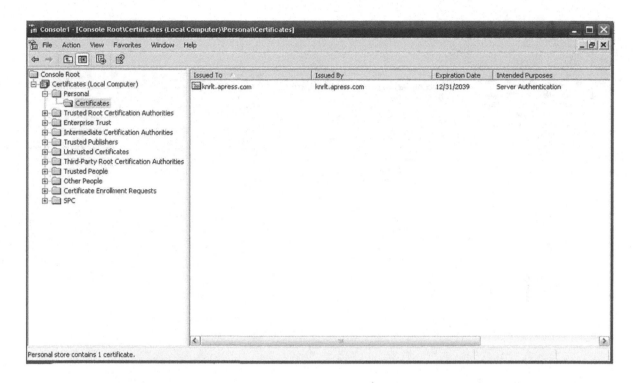

Figure 10-6. *Deployed self-signed certificate in MMC*

With the certificate now in place, we have several more options for secure channel communications with SQL Server than we have using the self-generated key SQL Server will create with each service restart. When SQL Server starts, it looks in the certificate store of the Windows system on which it runs for a valid certificate that can be applied in lieu of the self-generated certificate. If it finds one, it will apply it with no other options configured, which we will get to in the section "Enforcing Encryption between Server and Client."

With nothing more than the self-signed certificate deployed on the local server, let's restart SQL Server and see what happens. Since we will be using the SQL Server Configuration Manager throughout the chapter, it is a good time to go ahead and launch it. Click Start ➤ All Programs ➤ Microsoft SQL Server 2008 ➤ Configuration Tools ➤ SQL Server Configuration Manager. You can see in Figure 10-7 all of the services that are currently installed for one or more instances. Notice that the MSSQLSERVER instance of SQL Server is set to Logon as LocalSystem. I will discuss the importance of the logon account for SQL Server and how it works with different types of installed certificates next.

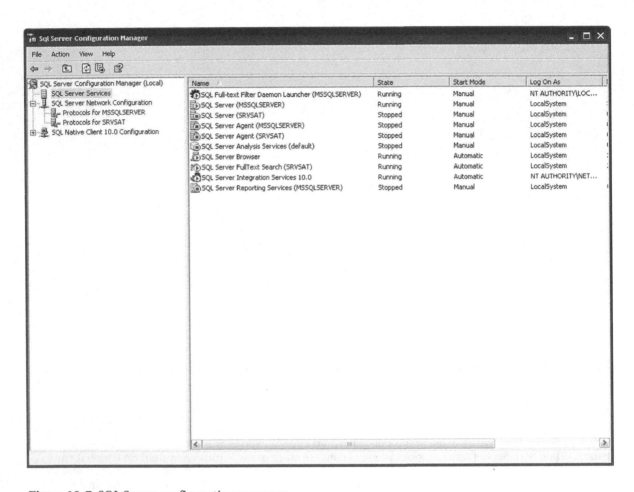

Figure 10-7. SQL Server configuration manager

Simply right-click on the SQL Server service for the default instance and select Restart. You can assign the certificate to more than one SQL instance per server. After the service has restarted, let's check the SQL Server Error Logs again to see if the newly provisioned certificate created via makecert.exe has been discovered and loaded by the default SQL Server instance. Figure 10-8 shows the new certificate SQL Server chosen from the local machines personal certificate store.

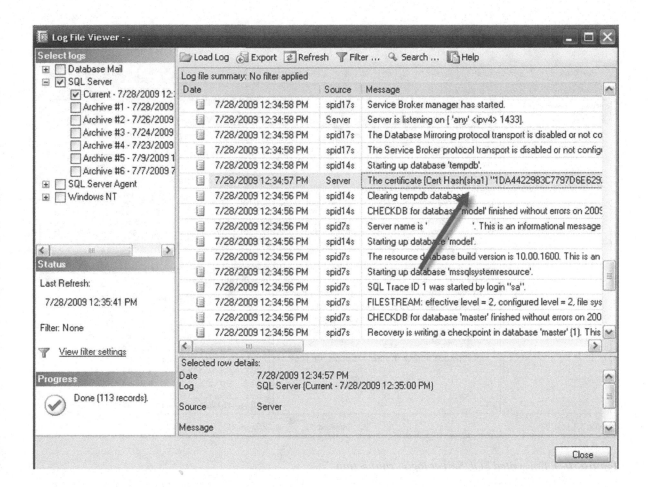

Figure 10-8. SQL Server errror log showing certificate

With this certificate now being used by SQL Server, we can be assured that, like with the self-generated certificate, all logon authentication attempts will be encrypted using the cipher strength of the certificate. You can see the actual hash code for the certificate listed in the SQL Server Error Logs as well. Though we did not explicitly select this certificate for use with SQL Server, it still loaded as a valid certificate. Later, we will explicitly select a certificate and show how to confirm the certificate that we specified is the one actually loaded by SQL Server. For now, know that with the self-signed certificate has been successfully applied. It is worth a look with Network Monitor to see what a logon packet may look like on the wire. Figure 10-9 shows a sample capture of a SQL Server logon attempt, encrypted as expected. Notice, too, the description of the captured packet is TDS: TLS SSL, which is the secure channel protocol we expect to see based on the cipher suite negotiated between the server and client.

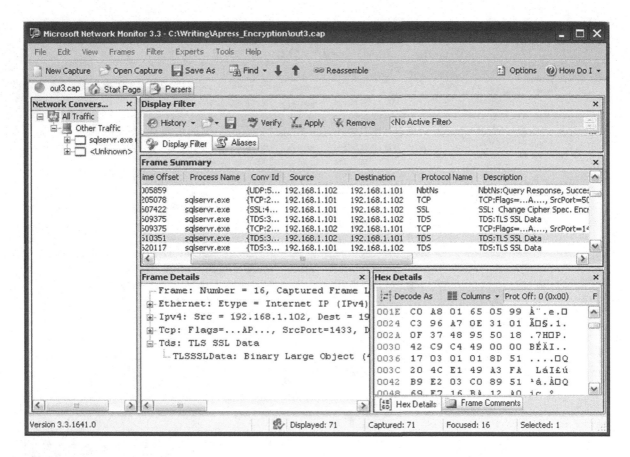

***Figure 10-9.** Encrypted SQL Server logon connection*

At this point, we could dive in and start forcing encryption for either the server or the client application, but that would be getting ahead of ourselves. We have successfully provisioned a self-signed certificate which we have verified is doing its job in securing logon authentication requests. The next step before utilizing certificate-based encryption to its fullest potential is to acquire a legitimate certificate from a certificate authority. The end result will be the same, in the sense that we will have a certificate provisioned for use with SQL Server. However, the biggest advantage is that by acquiring the key from a valid CA, the chain of trust will be established. After we acquire a valid certificate from a CA, we will then move on to testing client/server secure channel communications with and without certificates.

Requesting a Certificate from a Valid CA

Provisioning a server to use a certificate from a trusted CA is quite easy, assuming you have a CA sever inyour organization, which many do. By having a certificate that every client can validate by following the chain of trust back to the issuing authority, you can be assured that the connections to your SQL

Server, once configured to use this certificate, will be secure as all of the clients that connect to the server, assuming the server is internal to your private network, will trust the identity of the SQL Server and can establish secure channel communications without issue. For public connections to SQL Server via the Internet, a practice that is not as common, you can request a certificate from a trusted certificate authority such as Verisign or Thawte for a price. Both companies offer a free SSL trial certificate, generally for 14 days, for testing. While these certificates are often provisioned for web site security, applying a certificate for SQL Server secure channel communications would be just as important if the SQL Server instance was publicly facing on the Internet. ,

In this section, we are going to request a certificate from a Windows CA server. The first step in requesting a certificate is to open the Certificates MMC that we walked through in the previous section. This time, however, instead of reviewing the installed certificates, we are going to request one. Right click the Personal ➤ Certificates folder and select All Tasks ➤ Request New Certificate, as seen in Figure 10-10.

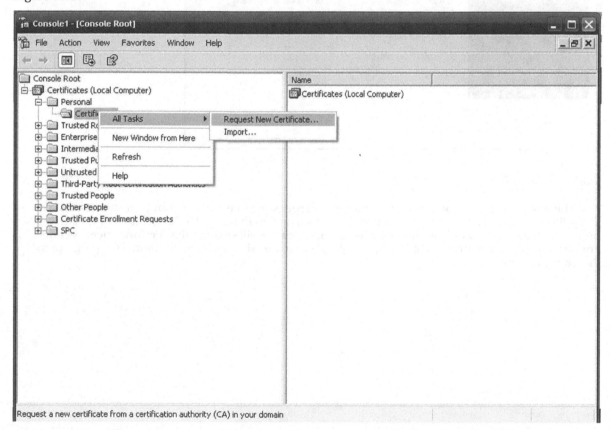

Figure 10-10. Requesting new certificate from CA

This will launch the Certificate Request Wizard, as seen in Figure 10-11.

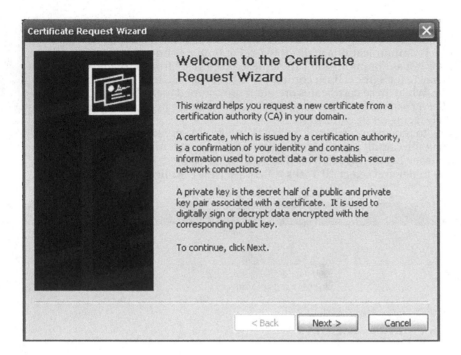

Figure 10-11. *Certificate request wizard*

The wizard will walk you through the process of requesting a certificate from your domain CA. You can select the type of certificate you want and the key length of that key. The longer the key length, the more overhead via CPU utilization will be incurred, which we will cover in the "Performance" section. For our purpose, a key strength of 1024 is acceptable from the Microsoft RSA SChannel Cryptographic Provider (see Figure 10-12).

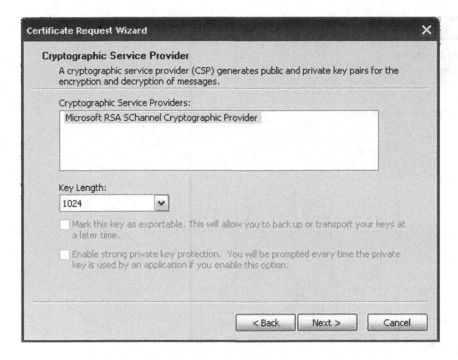

Figure 10-12. Requesting RSA X.509 certificate

Once you select the CA Server from the next dialogue, you have the option of selecting a friendly name for your certificate. Friendly names are useful when working with many similar types of certificates. These friendly names, by default, will show up in drop down list of certificates, for example, when assigning the certificate to SQL Server, which we will show next. We will name the requested certificate 4SQL_Dom, which Figure 10-13 shows.

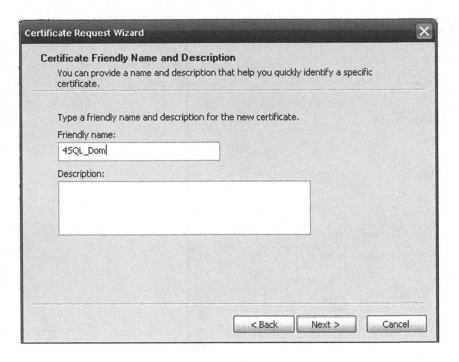

Figure 10-13. Naming requested certificate

When you click Finish, you should see the final message of the certificate request, which, if all worked, will be successful and we can then move onto applying the newly issued certificate to SQL Server, much like we did for the self-signed certificate with makecert. However, in this case, we are going to use the CA-issued certificate in the next section to demonstrate how to configure the SQL Server instance to utilize the provisioned certificate and enforce encryption for network requests other than for logons; there might be packets of data that contain employee salaries after all and we cannot have that floating about the network in plain view.

Enforcing Encryption Between Server and Client

To this point, we have provisioned out SQL Server for three different certificates: the self-generated certificate that SQL Server 2005 and beyond will use natively if no other "server authenticated" certificates have been loaded, a self-signed certificate using makecert.exe, and a certificate acquired from a CA server in the domain. What we have not done yet is enable secure channel encryption for anything other than logon negotiation whereby plain text passwords will be encrypted on the wire when authenticating from a client application. It is now time to explain the different options that are available to you for forcing encryption between server and client connections.

There are two basic scenarios that will force SSL/TLS connections to be made to SQL Server, either by forcing all connections to be encrypted at the server level or forcing connections at the client level. It is also possible for a user to simply request an encrypted connection from the client application, such as SQL Server Management Studio or a web application, but that is not a mandated process and relies upon the user or application owner to set the connection properly. We will cover the different types of applications and connections in the next section. For now, let's show how to configure both basic ways to force encrypted connections to SQL Server.

Forcing Encryption at the Server

SQL Server can be configured to force all connection packets to be encrypted. We will perform this step in the SQL Server Configuration Manger, which we previously used to restart SQL Services. In SQL Server Configuration Manger you will see SQL Server Network Configuration, which contains the different protocols that can be used for connections, like Shared Memory, Named Pipes, TCP/IP, and VIA (Virtual Interface Adapter). Of the four, the most commonly used protocols are Shared Memory and TCP/IP, the latter of which we are primarily concerned with. However, we will configure encryption at the individual protocol level but for all protocols. Right-click on "Protocols for <instancename>" and select Properties. As seen in Figure 10-14, the Force Encryption flag is shown, which by default is set to "No."

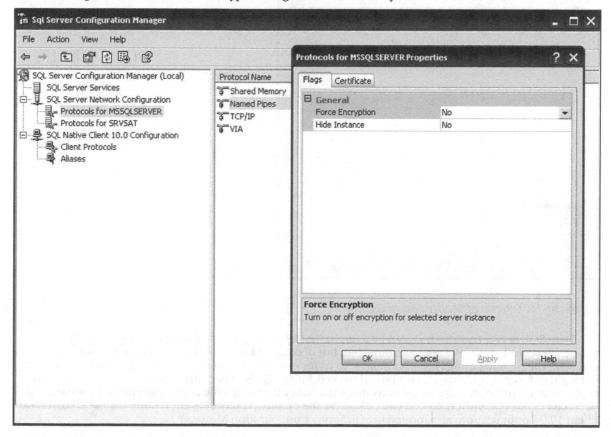

Figure 10-14. Setting force encryption flag

To force encryption, we will simply drop down on the Force Encryption flag value and select "Yes."

Also, in this Property windows you will see the Certificate tab. As we know, SQL Server will use a certificate if it has been provisioned on the server, even without specifying the certificate directly on the Certificate tab. However, you may have more than one certificate and can specify which one to use. Clicking on the Certificate tab, we can drop down and see the provisioned certificates for the server. You may recall that we had given the CA assigned certificate a friendly name of 4SQL_Dom. If a friendly name exists, we will see the image shown in Figure 10-15. We will select this certificate and click OK, which will prompt us to restart SQL Server for the changes to take effect.

Figure 10-15. Selecting friendly named certificate

With SQL Server restarted, we can be assured that all packets issued from and sent to SQL Server will be encrypted, right? We could assume that, but of course being thorough DBAs, we will test that and all of the myriad configurations available to us for encryption. Then, you may decide that you do not want to force secure channel encrypted packets for all SQL Server connections due to the potential performance overhead. Instead, you may make it a policy that a specific application or user base should be forced to use encryption. In that case, you have the option of enforcing encryption via the SQL Native Client 10.0 Configuration, also located in SQL Server Configuration Manager.

Forcing Encryption from Clients with SQL Native Client

To force encryption from client connections, we will stay in SQL Server Configuration Manager but instead of forcing the server network configuration we will right-click on the SQL Native Client 10.0 Configuration and select Properties. You can see that the options are similar to the server network configuration with the ability selected to the Force Protocol Encryption flag as "Yes." The key distinction is the "Trust Server Certificate" flag, as you can see in Figure 10-16. When enabled, this flag will allow the client to force encryption to a server even when the client does not have a chain of trust via a public key, such as it would have in a domain where a valid domain CA issued the certificate or if the certificate is self-generated. I had stated earlier in the chapter that it was possible to use the self-generated certificate, the default for SQL Server, to encrypt more than just logon credentials. The "Trust Server Certificate" combined with "Force Protocol Encryption" will accommodate that particular scenario.

Figure 10-16. SQL Native Client Properties

Creating and Testing Secure Connections

Now that we have taken the time to provision various types of SSL certificates for our SQL Server instance and started, restarted, and verified that indeed we can expect secure connections from our applications, either by forcing encryption via server or client, it is time to undo it all and start from scratch to show what can be expected from non-secure network communications. I think you will be surprised at what you see. Now, let's go back to default, no certificates provisioned and no forced encryption to where only a self-generated certificate exists for the sake of encrypting logon packets. This is what you can expect out of the box. As we all know, there are several types of applications that can connect to your SQL Servers. In this section, I will cover two: SQL Server Management Studio and SQL Server Reporting Services for demonstration. Both of these applications, like others you may be familiar with, share a common property and that is a connection string. We will build up from no encryption to full-blown secure channel enforcement via these application demos, which will lead to the final section on performance.

SQL Server Management Studio Example

Let's assume that we have sensitive data that is not encrypted by any other means. This could be the salary information mentioned earlier or credit card numbers or social security. Whatever data that you do not want to be passing about in unencrypted form counts. For sake of demonstration, let's look at the AdventureWorks2008 database, employee information. I have always wanted to work for Adventure Works and make an exceptional salary, but I doubt that will ever happen. The least I can do is protect the fake employees' salaries that work for the company fictitiously. So, back at default, self-generated certificate I open SSMS and issue the following query, with Network Monitor diligently capturing the packets.

```
SELECT TOP 1000 [BusinessEntityID]
      ,[NationalIDNumber]
      ,[LoginID]
      ,[OrganizationNode]
      ,[OrganizationLevel]
      ,[JobTitle]
      ,[BirthDate]
      ,[MaritalStatus]
      ,[Gender]
      ,[HireDate]
      ,[SalariedFlag]
      ,[VacationHours]
      ,[SickLeaveHours]
      ,[CurrentFlag]
      ,[rowguid]
      ,[ModifiedDate]
  FROM [AdventureWorks2008].[HumanResources].[Employee]
```

What I find is just salary information after all, though that can certainly be gleaned with a bit more probing. What we were able to capture, as you can see in Figure 10-17, is actually a username, among other data like the user's title, "Sales Representative." The bottom line is that the data was transferred across the wire with plain text. Also notice that in the Network Monitor capture, the protocol is TCP. Jillian0 is mine.

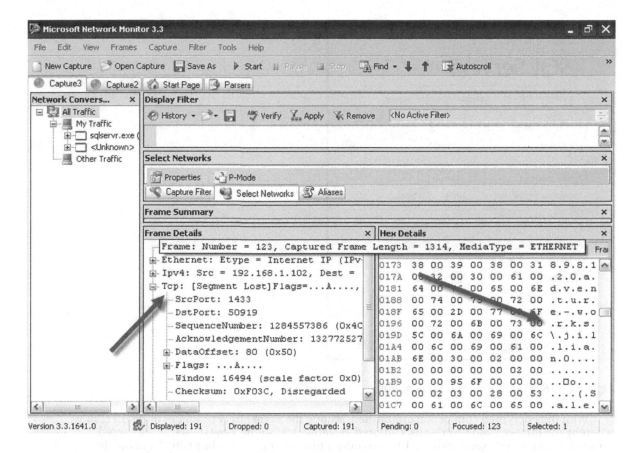

Figure 10-17. Capturing usernames in plain text with Network Monitor

The same query when issued form an application with encryption enabled will return much different results in the Network Monitor capture. Let's assume now that the Force Encryption option for the Server Network Configuration is set to "No," however a valid certificate has been applied to the server on the Certificate tab of SQL Server Configuration Manager. This will allow for a requested, not forced, encrypted connection to SQL Server. When connecting to the SQL Server within SSMS, you have the option of selecting "Encrypt Connection" from the Options menu, seen in Figure 10-18.

Figure 10-18. *SSMS force encryption option*

With the encrypted connection established, issuing the same query produces different results, whereby the former plain text results, captured in Network Monitor, now shown as encrypted, unintelligible packets (see Figure 10-19). Also notice that the protocol, while still TCP, now shows TLSSSL data, which proves the connection is being encrypted via secure channel communications.

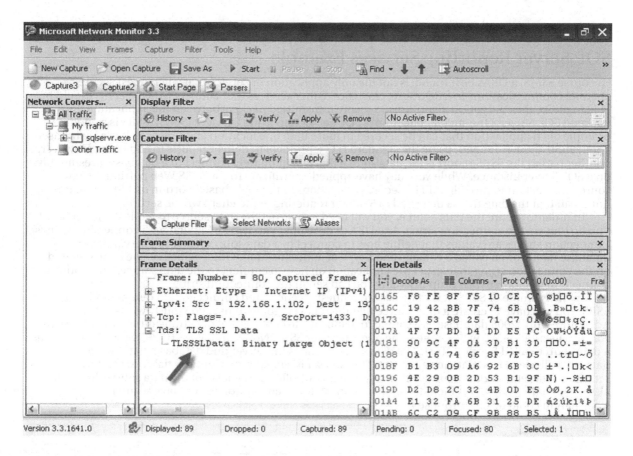

Figure 10-19. Encrypted employee information

There are other scenarios whereby encryption can be configured for SQL Server, either enforced or requested; SSMS only being one such application. All applications will request or be forced into encryption by SQL Server or the client configuration or connection strings.

SQL Server Reporting Services Example

Of course SSMS, a DBAs best friend, is not the only application or service that will request secure channel communications to a SQL Server instance. Other services that connect to SQL Server should be able to utilize the encryption algorithms to secure transmitted packets between the application and backend SQL Server. One such application is SQL Server Reporting Services (SSRS). SSRS is a good example of an application that can be secured in more than one location and protocol. It is a Web-based application at the front end, using the standard HTTP protocol to deliver reports to end users. However, another part of the SSRS report is the data source that will ultimately connect to a database, presumably on a SQL Server instance. While you may have applied a certificate to the SSRS Web portion the data source connection to provide HTTPS secure connections to the Web-based portion on SSRS, that does not mean that the data that is delivered to SSRS for rendering to the client will be secure.

In order to secure the data source, you will need to instruct the data source to request encryption. You do that via the connection string. As a DBA or developer you will be familiar with connection strings. Connection strings are values that define how to connect to a data source, such as a server name, database name, often called a catalog, and a type of authentication. Other values can be concatenated on the connection string to instruct the application on how to connect to the data source. Encrypting a connection is another such property value you can set on the connection string.

In the example of SSRS, it is quite easy to request an encrypted connection. In design mode for SSRS, you will have to create a data source that the report is going to use. Previously we used the AdventureWorks2008 database as a source to demonstrate confidential data transmitted on the wire by way of a username. We will use the same query here for SSRS. Notice in Figure 10-20, the SSRS report has a data source called Encrypt_Test. The data source defines the server and database that the query, or data set, will use to feed data to the report. The data set is called Emp_Confidential. You can have multiple data sets per data source. All encryption is controlled at the level of the data source. You can also see that the Login ID is included in the report. Without encryption, as we have seen, this information could be compromised.

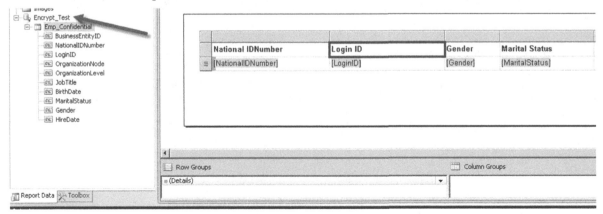

Figure 10-20. SSRS data source

To secure the data that is being fed to the report from the SQL Server instance, all that we need to do is configure the connection string that makes up the Encrypt_Test data source. Looking at the default properties of the Encrypt Test data source, it is not immediately evident how to force encryption from the report to the SQL Server instance. Figure 10-21 shows the default properties for the data source.

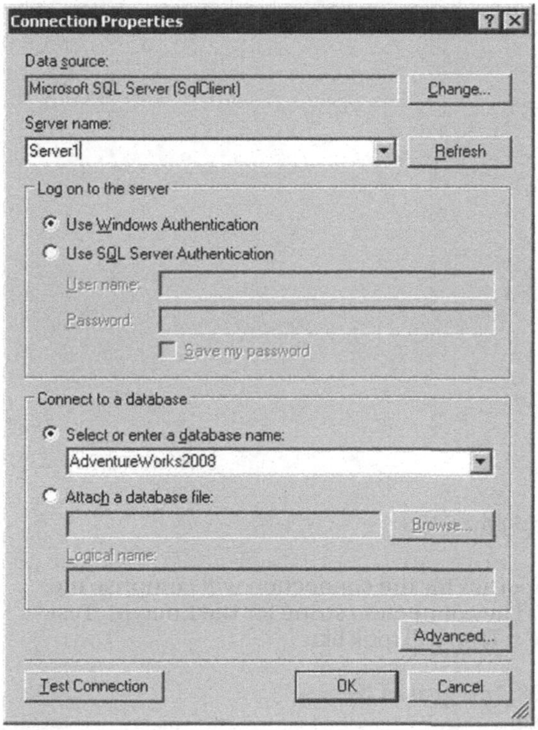

Figure 10-21. Default data source properties in SSRS

If we click on the Advanced tab of the Connection Properties, two additional property values become available, Encryption and TrustServerCertificate. These options, as discussed previously, will force an encrypted session and trust the server certificate on the SQL Server. You set the Encrypt value to True to force the encryption. However, if you select TrustServerCertificate, you must also select Encrypt to be True. Figure 10-22 shows the Advanced Properties of the data source connection.

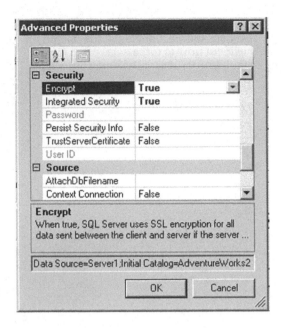

Figure 10-22. Advanced properties of a data source connection for SSRS

Ultimately, the options you select in the graphical properties for the connection will comprise the actual connection string, which will be represented in text. The connection string for the Encrypt_Test data source with Encrypt = True and TrustServerCertificate = True will look like:

```
Data Source=Server1;Initial Catalog=AdventureWorks2008;Integrated ↵
Security=True;Encrypt=True;TrustServerCertificate=True
```

Performance

Encrypting connections between the SQL Server instance and client application will require additional CPU resources. How much CPU will be required and the performance impact is dependent, as you can imagine, on the amount of data that is being encrypted as well as the cipher strength of the certificate. A 1024-bit RAS Public key, for example, is going to incur less processing overhead than an 8192-bit key. Another important factor is the number of connections requiring encryption as well as the amount of data transferred. The impact will not be relegated to the SQL Server, but will also appear on the client application which itself must participate in encrypting and decrypting packets sent to and from the SQL Server. Also, an additional round trip is required when connecting to SQL Server that is configured to use encryption. All of these combined may make DBAs think twice about configuring encryption. We would recommend that before enabling SSL/TSL encryption for SQL Server that you thoroughly test the circumstances that you may encounter in a non-production system. This way, you can be certain that the encryption levels you choose meet expectations for both application security as well as performance.

Summary

In this chapter, we focused on securing communications that occur between SQL Server client applications and SQL Server itself. By provisioning a server with a trusted certificate or even when a certificate is not available, it is possible to enforce secure channel communications so that there is not fear that a hacker may eavesdrop on your network and glean sensitive data, like we saw with user logon information. Differing form the physical storage of encrypted data, SSL and TLS, part of the overall Cryptographic Suite for network protocol security available in Windows Operating Systems, offers another level of security for confidential data.

■■■

Regulatory Requirements

Over the past decade, encryption of data at rest has quickly moved from being a tool reserved for governments and large organizations to a day-to-day business requirement for organizations of all sizes. As malicious hackers have increased their ability to steal sensitive information from database servers and laptop computers, pressure has increased on governments and businesses to counter the threat.

Increasing demands for better security has been met with a slew of new laws and regulations to force implementation of encryption and other countermeasures against data theft. Many industries have adopted, or are in the process of adopting, increased security standards. In some industries, it's not uncommon to see mandatory security measures and compliance steps detailed explicitly in contracts.

In this chapter, I'll discuss some of the different types of regulations, laws, and contractual obligations that you may face as a security officer, administrator, or data steward.

■ **Caution** Bear in mind that the penalties for noncompliance with laws, regulations, and contractual requirements are constantly changing and specific to the locales and industries involved. This is where I insert mydisclaimer: I am not a lawyer. For specific information about compliance and noncompliance penalties, consultqualified legal counsel.

Regulations

There are dozens of laws and regulations about data protection on the books, with more being added every day. In the United States alone, there are laws and rules being enforced by regulatory agencies at the federal level, laws at the state level, and the potential for even more regulation at the local level. In other countries, laws concerning data protection are in different stages of implementation at any given point in time. For companies that do business internationally the result can be a maze of regulations to navigate to ensure compliance. The following sections provide an overview of laws and regulations that require businesses to take steps to protect confidential data. While not comprehensive in depth, this survey gives an idea of the sweep and reach of these confidentiality laws. For specific answers about your organization's compliance obligations with these and other laws and regulations, consult professional legal counsel.

Health Insurance Portability and Accountability Act

The Health Insurance Portability and Accountability Act (HIPAA) is a federal law in the United States that pertains to the health care industry. HIPAA has two rules that are of interest to those charged withprotecting healthcare data. The first rule, the HIPAA Privacy Rule, requires certain "covered entities"—health plans, most health care providers, and health care clearinghouses—to put safeguards in place to protect health care information. These safeguards generally include some form of encryption of health care data, which includes health status, provision of health care, and payment for health care. Generally speaking, this is interpreted to include medical records, payment records, and other patient identifying information.

The HIPAA Security Rule requires encryption of certain electronically stored health care data, and also requires data corroboration (or data integrity validation). The data corroboration can be implemented via digital signatures, cryptographic hashing, and checksums.

Sarbanes-Oxley

The Sarbanes-Oxley Act (SOX) is a United States federal law that was enacted in response to several corporate accounting scandals that broke at the dawn of the 21st century. SOX was introduced to restore confidence in the securities markets after investors lost billions as a result of these scandals.

Two sections of SOX are of primary interest to those who must protect data. Sections 302 (Internal controls) and 404 (Assessment of internal controls) require implementation and auditing of internal controls. These sections of the act are meant to ensure effective internal control over financial reporting is exercised by management. Internal controls include those which are designed to prevent ordetect fraud. Encryption and cryptographic functions (such as digital signatures and cryptographic hashes) can be employed to prevent and detect tampering with financial data.

Fair and Accurate Credit Transactions Act

The Fair and Accurate Credit Transactions Act (FACTA) is a United States federal law that charges various government agencies with the task of instituting new rules and regulations for the protection ofconsumer credit data. These rules may require safeguarding confidential consumer information and credit data through a variety of methods, including encryption.

Federal Information Security Management Act

The Federal Information Security Management Act (FISMA) is specific to Federal government agencies and those vendors who work with government agencies. FISMA indicates that the security requirements of FIPS Publication 200 ("Minimum Security Requirements for Federal Information and Information Systems") must be followed. This publication defines rules that cover the areas of "media protection," "system and communications protection," and "system and information integrity."

Personal Information Protection and Electronic Documents Act

The Personal Information Protection and Electronic Documents Act (PIPEDA) is a Canadian federal law that requires private-sector organizations to take appropriate security measures to protect the personal information of individuals. Encryption is often considered an appropriate security measure when storage of personal information is involved. In addition to the federal PIPEDA law, Canada has provincial laws that may also mandate additional security of personal information.

Data Protection Act

The Data Protection Act of 1998 (DPA) is a United Kingdom law that requires appropriate technical and organizational measures be taken against unauthorized or unlawful processing of personal data. It also requires steps be taken to protect against "accidental loss, destruction, or damage to personal data." The appropriate technical measures often include encryption of personal data.

Data Protection Directive

One of the core principles of the Data Protection Directive (DPD, or Directive 95/46/EC) of the European Union (EU) is that collected personal data should be "kept secure from potential abuses." The Directive applies to all personal information collection and processing, whether done manually or via automation. Implementation specifics are implemented on a country-by-country basis, the DPD does require implementation of security measures which may include encryption. Transfer of personal data from within the EU to outside countries requires the country guarantee an "adequate level of protection."

California SB 1386 and AB 1298

In the United States, you may have to deal not only with federal laws, but also with state and local lawsconcerning privacy and consumer protection. California is notable because privacy is a right guaranteed under the state Constitution, and the right to privacy strongly shapes consumer privacy anddata protection laws there. California law SB 1386 requires reasonable protections for personal data, primarily to protect against identity theft. AB 1298 expands the definition of "personal information" in SB 1386 to include medical information and health insurance information. California also has requirements for notification of individuals in the event of a data breach.

Massachusetts Data Protection Law

The Massachusetts Data Protection Law is known as one of the toughest state data protection laws in the country. This law explicitly spells out that a minimum level of 128-bit encryption must be used for the encryption of personal data. The Massachusetts law also requires individual notification in the event of breaches or corruption of personal data.

Other State Laws

I mentioned California and Massachusetts state laws in this section because they are notable in their scope and toughness. However, every state in the United States has its own combination of consumer protection, data privacy, and notification laws. Likewise, Canadian provinces have their own provincial laws concerning consumer protection and personal data security. Data stewards should familiarize themselves with applicable laws to ensure compliance.

■ **Tip** When in doubt about the applicability or specifics of federal, state, or local laws governing data protection, consult with an attorney who specializes in the field.

The Cost of Data Loss

The cost of noncompliance with applicable laws that require personal, medical, and credit data protection can be very steep—and not just in dollars. Consider the following generalized costs that can be incurred by an organization in the event of a data breach:

- Many states, countries, and local governments have implemented laws that require notification of individuals in the event of a data breach. California law, for instance, requires notification of consumers in the event of breaches in security, confidentiality, or integrity of confidential data.

- Data breaches can result in lowered customer confidence in your ability to protect personal information, resulting in fewer customers willing to do business with your organization. When CardSystems Solutions, a credit-card processing company, exposed 40 million credit card numbers to hackers they were dropped by Visa and American Express as a processor. CardSystems Solutions no longer exists.

- Data loss can cause injured parties, including individuals, organizations that you do business with, and even state Attorneys General to launch civil suits against your organization. A class-action lawsuit was brought against TD Ameritrade in 2007 when it became clear that account holders' personal information was leaked.

None of this includes the additional incidental costs associated with a data breach, such as consulting costs associated with bringing in third-party auditors to investigate after the fact, business interruption costs, loss of hardware (such as stolen laptops), and lost productivity after a data loss incident.

Contracts

Many industries have enacted standards that they implement through contracts. Credit card companies include standard security clauses in their contracts with credit card processing companies, for instance. The security clauses mandate what data pertaining to credit card processing can be stored, what data needs to be encrypted, and often the encryption algorithm that has to be used.

Government contractors often have to implement mandated encryption standards as well. When you do contract work for government departments, such as the Department of Defense (DoD), you have to comply with federal rules and departmental regulations concerning data protection. No matter what industry you're in, it's important to research your contractual obligations and industry-wide standards for data protection.

What to Encrypt

How do you know what data to encrypt? Although there are some data elements that you should always encrypt, such as social security numbers and credit card numbers, the data elements that require encryption are not always so clear-cut. There are, however, data elements that should serve as "red flag" indicators—meaning you should consider them as candidates for encryption and additional protection whenever you see them.

As a general rule, the data elements you need to encrypt can be divided into four categories: (1)personal identification, (2) personal credit and financial data, (3) health and medical records, and (4)sensitive corporate data. Protection of data that falls into the first three categories of data is dictated by laws and regulations. The following sections discuss some of the data elements that should serve as red flag indicators whenever you store them.

■ **Note** This list is not exhaustive. There are often many industry-specific data elements that can be identified, but which require specific knowledge of the business.

Personal Identification

Data elements that can be used to personally identify an individual should always be treated as sensitive. In some instances, a single data element should be treated as confidential, while in other cases combinations of elements are required to identify a person. The following is a list of data elements that can be used for personal identification.

- *Social Security Number/Tax Identification Number*: Social security numbers, tax identification numbers, and equivalents from non-U.S. countries, should always be encrypted whenever they need to be stored. Generally speaking, you will not need to search on these ID numbers and only rarely will you need to report specifically on these numbers. When these ID numbers are retrieved from a database it's usually for identity verification or tax reporting purposes.

- *Drivers License Number/Government ID Number*: Encryption is strongly recommended for government-assigned ID numbers, such as driver's license numbers. This information can be used in concert with other data elements to personally identify individuals.

- *Name and address*: These data elements are often left unencrypted in databases; however, these two elements combined can be used with other elements to piece together a complete identity of a person. Whether these elements are encrypted or not, care should be taken to protect this information from unauthorized persons.

- *Email address*: Like name and address, email addresses are often left unencrypted. You should also protect this data to prevent unauthorized access. Remember, many a spammer would love to get access to your corporate email list to contact your customers directly.

- *Identity verification questions*: Many web sites ask questions to verify the identity of a user prior to sending or resetting a password. These questions, like "What's your mother's maiden name?" and their associated answers should always be secured.

Personal Credit and Financial Data

Data elements that include personal credit and financial data are always strong candidates for encryption.

- *Credit card numbers*: Whenever you see a business requirement to store credit and debit card numbers, you should first ask whether you really need to store this information. If you use a credit card processor you may not even need to deal with the responsibility of storing credit card numbers in your database. If you absolutely do need to store credit card data, it always needs to be encrypted. Although some people store the last 4 or 5 digits of credit card numbers in an unencrypted field, for display or search purposes, this is not a good practice. This may also be a violation of your contractual or regulatory requirements. If you need to store the last 4or 5 digits in another field for searches, consider using a keyed hash to secure it.

- *Bank account number*: How many times have you received a spam email from a scammer asking you to send your bank account number, so you could help them sneak millions of dollars out of their country? There's a reason they want your bank account number—it makes it a lot easier for them to steal your money. Always encrypt bank account numbers.

Health and Medical Records

Health and medical records are, without a doubt, sensitive information. Depending on the type of business you are in and the state in which you're doing business, the requirements for data protection may vary by country and state.

- *Medical records*: Medical records generally are broadly defined to include any treatment records, medical test results, and other related records. Medical records should, as a rule, always be treated as confidential. The level of security that must be applied to these types of records depends on applicable laws of the countries and states in which you do business.

- *Health payment records*: Records and receipts for payment of medical services and treatment must be treated as confidential as well. Again, the level of security that must be applied depends on applicable laws.

- *Health insurance information/applications*: Health insurance information and health insurance applications must be treated as confidential in a variety of cases. The level of security that must be applied depends on applicable federal and state laws.

Sensitive Corporate Data

Protection of sensitive corporate data is a safeguard against corporate espionage. Taking adequate precautions with your sensitive data will help your organization maintain its competitive edge. To determine which data elements fall into this category, just answer the simple question "Which data, if it were obtained by our competitors, would give them a competitive advantage?" Determining which data elements would hurt your company if they were exposed to the competition is the key to rounding out your security requirements.

- *Compensation data*: The competition could do serious damage if they were to get hold of your organization's complete compensation data, including salary, wage, and bonus information. Compensation records are considered sensitive information and should be treated as such by your organization.

- *Financial data*: Sensitive organizational financial data can be a damaging tool if it leaked out of your company and got into the hands of miscreants and corporate spies. This data should be protected. Note that this is considered separate from consumer financial data, the exposure of which could lead you afoul of the regulators.

- *Client lists*: Lists of clients and customers in the wrong hands can deal a serious blow to your competitive advantage. These should be protected like other corporate secrets.

- *Contracts*: Corporate contracts often contain sensitive information and should be encrypted when stored electronically, to guard against unauthorized access.

- *Secret formulas*: Some companies have been built on the success of their secret formulas. Consider Coca-Cola and Kentucky Fried Chicken (KFC). If the success of your company is dependent on guarding secret formulas like KFC's "11 secret herbs and spices," encryption is a no-brainer.

- *Plans and schematics*: Plans and schematic drawings are often extremely sensitive confidential corporate property. When these are stored, they should be encrypted to guard against corporate espionage.

- *Performance tests*: Performance test data, particularly during development stages, is often considered extremely sensitive. Again, these should be encrypted to protect against theft and unauthorized dissemination.

Example: From $15 Billion to Bankruptcy

In 2001, the major credit card companies began incorporating compliance with a standard known as Payment Card Industry Data Security Standard (PCI DSS) into their standard contracts for credit card processors. PCI DSS is the credit card industry security standard, created to "proactively protect customer account data"[1]. In June 2004, Visa Inc. certified CardSystems Solutions, a large credit card processor, as compliant with PCI DSS.

A year later CardSystems Solutions' network was hacked, exposing 40 million credit card and debit card numbers[2]. CardSystems went from processing $15 billion worth of credit card transactions per year to bankruptcy when both Visa and MasterCard denied CardSystems the ability to process credit card transactions. Less than six months after the incident, CardSystems' assets were bought by another doomed company, Pay By Touch, which went out of business in 2008[3].

PCI DSS

The PCI DSS is a 70 plus page standard that details security requirements for merchants and processors. The centerpieces of this standard include 12 requirements that cover everything from building and maintaining a secure network to encrypting cardholder data at rest and in transit. You can access the full PCI DSS version 1.2 at https://www.pcisecuritystandards.org/security_standards/pci_dss_download.html.

Some People Never Learn

You might think the security failures of CardSystems Solutions, which ultimately drove it out of business, would have served as sufficient warning to other companies. The Princeton, N.J.-based credit-card processor Heartland Payment Systems, however, was hacked in January 2009—a mere seven months

---

[1] PCI DSS—PCI Security Standards Council web site: https://www.pcisecuritystandards.org/security_standards/pci_dss.shtml
[2] Wired.com, "Card Systems' Data Left Unsecured," 6/22/2009, http://www.wired.com/science/discoveries/news/2005/06/67980
[3] New York Times, "Card Center Hit By Thieves Agrees to Sale," 10/17/2005, http://query.nytimes.com/gst/fullpage.html?res=9B07E2DF153FF934A25753C1A9639C8B63

after the American Business Awards conferred the honor of "Best Sales Organization in America" on them[4, 5]. The fallout from the Heartland Payment Systems breach included the following:

- Plenty of negative publicity surrounding what many speculated might be "the largest security breach in the [credit card] industry's history,"[6] possibly eclipsing the massive TJX breach of 2007.

- Investigations by federal government agencies, including the Securities and Exchange Commission and the Federal Trade Commission.[7]

- A class-action lawsuit filed by Heartland Payment Systems' own shareholders, who cited "failure to disclose" and misrepresentation of "materially adverse facts" relating to the security of Heartland's systems.[8]

- Lawsuits by banks and credit unions affected by the data breach for "violating the state's [New Jersey's] consumer protection laws" and for "breach of implied contract."[9]

- Even more lawsuits from affected consumers for failure to promptly notify individuals of the data breach in a timely manner.[10]

In addition, the attorney general from several states began requesting information from Heartland Payment Systems concerning the data breach and its handling. Only recently has Heartland Payment Systems been added back into Visa's Global List of PCI DSS Validated Service Providers[11], with an indication that their annual "report on compliance" is between one and sixty days late.

In all, Heartland Payment Systems appears to be in the early stages of recovery mode. And they appear to be making progress in regaining the confidence of Visa; but as of this writing it's still too early to tell if they will regain the trust of investors, banks, credit unions, and most importantly, customers.

CardSystems Solutions and Heartland Payment Systems both could have avoided their security nightmares and minimized their legal exposure by properly implementing the industry security standards. At best, both of these utter failures of security management should serve as high profile warnings to other organizations.

---

[4]   Heartland Payment Systems, "Heartland Payment Systems Named Best Sales Organization in America by American Business Awards," 6/23/2008, http://www.heartlandpaymentsystems.com/article.aspx?id=438

[5]   Information Week, "Heartland Payment Systems Hit By Data Security Breach," 1/20/2009, http://www.informationweek.com/news/security/attacks/showArticle.jhtml?articleID=212901505&pgno=1&queryText=&isPrev=present

[6]   Columbus Dispatch, "Breach Prompts Reissue of Bank Cards," 2/25/2009, http://www.columbusdispatch.com/live/content/local_news/stories/2009/02/25/CREDIT_CARD_REISSUE.ART_ART_02-25-09_A1_V2D1ENE.html?sid=101

[7]   PC World, "SEC, FTC Investigating Heartland After Data Theft," 2/25/2009, http://www.pcworld.com/businesscenter/article/160264/sec_ftc_investigating_heartland_after_data_theft.html

[8]   MarketWatch, "Shareholder Class Action Filed Against Heartland Payment Systems Inc.," 4/3/2009, http://www.marketwatch.com/story/shareholder-class-action-filed-against-heartland

[9]   PC World, "Banks, Credit Unions Begin to Sue Heartland Over Data Breach," 3/3/2009, http://www.pcworld.com/businesscenter/article/160543/banks_credit_unions_begin_to_sue_heartland_over_data_breach.html

[10] cnet News, "Heartland Sued Over Data Breach," 1/28/2009, http://news.cnet.com/8301-1009_3-10151961-83.html?tag=mncol;txt

[11] Visa Inc., "Global List of PCI DSS Validated Service Providers," as of 6/4/2009, http://usa.visa.com/download/merchants/cisp-list-of-pcidss-compliant-service-providers.pdf

And It Goes On

In between the time that CardSystems Solutions and Heartland Payment Systems each dropped the balland exposed millions of credit card numbers to hackers, several other organizations failed their customers. In 2007, for example, TJX (the parent company of TJ Maxx stores) exposed 45 plus million customer credit and debit cards to hackers.[12] Their failure to properly secure sensitive communications from the point of sale, and their policy of collection "too much personal information" from customers, resulted in one of the worst retail hacks in history.

In 2006, a laptop containing names and social security numbers of 230,000 customers and advisers was stolen from Ameriprise Financial, an investment advisory company spun off from American Express. Though Ameriprise had previously instituted a policy of encrypting personal data stored on laptops, the policy went unenforced in this case. All of the customer data on the computer's hard drive was unencrypted.[13]

In 2009, a data storage company lost NY Mellon Bank's unencrypted backup data tapes with information including customer names, birth dates, bank account information, and social security numbers. In a strange case of déjà vu, NY Mellon Bank lost another unencrypted backup tape with customer financial and personal data on it just a couple of months later.[14]

I mention these shining security failures not to beleaguer the point or to dredge up news stories these companies probably wish would just go away. Rather, these examples of utter failure are great learning tools, and are notable for a variety of reasons, including the following:

- These failures were fairly large, exposing tens of millions of these organizations' customers to potential fraud and abuse.

- Many security failures of this type result in the additional expenses associated with legal defense in civil court, payment for customer credit monitoring, and additional compensation settlements.

- These well-known organizations hurt their reputations and in some cases are still trying to rebuild trust and confidence around their brands.

- All of these failures were not just technical failures of data stewards; they were also complete and utter failures of every level of organizational management, from the top down.

- Every one of these organizations should have seen themselves as potential targets. Any organization that stores, transmits, or processes large amounts of personal, credit, financial, ormedical data is automatically a high-value target for hackers. Organizations that engage inthe handling of large volumes of this type of information need to keep this in mind when designing a security strategy.

- All of these security failures fall into the category of "they should have known." At the very least these organizations had access to the same news stories of the security failures of their competitors and sister organizations to study.

---

[12] USA Today, "Encryption Faulted in TJX Hacking," 9/26/2007, http://www.usatoday.com/tech/news/computersecurity/infotheft/2007-09-26-tjx-encryption-breach_N.htm

[13] NY Times, "Ameriprise Says Stolen Laptop Had Data On 230,000 People," 1/6/2006, http://query.nytimes.com/gst/fullpage.html?res=9F02E6D9103FF935A15752C0A9609C8B63

[14] Pittsburgh Post-Gazette, "Another Breach at Mellon," 5/31/2008, http://www.post-gazette.com/pg/08152/886254-28.stm

The most shocking aspect to all of these security failures is that every single one of these security failures was 100% preventable. Simply by defining a proper security strategy, defining organizational security policies, and proper enforcement would have prevented every single one ofthesehacks. Remember, when your organization implements proper security the vast majority of hackers will give up on you as a target and move on to search for softer targets.

Summary

The first decade of the 21st century is literally oozing with the security failures of hundreds of organizations. This includes small businesses, national firms that we trust with our personal and creditdata, and large international firms with brand names we see on commercials every night. Many businesses don't take the threat seriously, even when it happens to their competition. Others don't take it seriously until it happens to them. There are even those who don't consider taking precautions until it happens to them twice.

Any organization that processes personal information, credit information, or financial information tied to a person or medical data needs to protect itself. This first step is to recognize thatyour company is a potential target. Even if you have a small business, keep in mind that as larger organizations harden their systems hackers will move on to smaller, softer targets. As I mentioned in Chapter 1, encrypting your data at rest is the last line of defense in hardening your company infrastructure. Encryption is not a complete security solution by itself, but it works well to complement a total security strategy.

■ ■ ■

SQL Server 2008 Encryption Glossary

In this book, I've introduced several concepts and used terminology that may be new to many readers. In this appendix, I've rounded up many of the terms used to provide a quick reference to their definitions.

A

AES

AES, the Advanced Encryption Standard, is the encryption standard adopted by the National Institute of Standards and Technology (NIST) for use by the US government for use in securing information classified as Secret and Top Secret. AES is a 128-bit block symmetric encryption cipher with key lengths of 128, 192, or 256 bits. AES is a subset of the Rijndael algorithm, which supports a larger number of key lengths. AES was selected to be a Federal Information Processing Standard (FIPS) in FIPS PUB 197 on November 26, 2001. AES replaced the older DES.

algorithm

An algorithm is a finite sequence of instructions for solving a particular problem or performing a task. In terms of cryptography, an algorithm is a step-by-step procedure for encrypting, decrypting, or calculating cryptographic hashes from data.

asymmetric encryption

Asymmetric encryption is an encryption model in which the encryption and decryption processes use different keys. Modern asymmetric encryption algorithms are based on the public key/private key pairs, in which the encryption and decryption keys are different but nontrivially related. The public key is widely known and distributed for encryption while the private key is kept secret and used for decryption. Although the keys are related, it is considered infeasible to try to derive the private key from the public key.

authenticator

The authenticator is a binary string that is combined with the encryption key or plaintext during encryption to further obfuscate the resulting ciphertext. Authenticators are used with SQL Server encryption functions to prevent wholesale substitution attacks of encrypted data in a table.

B

Base64

Base64 is a character encoding designed for transfer of Multipurpose Internet Mail Extensions (MIME) content. It is designed to use a subset of symbols that can be represented using printable 7-bit characters. It was originally designed to prevent problems with modification of email data in transit. Base64 uses the letters A–Z, a–z, 0–9, and the special symbols + and / to represent a 6 bit group from an input stream. The symbol = is used to pad the result.

binary

Binary data is computer data that is encoded in binary form for storage and processing purposes. SQL Server stores binary data using the binary and varbinary data types.

BitLocker Drive Encryption

BitLocker Drive Encryption is a feature introduced in Windows Vista and Windows Server 2008 to provide full volume encryption and integrity checking when a TPM is present.

BLOB

Binary large object (BLOB) data is data that is stored using the varbinary(max) data type. A BLOB column or variable can hold up to 2.1 GB of data, as opposed to a regular non-LOB varbinary or binary column or variable, which can max out at 8,000 bytes of data.

block

A block is a fixed-length group of bits that an encryption algorithm operates on at a given time. The DES family of ciphers operate on 64 bit blocks. AES operates on 128-bit blocks.

brute force attack

A brute force attack attempts to defeat a cryptographic algorithm by trying a large number of possibilities. A brute force attack on a cipher might include trying a large number of keys in the key space to decrypt a message. Brute force attack is the most inefficient method of attacking a cipher, and most cryptanalysis is concerned with finding more efficient means of defeating ciphers.

C

Caesar Cipher

The Caesar cipher is one of the simplest known monoalphabetic substitution ciphers. In this type of cipher, each letter of a plaintext is replaced by another letter that is a fixed number of positions down the alphabet. Because of its simplicity, Caesar cipher is considered insecure and, in modern times, it is generally only used in games and toys.

CAST

CAST is a 64-bit block symmetric encryption algorithm with support for key sizes that range from 40 bits up to 256 bits, depending on which variant of CAST is used. CAST gained popularity initially as the symmetric cipher used in PGP.

CBC

Cipher Block Chaining is a mode of operation in which each block of plaintext is combined (via exclusive-OR operations) with the previous block of ciphertext prior to its being encrypted.

certificate

A certificate is an electronic document that uses a digital signature to bind an asymmetric key with a public identity. In its simplest form, a certificate is essentially an asymmetric key which can have additional metadata, like a certificate name, subject, and expiration date. A certificate can be self-signed or issued by a certificate authority.

certificate authority

A certificate authority (CA) is an entity that issues digital certificates for encryption and identity verification. CAs can also provide verification services for certificates that they issue.

checksum

A checksum is a fixed-length value generated from an arbitrary block of data by a checksum or hash function. A checksum is used to verify the integrity of a block of data.

cipher

A cipher is an algorithm that performs encryption and decryption of data. Although a cipher operates by systematically rearranging and obfuscating text on a character-by-character basis, in nontechnical usage the term cipher is often used interchangeably with the term code.

Cipher Block Chaining

Cipher Block Chaining (CBC) mode defines a block cipher mode of operation in which each block of plaintext is combined with the previous block of encrypted ciphertext prior to encryption. CBC mode requires an initialization vector to combine with the first block of plaintext.

Cipher Feedback

Cipher Feedback (CFB) mode is a block cipher mode of operation that turns a block cipher into a self-synchronizing stream cipher. The operation of CFB is similar to CBC mode.

cipher mode

A block cipher mode, or mode of operation, helps provide additional obfuscation for messages of arbitrary length. Cipher modes, like CBC, define methods for using previously encrypted blocks of data to obfuscate subsequent blocks of data. This makes it less likely that the same block of data contained in the same plaintext will encrypt to different ciphertext blocks.

ciphertext

Ciphertext is the enciphered data that results from an encryption operation. Compare *plaintext*.

CLR

The Common Language Runtime (CLR) is the core component of the Microsoft .NET Framework. The CLR uses just-in-time compilation to convert the Common Intermediate Language (CIL) instructions into native code at runtime. SQL Server provides CLR integration via the SQL CLR.

compression

Compression is the science of encoding data to use fewer bits than a noncompressed encoding of the same data would require. When compressing data which cannot handle a loss of fidelity or integrity (database backups, for instance) methods of lossless compression are used. Generally when compressing textual data compression algorithms utilize redundancies to reduce the amount of space required to store the same information.

confusion

Confusion is a property of secure cipher systems as defined in Information Theory. Confusion makes the relationship between the plaintext and the encryption key as complex as possible. The concept of confusion makes it difficult to reverse engineer the key from the ciphertext, even when presented with plaintext and ciphertext pairs produced by the same key.

countermeasures

Countermeasures are steps that can be taken, and systems that can be implemented, to prevent internal and external threats from accessing your data and causing issues.

CRC

Cyclic Redundancy Check (CRC) is a type of hash function often used to detect integrity issues in stored data.

cryptanalysis

Cryptanalysis is the science of analyzing cryptographic methods and algorithms, generally probing them for weaknesses. Cryptanalysts devise new methods of defeating cryptographic algorithms.

CryptoAPI

The Cryptographic Applications Programming Interface (CryptoAPI or CAPI) provides access to Windows-based cryptographic and security services.

cryptography

Cryptography is the science of hiding information through ciphers and codes. Cryptographers devise new cryptographic algorithms.

cryptology

Cryptology is the science of hidden information, and encompasses cryptography, cryptanalysis, and other methods of obfuscating plaintext.

D

data key

A data key (KD) is an encryption key used to encrypt data directly. Compare to *key encrypting key* and master key.

database encryption key

A database encryption key (DEK) is a symmetric key used by SQL Server to encrypt an entire database when transparent data encryption (TDE) is used.

DBA

A database administrator (DBA) is a person responsible for the installation, maintenance, security, and other administrative concerns relating to databases.

DBMS

A database management system (DBMS) is a software program, or set of programs, designed to control organization, management, security, updates, and retrieval of data from organized storage structures.

DES

DES, the Data Encryption Standard, is a 64-bit block cipher that was adopted by the National Bureau of Standards (NBS; now NIST) as a FIPS in 1976. DES is a symmetric encryption cipher that uses a 56-bit key. The DES algorithm is based on the Lucifer cipher, developed at IBM in the 1970s. The DES family of algorithms relies on a Feistel network to encrypt and decrypt data. DES opened the door to a greater understanding of block ciphers and cryptanalysis due to widespread academic scrutiny of the algorithm. DES is now considered inadequate for secure applications, and has been replaced by Triple DES and AES.

DES-X

DES-X is a variant of the DES block cipher that was devised to increase the complexity of brute force attacks. The DES-X algorithm combines additional key material to blocks of plaintext before encryption and to ciphertext blocks after encryption.

deterministic function

A deterministic function is one which, given a specific set of inputs, will always produce the same result. The SQL Server decryption functions are an example of deterministic functions. SQL Server's symmetric encryption functions, however, generate a random IV so the result is nondeterministic.

differential cryptanalysis

Differential cryptanalysis is primarily concerned with the study of how differences in input affect the output of a cryptographic algorithm. The key to differential cryptanalysis is discovering where an algorithm exhibits nonrandom properties or predictable behaviors that can be exploited.

Diffie-Hellman Key Exchange

Diffie-Hellman (D-H) Key Exchange is a cryptographic protocol that allows two parties with no shared information to establish a shared secret key over an open communications channel. The key can subsequently be used to encrypt communications between the parties.

diffusion

Diffusion is one of the properties of a secure cryptographic algorithm as defined in Information Theory. Diffusion refers to dissipating non-uniform statistical distributions of letters in a given plaintext. Diffusion provides protection against statistical analysis of ciphertext.

digest

See *hash*.

DLL

A dynamic link library (DLL) is a file that consists of a shared executable library of functions. SQL Server uses a DLL to allow access to third-party hardware security modules (HSMs) through extensible key management (EKM).

DMF

Dynamic Management Functions (DMF) are system functions that provide access to SQL Server state information.

DMK

A Database Master Key (DMK) is a symmetric key that is used to encrypt other keys within a database. Each database can have only one DMK.

DMV

Dynamic Management Views (DMV) are system views that provide access to SQL Server state information.

DPAPI

The Data Protection Application Programming Interface (DPAPI) is a cryptographic API that is designed to use Windows user credentials or machine keys to protect asymmetric private keys.

E

EDE

Encrypt-Decrypt-Encrypt (EDE) indicates a strategy for increasing the strength of an encryption algorithm by applying multiple passes to a plaintext. Triple DES uses an EDE strategy in which one key is used to encrypt a plaintext using DES, a second key is used to decrypt the encrypted data, and a third key (or the first key again) is used to perform another encryption on the data. This type of strategy can effectively double or triple the effective key length without changing the underlying algorithm.

EFS

Encrypting File System (EFS) is a Microsoft Windows feature that performs encryption of files and folders at the operating system level.

elliptical curve cryptography

Elliptical curve cryptography (ECC) is an efficient public key encryption technique based on elliptic curve theory. SQL Server does not support ECC.

encipher

To encipher means to convert plaintext into an unintelligible form using cryptographic encryption algorithms.

encode

To encode means to convert data from one format to another. The purpose of encoding is not to hide information, but rather to convert it to another form, such as converting text from UTF-8 format to Unicode format.

encrypt

See *encipher*.

Enigma

Enigma was the cipher used by the German military during World War II to encrypt sensitive communications. The Enigma machine was used to encrypt and decrypt secret messages.

ETL

Extract, Transform, and Load (ETL) is the name of a process by which data is extracted from source systems or files, put through various transformation processes, and loaded into a destination database.

extended stored procedures

Extended stored procedures, or XPs, are functions exposed through unmanaged binary DLLs that are designed to run within the SQL Server process space. XPs were used in SQL Server 2000 and prior to programmatically extend the functionality of SQL Server using languages like C and C++ that compile to native code. XPs have been deprecated and SQL CLR functions and procedures are preferred over XPs.

Extensible Key Management

Extensible Key Management (EKM) is a SQL Server 2008 feature that allows you to take advantage of third-party hardware security modules (HSMs) to perform off-box encryption, decryption, and key management.

F

FACTA

FACTA is the Fair and Accurate Credit Transactions Act of 2003, a US federal law that amends the previously enacted Fair Credit Reporting Act (FCRA). FACTA, in addition to other laws and regulations, requires organizations to implement special handling of sensitive consumer credit data.

factor

A factor is a non-trivial divisor of a composite number. The presumed difficulty of factoring large numbers (breaking large composite numbers into their factors) is critical to the security of many common asymmetric encryption algorithms. Large semiprime numbers (the product of two prime numbers) are considered to be among the hardest to factor.

Feistel network

Feistel networks are iterated symmetric encryption structures that contain an internal round function. The DES family of algorithms, and related algorithms, use Feistel networks to perform encryption and decryption. A Feistel network has the advantage that encryption and decryption operations are very similar, often identical to one another.

filestream

The filestream option allows developers to store, manipulate, and query large object (LOB) data in the file system. Filestream leverages the efficiency of Windows NTFS file streaming technology for storage and management of large files.

fingerprint

Collision-free, one-way hash codes are often compared to human fingerprints, as the odds of two different source texts generating the same hash codes are extremely small.

FIPS

Federal Information Processing Standards (FIPS) are standards adopted by the United States government for use by government agencies and government contractors. Adopted FIPS include information management, information security, data standardization, and other aspects of information processing and intragovernmental communications.

firewall

A firewall is part of a computer network or system that is designed to block unauthorized access over communications lines.

frequency analysis

Frequency analysis was one of the first published methods for defeating classical cipher-based security. Frequency analysis relies on statistical patterns based on the relative occurrences of letters in large bodies of text.

G

GUID

A GUID is a globally unique identifier, which is a special type of identifier that has an infinitesimally small probability of being generated more than once in any circumstance.

H

hash

A cryptographic hash is a fixed-size bit string that is generated by applying a hash function to a block of data. Secure cryptographic hash functions are collision-free, meaning there is a very small possibility of generating the same hash for two different blocks of data. A secure cryptographic hash function should also be one-way, meaning it is infeasible to retrieve the original text from the hash.

hierarchy

SQL Server 2008 has a built-in encryption key hierarchy, in which all encryption keys and certificates can be protected by higher level keys. The highest level key in the SQL Server encryption key hierarchy is the Service Master Key (SMK), which is secured by the DPAPI.

HMAC

A hash message authentication code (HMAC) is a special code used to validate the integrity of data. An HMAC is generated via application of a cryptographic hash function, combined with a secret key, to a block of data.

HSM

Hardware Security Modules (HSMs) are third-party hardware devices that provide encryption, decryption, and key management services.

I

initialization vector

An initialization vector (IV) is a block of bits required for many block cipher modes of operation. The IV is combined with the initial block of plaintext prior to encryption in modes like CBC, after which each encrypted block is combined with the subsequent block of plaintext.

ISO

The International Organization for Standardization (ISO) is an international standards body composed of representatives from standards organizations from several countries. ISO promotes standards that include the SQL standard and information security and management standards.

iteration

An iteration is a repetitive process in an algorithm. Cryptographic algorithms often employ many successive iterations to encipher plaintext.

K

key encrypting key

A key encrypting key (KEK) is an encryption key used to encrypt other keys in an encryption key hierarchy. Compare to *data key* and *master key*.

key expansion

Key expansion is a process by which a larger key, or a set of sub-keys, is made from a smaller key via a cryptographic algorithm's key schedule.

keyed hash

A hash generated by applying a hash algorithm with a secret key to a block of data. See *HMAC*.

key length

The length of encryption keys is measured in bits. The security of an algorithm cannot exceed its key length, although the effective security of an algorithm can be smaller than its key length.

key schedule

A key schedule is an algorithm that calculates a set of sub-keys from a given source key material.

L

leakage

Leakage in cryptography is a phenomenon that occurs when statistical or other information about encrypted data is exposed. Leakage can occur when data is decrypted and artifacts of the data are left in memory, in durable storage, or when other methods, such as non-keyed hashes of plaintext are used to make searches of encrypted data more efficient.

Lucifer

Lucifer was the name of one of the first modern civilian block ciphers. It was developed by Horst Feistel of IBM in the 1970s for commercial use in banking applications. DES is a direct descendant of Lucifer.

M

master key

A master key (KKM) is the highest-level key in an encryption key hierarchy. The master key protects all lower-level keys in the hierarchy, either directly or indirectly. Compare to *key encrypting key* and *data key*.

Message Digest Algorithms

The Message Digest Algorithms are a family of related cryptographic hash algorithms invented by Ron Rivest. The Message Digest Algorithms include MD2, MD4, MD5, and others.

monoalphabetic cipher

A monoalphabetic cipher is a simple substitution cipher using only one substitution alphabet. Monoalphabetic ciphers, like the Caesar Cipher, are considered insecure by modern cryptographic standards. Compare *polyalphabetic cipher*.

Morse Code

Samuel Morse invented Morse code in the 1840s as a means of transmitting information over telegraph lines. Morse code uses a standardized sequence of short and long elements (dots and dashes) to encode alphabetic messages.

N

Null

Null is a special marker used to indicate an unknown value or the absence of a value within a database.

O

Ouput Feedback

Output Feedback (OFB) mode is a block cipher mode that essentially turns a block cipher into a synchronous stream cipher. OFB generates keystream blocks which are combined with plaintext blocks to generate ciphertext.

P

padding

Because block ciphers encrypt only fixed-length blocks of data, plaintext must often be padded to the proper length. There are several methods of padding, but all include adding additional bytes of data to the end of a plaintext and stripping those additional bytes from the data during decryption.

PBKDF2

The Password-Based Key Derivation Function #2 (PBKDF2) iteratively applies a cryptographic keyed hash or other function to a password in order to generate a cryptographic encryption key.

Pin Entry Device

A Pin Entry Device (PED) allows users to authenticate themselves by entering a PIN code via an input device. Some hardware security modules or other security devices may require a PED to be used. See *hardware security module*.

PGP

Pretty Good Privacy (PGP) is a program created by Philip Zimmerman to provide personal security, privacy, and authentication services. PGP is often used to encrypt email and other personal communications.

PIN

A Personal Identification Number (PIN) is a secret, often numeric, code that is often used to authenticate a person in the context of multifactor authentication. Generally, when a PIN is used to for personal authentication it is done in conjunction with another form of authentication. For instance, bank automated teller machines (ATMs) require both an ATM card and a PIN.

PKCS

PKCS represents a set of Public Key Cryptography Standards that are published by RSA Security.

plaintext

Plaintext is data which is not encrypted. Compare *ciphertext*.

polyalphabetic cipher

A polyalphabetic cipher is a substitution cipher that relies on multiple substitution alphabets. The Vigenère cipher is an example of a polyalphabetic cipher. Compare *monoalphabetic cipher*.

public key

A public key is an asymmetric encryption key that is publicly known and may be widely distributed without compromising the security of an asymmetric encryption algorithm. See *asymmetric encryption*.

private key

A private key is an asymmetric decryption key that is kept secret and is nontrivially related to the public key. The security of the asymmetric encryption relies on maintaining the secrecy of the private key. See *asymmetric encryption*.

R

RACE

RACE is the Research and Development in Advanced Communications Technologies in Europe program. This program was launched in 1988 to promote high speed communications services in Europe. RACE created the RIPEMD family of hash algorithms.

RC2

RC2, Rivest Cipher 2, is 64-bit block cipher designed by Ron Rivest in 1987. RC2 was originally supposed to be incorporated into Lotus Notes software for export. The National Security Agency (NSA) approved a 40-bit version of RC2 for export to foreign countries. RC2 uses a variable size key with 18 rounds arranged in a Feistel network. RC2 has proven vulnerable to various cryptanalytic attacks.

RC4

RC4, Rivest Cipher 4, is a stream cipher used in protocols, such as Secure Sockets Layer (SSL) and Wired Equivalent Privacy (WEP). RC4 is simple and fast, but it suffers from known weaknesses that can compromise security.

refactor

To clarify and simplify computer code.

register

A register is a specially designated storage area for binary data in a computer. TPM chips have special registers that are used for hardware validation calculations.

RFC

An RFC is a Request for Comments, as published by the Internet Engineering Task Force (IETF). The RFC format is used to innovations, research, and behaviors of applications which provide Internet connectivity. RFC 2898, for instance, describes password-based cryptography methods for Internet applications.

Rijndael

Rijndael is a 128-bit block cipher that supports key lengths of 128, 160, 192, 224, and 256 bits. A subset of Rijndael, consisting of the algorithm with 128, 192, and 256-bit key lengths was selected as the AES in 2001. The Rijndael algorithm consists of a specific number of repetitions, determined by the key length, of transformation rounds that encipher plaintext.

RIPEMD

RIPEMD (RACE Integrity Primitives Evaluation Message Digest) is a cryptographic hash algorithm. RIPEMD comes in several forms, including RIPEMD-128, RIPEMD-160, RIPEMD-256, and RIPEMD-320, which represent 128, 160, 256, and 320-bit versions, respectively. RIPEMD was originally based on the design of the MD4 hash algorithm.

RSA

RSA is a widely used asymmetric encryption algorithm. The name RSA is derived from the surnames of the men who first published a paper describing the algorithm: Rivest, Shamir, and Adleman. British mathematician Clifford Cocks invented asymmetric encryption independently prior to the Rivest, Shamir and Adleman discovery; however, Cocks's work was classified Top Secret and his work was not published until decades later.

S

salt

Salt is a string of bits provided as input to a key derivation function. A salt can be a randomly generated value, or in many cases it can be a previously generated initialization vector bit string.

session

A cryptographic session is a SQL Server session in which an encryption key is accessed.

SHA

The Secure Hash Algorithm (SHA) family of cryptographic hash functions were designed by the National Security Agency (NSA) and published by NIST as a FIPS. SHA-0 and SHA-1 are very similar hash functions that return 160-bit hash values for any given block of input data. The SHA-2 group of hash functions generate a 224, 256, 384, or 512-bit hash for any given block of input data.

SMK

The Service Master Key (SMK) is the encryption key that sits at the top of the SQL Server encryption key hierarchy. The SMK is protected by the DPAPI.

SQL

SQL is the basis for the query language supported by SQL Server. SQL is defined as an ISO standard.

SSH

Secure Shell (SSH) is a network protocol that allows devices to communicate securely.

SSL

SSL, or Secure Sockets Layer, is a protocol used to provide security and ensure data integrity over networks and on the Internet. See *TLS*.

T

temporary key

A temporary key, sometimes called a session key, is a transient key that exists only temporarily to perform encryption and decryption functions. Temporary keys are dropped once they are no longer needed, often at the end of the current session.

TLS

Transport Layer Security, or TLS, is an updated cryptographic protocol that provides security and ensures data integrity for network or Internet-based communications. TLS provides additional options over its predecessor, SSL. See *SSL*.

trie

A trie is an ordered tree-like data structure that is used to store an associative array.

Triple DES

Triple DES was developed as a low-cost interim replacement for the DES algorithm. Triple DES increases the key size, and security, of DES without requiring a complete overhaul of the algorithm. Triple DES works by performing three DES passes on the same data, using either 2 or 3 different keys. Triple DES commonly uses an encrypt-decrypt-encrypt strategy to effectively increase the encryption key length.

trivial

In mathematics, trivial often refers to the simple and obvious solutions to mathematical problems. Asymmetric encryption algorithms rely on mathematical problems with no trivial solutions.

trust

Trust is central to the authentication and verification of identity and bindings between public keys and private keys in asymmetric encryption. Certificates may be validated via a trusted third party (TTP) like an issuing certificate authority (CA), or identity can be validated using a Web of Trust methodology, in which each user identifies core groups of people whom they trust. The Web of Trust methodology was implemented in PGP.

Z

Zimmerman Telegram

The Zimmerman Telegram was an enciphered telegram sent by the Foreign Secretary of the German Empire prior to the United States' entry into World War I. The Zimmerman Telegram advised the Mexico government that Germany would materially support Mexico in a declaration of war against the United States, including reclamation of territories lost to the United States during the Mexican-American War. The telegram was intercepted and decrypted by British cryptanalysts. It was later made public and caused an outcry that precipitated the United States' entry into World War I.

APPENDIX B

■■■

Encryption Checklist

I briefly discussed threat modeling as a means of mitigating the risks to your databases and other critical assets back in Chapter 1. In this chapter, I'll explore this concept more fully and provide a checklist for determining whether your organization could benefit from implementing encryption.

Threat Modeling

The first step to determining your security risks is to identify threats to your corporate assets. You can use the threat modeling worksheet shown in Figure B-1 as a starting point to identifying those threats.

Threat	Source	Estimated Threat	Capabilities	Data Arsenal	Remediation	Remedial Threat Level

Figure B-1. Threat modeling worksheet

When completing this worksheet you identify one distinct threat per row, with the following information in each column:

1. The *Threat* column of the worksheet is the name of the threat you're identifying. DBAs, developers, business users, and hackers are some of the examples I gave back in Chapter 1. You can refine these to a more granular level if you choose, identifying different levels of business users or different communities of hackers.

2. The *Source* column indicates whether the threat is an internal threat, an external threat, or possibly a mixed source-type threat. An employee might be an internal threat while a hacker would be considered an external threat. A subcontractor for your company with systems that interface directly with your internal network might represent a mixed internal/external threat.

3. The *Estimated Threat* is your estimate of the level of danger the specified threat poses to your assets. The estimated threat level should reflect several variables, such as the following:

   a. *Criticality of the assets that are at risk*: The question to ask here is whether or not the asset is mission-critical. When hacked, a database that stores customer orders could potentially bring business to a screeching halt while a management reporting database might not be so critical.

   b. *The likelihood that the asset will be targeted*: The simple fact is that some assets make juicier targets than others. A database with millions of credit card numbers stored in it might make a much more enticing target to a broader audience than a database containing bills of materials for your products.

   c. *The security precautions currently employed to protect the asset*: A production database that is already properly firewalled and on which accounts and permissions are tightly controlled already will represent a lower risk than a development database that is not so strictly managed.

   d. *Paths of access from the asset to other assets*: A given noncritical asset might be interconnected via your organizational network to several far more critical assets. A knowledgeable hacker will seek out the weakest link in the chain and exploit it to launch attacks on other more critical interconnected systems.

I use a threat level scale that includes the following threat levels:

   • *Low*: The odds of the threat accessing the asset and causing harm are extremely unlikely.

   • *Limited*: The threat may be able to access an asset and could potentially cause limited damage to noncritical systems. This might represent situations that are beyond your control, like flaws in off-the-shelf software or invention of new hacker tools.

   • *Moderate*: The threat has some access to an asset and could potentially cause damage. A DBA with administrative access might represent a moderate threat level, for instance.

- *High*: The threat can access an asset and could cause a considerable amount of damage to the asset and to the organization as a whole.

- *Significant*: A significant threat is one with the means, motive, and opportunity to access assets and cause severe damage that could cause crippling damage to your organization. Significant threats represent the worst of the worst and need to be dealt with immediately.

Again, this column represents your best estimates as to the level of danger posed to your assets by a particular threat based on the best available data at the time.

4. The *Capabilities* column is intended to measure the skill with which a threat can attack your organizational asset as well as the level of access the threat has to your asset. A highly-skilled DBA might represent a level of 5.0 (extremely high) in this column since the DBA has access and the skill to carry out threats against your assets. A less skilled end user with highly restricted access, however, might represent a significantly lower level of access (1.0, extremely low). The scale goes from 1.0 to 5.0.

5. The *Data Arsenal* column represents the threat's ability to obtain and utilize automated and high-tech weapons to attack your databases. An internet-based hacker might rate a high 5.0 (extremely high) on this scale since she would be able to obtain the most high-tech tools available and employ them with skill and precision. A less-sophisticated business user, on the other hand, might be able to obtain high-tech hacking tools, but probably won't have the training and experience to use them to great effect against your assets. This scale also goes from 1.0 to 5.0.

6. The *Remediation* column represents a summarized plan of action, steps you can take to lower the ability of a threat to access and cause damage to your assets. The remediation steps might include hardening your servers by tightening down access and permissions, adding hardware to increase security, implementing new security protocols, adding auditing and other controls, employee background checks, training, encryption, and numerous other possible steps.

7. The *Remediated Threat Level* column is another estimate of the threat level. While the *Estimated Threat* column represents the current threat level, under existing circumstances, the *Remediated Threat Level* represents your estimate of the reduced threat level after implementing the plan of action outlined in the *Remediation* column.

After you've identified the threats to your organizational assets and identified overarching steps you can take to remediate them, you'll need to drill deeper into each step to drive the specific implementation details.

For instance, if database encryption is one of your remediation steps for a specific threat you'll need to determine the granularity of encryption, the algorithms you'll use and other details. There may be external factors driving these decisions, as we'll discuss in the following section.

Driving Encryption Design

If you determine that encryption is a remediation step that will benefit your organization, you'll need to drive a detailed design. Some of the factors you'll need to consider include the following:

- *Internal organizational policies*: You may already have IT policies indicating which data needs to be encrypted and which algorithms are acceptable, for example.

- *Regulatory requirements and contractual obligations*: As discussed in Chapter 11, you may have regulatory requirements or contractual obligations requiring you to encrypt certain data. Government contractors and subcontractors who work on Department of Defense projects, for instance, have stringent contractual obligations to encrypt data stored on their systems.

- *Determining which data needs to be encrypted*: Depending on your business you may be storing classified government information on your systems, sensitive medical records, consumer credit data, or any of a wide variety of other sensitive data. You may only need to encrypt a small portion of your data or you may need to encrypt the majority of the data you're storing. In many cases, you'll need to do an element-by-element analysis of your data to determine which data elements need to be encrypted and which don't.

- *Deciding the granularity at which to encrypt your data*: If you have very small amounts of data to encrypt you may be able to effectively utilize cell-level encryption. If you need to encrypt large amounts of data, database-level or file-level encryption might be a better option. In some instances, a combination of the two might be most effective.

- *Estimating the effort to implement encryption*: It's definitely a lot easier to build security, including encryption, into new systems when they're still in the design stage than to add it to legacy systems retroactively. In many cases though, you'll face the task of retrofitting encryption into existing databases and applications. The effort required may determine, to some extent, the prioritization of elements to be encrypted as well as the overall strategy for implementing encryption. You might, for instance, implement database-level encryption immediately for some systems and address cell-level encryption using a strategy of iterative refinement.

- *Encryption key management*: Your encryption key management policies and procedures play an integral role in your encryption planning. You will have to ensure that your encryption key management plan offers proper levels of security and that it aligns with company policies, regulatory requirements, and contractual obligations.

Security Review

The Department of Defense's Defense Information System Agency (DISA) has issued some of the most comprehensive security auditing checklists and guidelines available anywhere. In particular, their database security checklists are designed to target "conditions that undermine the integrity of security, contribute to inefficient security operations and administration, or may lead to interruption of production operations." The DISA review process also "ensures the site has properly installed and implemented the database environment and that it is being managed in a way that is secure, efficient, and effective. (Database Security Readiness Review Checklist, DISA, 2007)."

The Abbreviated Security Review checklist in Table B-1 consists of a summarized version of the DISA Database Security Readiness Review (DSRR) checklist targeted specifically for SQL Server 2008. You can leverage this checklist to review your SQL Server system security.

Note This is not a replacement for the full DISA DSRR. If you do business with the Department of Defense or other government agencies, you will need to properly apply their complete review and audit processes.

The Abbreviated Security Review checklist in Table B-1 consists of five columns, listed as follows:

1. *Test Method*: This column indicates the method used to test. It can be one of the following:

    - Auto for automated testing, which can be performed using the DISA SRR automated testing script available from http://iase.disa.mil.

    - *Interview* for results gathered through interviews with information assurance managers (IAMs), DBAs and others, as well as reviews of available documentation.

    - *Manual* for results gathered through manual technical procedures.

    - *Verify* for results returned by the SRR test script that must be verified by the reviewer.

2. *Pass/Fail/NA*: This column is a simple pass/fail indicator for each test. Simply circle *P* for pass, *F* for fail, or *NA* for not applicable as necessary for each item.

3. *Group*: The Group column is a grouping I've applied to bring together related checklist items.

4. *Details*: This column is a summary description of the checklist item being reviewed.

5. *Category*: The Category column indicates the ranking applied by DISA as a severity level of the vulnerability. The categories assigned by DISA include the following:

    - *Category 1 findings* are the highest risk vulnerabilities that DISA feels "provide an attacker immediate access into a machine, superuser access, or access that bypasses a firewall."

    - *Category 2* findings encompass vulnerabilities that "provide information that has a high potential of giving access to an intruder."

    - *Category 3 findings* are the remaining "vulnerabilities that provide information that potentially could lead to compromise."

Although the checklist in Table B-1 is based largely on the DISA SRCC, I've adapted items to be SQL Server specific, added some additional SQL Server-specific security items, and grouped the items. Note that this abbreviated security review checklist is not exhaustive, nor is it encryption-specific although there are several encryption-related items listed.

Table B-1. *Abbreviated Security Review Checklist*

Test Method	Pass/Fail/NA	Group	Details	Category
Auto	P F NA	Accounts	sa account has been renamed.	CAT 3
Auto	P F NA	Accounts	sa password has been changed from default.	CAT 1
Interview	P F NA	Accounts	All DBA accounts that are used to support non-DBA activity are documented.	CAT 2
Interview	P F NA	Accounts	DBMS installation account is restricted to authorized users.	CAT 2
Interview	P F NA	Accounts	No unapproved inactive or expired user accounts have been found in the database.	CAT 2
Interview	P F NA	Accounts	Privileges assigned to DBA roles are monitored to detect assignment of unauthorized or excess privileges.	CAT 2
Interview	P F NA	Accounts	Use of the DBMS installation account is logged.	CAT 2
Interview	P F NA	Accounts	Use of the DBMS software installation account is restricted to DBMS software installation, upgrade, and maintenance.	CAT 2
Interview	P F NA	Accounts	User privilege assignment is reviewed monthly or more frequently to ensure compliance with least privilege and documented policy.	CAT 2
Manual	P F NA	Accounts	DBMS processes and services run under custom, dedicated accounts.	CAT 2
Manual	P F NA	Applications	Database applications are restricted from using static DDL statements to modify the application schema.	CAT 3
Interview	P F NA	Audit	Audit trail data is reviewed daily or more frequently.	CAT 2
Interview	P F NA	Audit	Audit trail is reviewed regularly to detect unauthorized database access.	CAT 2
Interview	P F NA	Audit	Automated tools are used to provide audit trail reports.	CAT 2

Table B-1. *Continued*

Interview	P F NA	Audit	Automated tools to monitor audit data and immediately report suspicious activity has been employed for the DBMS.	CAT 2
Interview	P F NA	Audit	The DBMS is periodically tested for vulnerability management and IA compliance.	CAT 3
Manual	P F NA	Audit	Audit records are restricted to authorized individuals.	CAT 2
Manual	P F NA	Audit	DBMS audit logs are included in backup operations.	CAT 2
Verify	P F NA	Authentication	SQL Server authentication mode is set to Windows authentication.	CAT 2
Auto	P F NA	Encryption	Asymmetric private key encryption uses an authorized encryption type.	CAT 2
Auto	P F NA	Encryption	Symmetric keys are protected with approved key management methodologies, such as NIST or NSA approved methods.	CAT 2
Auto	P F NA	Encryption	Symmetric keys use only approved encryption algorithms. No use of RC2, RC4, or plain DES.	CAT 2
Interview	P F NA	Encryption	All sensitive data stored in the database has been identified in the AIS Functional Architecture.	
Interview	P F NA	Encryption	Certificates and asymmetric keys are backed up and stored securely off-site.	CAT 2
Interview	P F NA	Encryption	Database Master Keys are backed up and stored securely off-site.	CAT 2
Interview	P F NA	Encryption	Symmetric keys can be recreated; key material and key generation process are documented and stored securely off-site.	CAT 2
Interview	P F NA	Encryption	The Service Master Key is backed up and stored securely off-site.	CAT 2
Manual	P F NA	Encryption	Database data files are encrypted.	CAT 2

Manual	P F NA	Encryption	Sensitive data, as identified by the Information Owner, is encrypted within the database.	CAT 2
Manual	P F NA	Encryption	Sensitive information stored in the database has been identified and protected by encryption.	CAT 2
Verify	P F NA	Encryption	Database Encryption Key is backed up and stored securely off-site.	CAT 2
Verify	P F NA	Encryption	Database Master Key access is granted only to authorized users.	CAT 2
Verify	P F NA	Encryption	Database Master Key encryption password meets complexity requirements.	CAT 2
Verify	P F NA	Encryption	Symmetric keys do not use a master key, certificate or asymmetric key to encrypt the key.	CAT 2
Verify	P F NA	Endpoints	No unauthorized HTTP SOAP endpoints are configured on the server.	CAT 2
Verify	P F NA	Endpoints	No unauthorized Service Broker endpoints are configured on the server.	CAT 2
Interview	P F NA	Extensions	No undocumented/unsupported DBMS procedures and features are used in code that accesses the database.	CAT 2
Manual	P F NA	Extensions	If SQL CLR is in use, only properly signed modules with least privileges are installed.	CAT 3
Manual	P F NA	Extensions	No third-party extended procedures are used.	CAT 2
Manual	P F NA	Extensions	SQL CLR is disabled; if enabled, only CLR modules approved by the Information Assurance Officer are installed.	CAT 3
Manual	P F NA	Extensions	xp_cmdshell extended procedure is disabled.	CAT 2
Verify	P F NA	Extensions	Access to registry extended stored procedures are restricted to sysadmin access.	CAT 2
Verify	P F NA	Extensions	Database TRUSTWORTHY status bit is set to off.	CAT 2
Verify	P F NA	Extensions	OLE Automation extended procedures are restricted to sysadmin access.	CAT 2

Table B-1. *Continued*

Manual	P F NA	Network	Sensitive data accepted and returned by the DBMS is protected by encryption when transmitted across the network.	CAT 1
Auto	P F NA	Password	Account passwords expire every 60 days or more frequently.	CAT 2
Auto	P F NA	Password	Account passwords meet complexity requirements.	CAT 2
Auto	P F NA	Password	No accounts have blank passwords.	CAT 1
Interview	P F NA	Password	Applications that access the database do not echo or display the clear text of passwords.	CAT 2
Interview	P F NA	Password	Applications that access the database do not transmit passwords over the network in cleartext.	CAT 2
Interview	P F NA	Password	Database passwords used by batch and/or job processes are stored in encrypted format.	CAT 1
Interview	P F NA	Planning	The DBMS is included in, and hasdefined for it, a System SecurityPlan.	CAT 3
Interview	P F NA	Policy	DBMS Information Assurance policies and procedures are viewed annually or more frequently.	CAT 3
Manual	P F NA	Policy	Procedures and restrictions for importing production data to development databases are well-defined, implemented, and followed.	CAT 2
Interview	P F NA	Privileges	Privileges assigned to developers onshared production and development DBMS hosts and the DBMS are monitored every three months or more frequently for unauthorized changes.	CAT 2
Manual	P F NA	Privileges	No unnecessary privileges to the host system have been granted to DBA OS accounts.	CAT 2
Manual	P F NA	Privileges	Sensitive information stored in the database has been identified and protected through access restrictions.	CAT 2

Manual	P F NA	Production	Developers are not assigned excess privileges on production databases.	CAT 3
Manual	P F NA	Production	Production databases are protected from unauthorized access bydevelopers on shared production/development host systems.	CAT 2
Interview	P F NA	Remote Access	Remote administrative access to the database is monitored by the Information Assurance Officer or the Information Assurance Manager.	CAT 2
Interview	P F NA	Remote Access	Remote administrative connections to the database are encrypted.	CAT 2
Interview	P F NA	Remote Access	The database is accessible to internet users and is not located in a DMZ.	CAT 2
Interview	P F NA	Roles	Information Assurance Manager reviews changes to DBA role assignments.	CAT 2
Interview	P F NA	Roles	Information Assurance Officer assigns and authorizes DBA roles and assignments.	CAT 3

Encryption Planning Checklist

Figure B-2 is a representative high-level encryption checklist that can be used as a quick reference to help plan encryption implementations. Note that this checklist is not exhaustive, but it is representative of the factors affecting encryption implementations that I've discussed throughout this book.

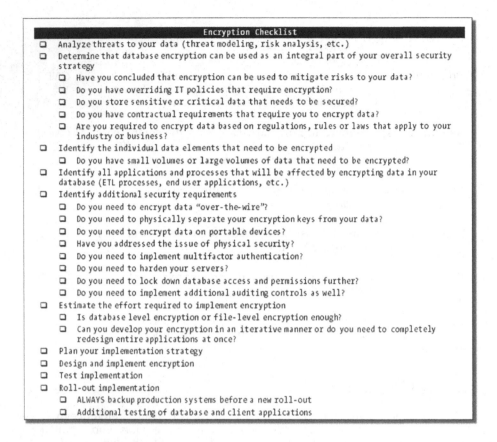

Figure B-2. *Quick encryption checklist*

APPENDIX C

■ ■ ■

Luna EKM Setup

In Chapter 5, I described how SQL Server 2008 EKM works to extend the functionality of SQL Server encryption by offloading encryption key management and data encryption and decryption duties to a dedicated HSM appliance. The HSM I used in developing that chapter was the SafeNet Luna SA, one of the first EKM providers approved for use with SQL Server 2008. In this appendix, I'll describe the vendor-specific setup and configuration required to prepare the Luna SA for use with SQL Server 2008. This appendix is specific to the Luna SA appliance that we used to demonstrate EKM in Chapter 5, but also provides an idea of the level of detail involved in setting up and configuring an HSM in general.

Prerequisites

The Luna SA HSM is a rackmount device with a 1U (or 2U in some models) profile. The hardware setup instructions are provided with the CD that comes with the appliance, so I won't go into detail here other than to point out a few key components. The Luna SA appliance comes with a PED (Pin Entry Device), USB PED keys, and cables. Once you've set up the hardware, the PED and PED keys are used to log into the HSM. The Luna SA PED and USB PED keys are shown in Figure C-1.

■ **Note** You can find out more about the SafeNet Luna SA HSM at www.safenet-inc.com.

Figure C-1. Luna SA PED and USB PED keys

The Luna SA HSM (v4.3.2) requires the following software to work with SQL Server 2008 EKM:

- SQL Server 2008 Enterprise Edition
- Windows XP (SP3), Windows Server 2003 (SP2), Windows Vista, or Windows Server 2008
- Luna SA client and EKM client software (distributed with HSM)

Installing Client Software

When using EKM your SQL Server instance acts as a client to the HSM. To prepare your SQL Server toaccess the Luna HSM, you'll need to install the Luna SA client software on the client computer. The32-bit and 64-bit versions of the setup.exe file for the Luna SA client software is located in the windows\32 and windows\64 directories, respectively.

After following the onscreen prompts and completing the client installation, the Luna SA client software will be located in a directory on your machine. The default installation directory is Program Files\LunaSA. Various utility programs, like the Putty terminal client and the vtl utility are located in this directory.

Configuring the HSM

You will need to follow the Luna SA setup steps outlined in the documentation to configure your HSM to communicate over the network with your server. Initially, you'll want to connect via serial connection using the supplied null modem serial cable that comes with the device. This ensures that your server maintains a connection while configuring the device for network use. You can use any terminal emulation package, including the Windows-supplied HyperTerminal, or the Putty application supplied with the Luna SA.

■ **Tip** The terminal settings for this connection are 115200 serial port baud rate, no parity/8 bits/1 stop bit, VT-100 terminal emulation and hardware flow control.

Once you've connected to the Luna SA appliance, you'll be faced with a login screen, as shown in Figure C-1. On the first login, you'll use a username of *admin* and the initial password which is supplied in the Luna SA documentation. You will be immediately prompted to change the password from the factory default on the first *admin* login.

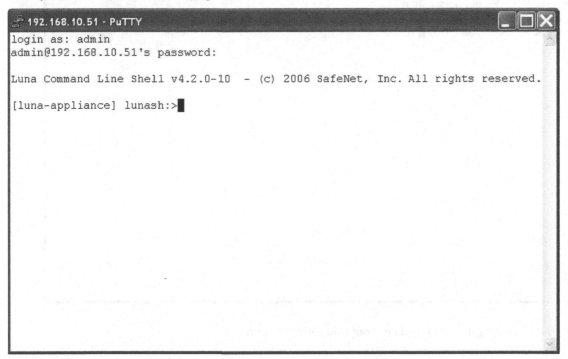

```
192.168.10.51 - PuTTY

login as: admin
admin@192.168.10.51's password:

Luna Command Line Shell v4.2.0-10  - (c) 2006 SafeNet, Inc. All rights reserved.

[luna-appliance] lunash:>
```

Figure C-2. Luna SA appliance login screen

The Luna SA provides a Unix-style command-line shell interface for performing administrative tasks. Once you've logged in, you'll use the command-line to perform the initial setup, which includes setting system time, network configuration, and partition setup. The following sections describe this process.

Setting System Time

Your first task after logging in for the first time and changing the admin password is to set the system date and time for the Luna SA. You can use the status date command to see if the date, time, or time zone settings need to change. Figure C-3 shows the status date command.

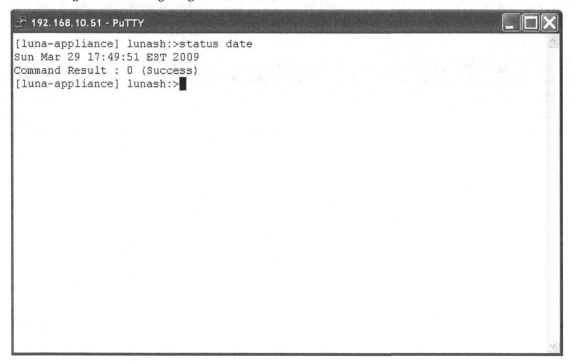

Figure C-3. Checking the Luna SA date, time, and time zone settings

If you do need to change these settings, use the sysconf command to make the necessary changes. The sysconf command has options to set the date, time, time zone, and to set a network time protocol (NTP) server to keep your appliance time in sync automatically.

■ **Tip** Use the help command at any time to get help about all commands or a specific command.

Network Configuration

The next step in the Luna SA setup is the network configuration. You'll need to configure your HSM to communicate with your local network. This means binding the network interface cards, setting the hostname, name servers, and so forth. You can use the net show statement to get the initial settings from the device. In Figure C-4, I've already set the HSM for configuration on my local network and am using the net show command to show my settings.

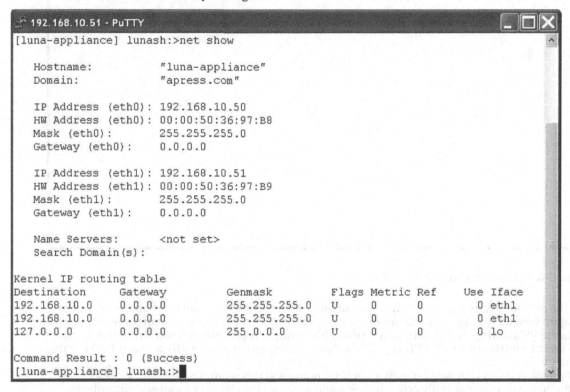

```
192.168.10.51 - PuTTY
[luna-appliance] lunash:>net show

   Hostname:            "luna-appliance"
   Domain:              "apress.com"

   IP Address (eth0): 192.168.10.50
   HW Address (eth0): 00:00:50:36:97:B8
   Mask (eth0):         255.255.255.0
   Gateway (eth0):      0.0.0.0

   IP Address (eth1): 192.168.10.51
   HW Address (eth1): 00:00:50:36:97:B9
   Mask (eth1):         255.255.255.0
   Gateway (eth1):      0.0.0.0

   Name Servers:        <not set>
   Search Domain(s):

Kernel IP routing table
Destination     Gateway         Genmask          Flags Metric Ref    Use Iface
192.168.10.0    0.0.0.0         255.255.255.0    U     0      0        0 eth1
192.168.10.0    0.0.0.0         255.255.255.0    U     0      0        0 eth1
127.0.0.0       0.0.0.0         255.0.0.0        U     0      0        0 lo

Command Result : 0 (Success)
[luna-appliance] lunash:>
```

Figure C-4. Reviewing network settings with the net show command

You can use the net hostname, net dns, and net interface commands to configure your network settings. You can use the net show command at any time to verify your settings. Once you are satisfied with the settings, connect your HSM to the network with an Ethernet cable and open an SSH connection to it from your server.

Generating a New Certificate

After you've connected your HSM to the network, you can use the sysconf regenCert command to regenerate a new certificate for your HSM and bind the Network Trust Link (NTLS) service to an adapter with the ntls bind command. The sysconf regenCert command is shown in Figure C-5.

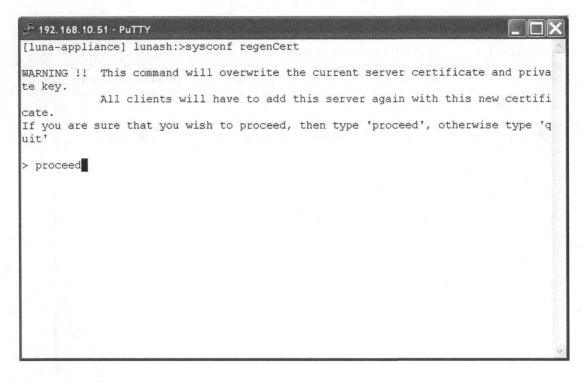

Figure C-5. *Regenerating the HSM certificate*

The next step is to run the `hsm-init` command, which will initialize the HSM and allow you to configure various settings, as documented in the Luna SA documentation. Most of these settings will be set via the PED during the initialization process. It's during this process that you'll initialize a "blue PED key," the administrator's USB PED key. You'll also have the option to set a PIN for each PED key that youcreate.

Finally, you can view and set individual HSM policies at this point. Use the `hsm showPolicies` command to view the currently active policies, and use `hsm changePolicy` to set specific policies.

Creating Partitions

The Luna SA HSM subdivides its resources into separate workspaces called partitions. When you configure SQL Server to communicate with the HSM via the EKM interface, the appliance will perform cryptographic tasks within the confines of designated partitions. To create a partition you'll need to first connect to the HSM using SSH. Then you'll need to issue the `hsm login` command and login using the PED and the blue administrator's PED key. This lets you login as an administrator, allowing you to perform administrative tasks like creating and managing partitions.

To create a partition, you'll enter the `partition create` command at the command prompt, as shown in Figure C-6.

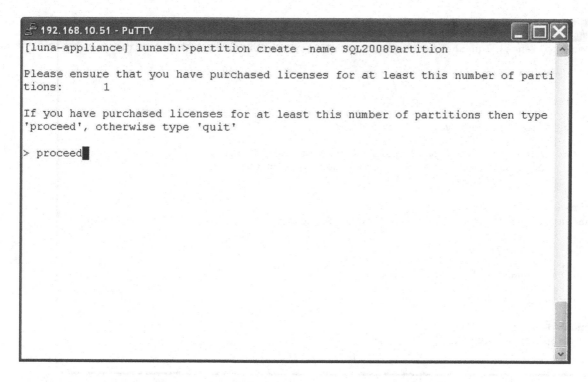

Figure C-6. Creating a new partition on the HSM

During the partition creation step the Luna SA will prompt you to enter a "black PED key," or partition owner key, into the PED. You'll have an opportunity to assign a PIN to the PED key and to make duplicates of the black PED key at this time.

After you create a new partition the PED display on the HSM will display a secret value, the client partition password. You'll need to write the client partition password down somewhere and secure it—it will never be displayed again. This password is vital to connecting to the Luna SA from SQL Server. Figure C-7 shows an example PED displaying the client partition password.

```
Login secret value
x9SP-PH9C-L/FK-q/TW
Please write it down.
(Press ENTER)
```

Figure C-7. PED display with secret value

On the Luna SA, there are a couple of partition policies that you'll need to change upon setup. You'll want to turn on the *Allow activation* and *Allow auto-activation* policies using the partition changePolicy command, as shown in Figure C-8.

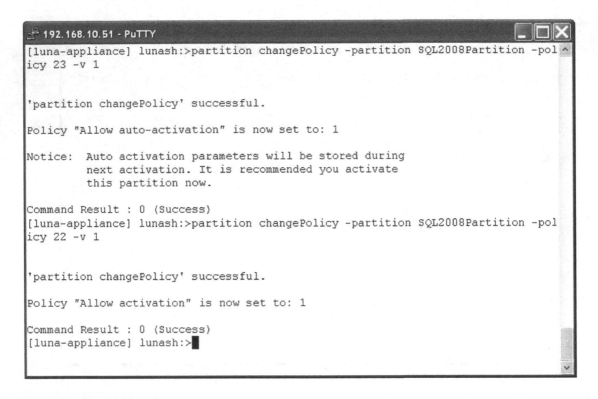

```
192.168.10.51 - PuTTY                                              _ □ X
[luna-appliance] lunash:>partition changePolicy -partition SQL2008Partition -pol
icy 23 -v 1


'partition changePolicy' successful.

Policy "Allow auto-activation" is now set to: 1

Notice:   Auto activation parameters will be stored during
          next activation. It is recommended you activate
          this partition now.

Command Result : 0 (Success)
[luna-appliance] lunash:>partition changePolicy -partition SQL2008Partition -pol
icy 22 -v 1


'partition changePolicy' successful.

Policy "Allow activation" is now set to: 1

Command Result : 0 (Success)
[luna-appliance] lunash:>█
```

Figure C-8. Changing partition policies

Configuring Client Access

After you create one or more partitions on the Luna SA, you'll need to configure your SQL Server to access the HSM. You'll need to prepare your server to create a network trust link between it and the HSM by exchanging certificates.

Registering HSM Certificate

You can use the ctp utility in the Program Files\LunaSA directory to copy the HSM's server certificate to the SQL Server computer. Then use the vtl utility's addServer command to register the certificate with your SQL Server. Figure C-9 demonstrates copying the HSM server certificate and registering it on the SQL Server with the ctp and vtl utilities.

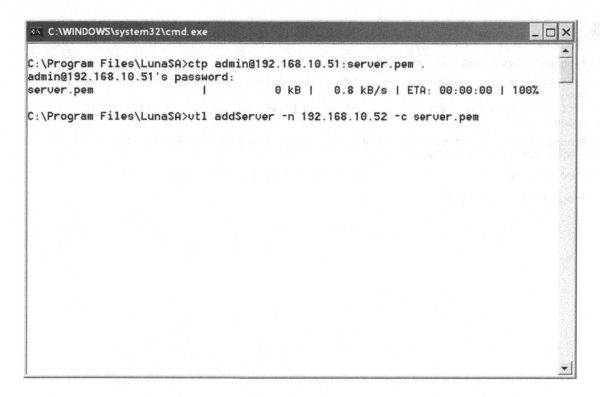

```
C:\WINDOWS\system32\cmd.exe                                    _ □ X

C:\Program Files\LunaSA>ctp admin@192.168.10.51:server.pem .
admin@192.168.10.51's password:
server.pem                 |           0 kB |   0.8 kB/s | ETA: 00:00:00 | 100%

C:\Program Files\LunaSA>vtl addServer -n 192.168.10.52 -c server.pem
```

Figure C-9. Using ctp utility to copy HSM certificate to SQL Server

Creating and Upload Client Certificate

The next step to preparing the client for the network trust link is to create a client certificate and upload it to the HSM. The vtl utility's createCert command generates a client certificate and places it in the cert\client subdirectory. The ctp utility can be used to upload the client certificate to the HSM. Creation and upload of the client certificate with these utilities is shown in Figure C-10.

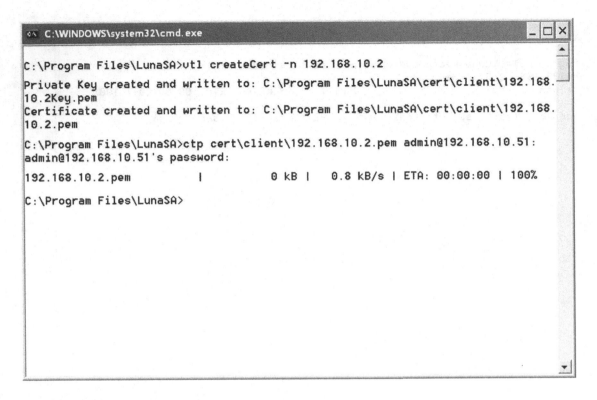

Figure C-10. Create and upload a client certificate

After you've uploaded the client certificate to the Luna SA, you have to register the client certificate with the HSM. For this, you'll need to use your terminal emulation utility to log back into the Luna SA shell. Use the client register command on the HSM, as shown in Figure C-11, to register the client certificate. You can use the client list command, also shown in the figure, to verify the client was successfully registered.

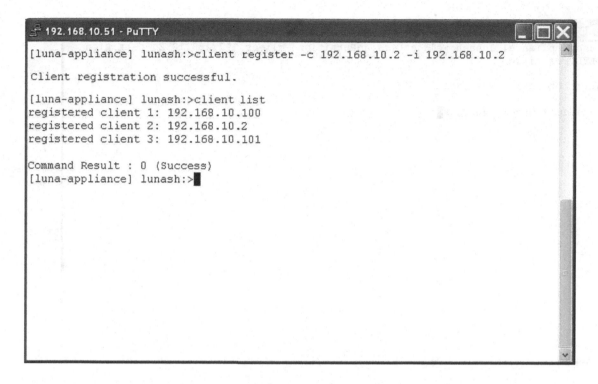

```
192.168.10.51 - PuTTY                                           _ □ X
[luna-appliance] lunash:>client register -c 192.168.10.2 -i 192.168.10.2

Client registration successful.

[luna-appliance] lunash:>client list
registered client 1: 192.168.10.100
registered client 2: 192.168.10.2
registered client 3: 192.168.10.101

Command Result : 0 (Success)
[luna-appliance] lunash:>█
```

Figure C-11. Registering the client with the HSM

After you've registered a client, you can assign it to the previously created Luna SA partition with the
client assignPartition command, as shown in Figure C-12.

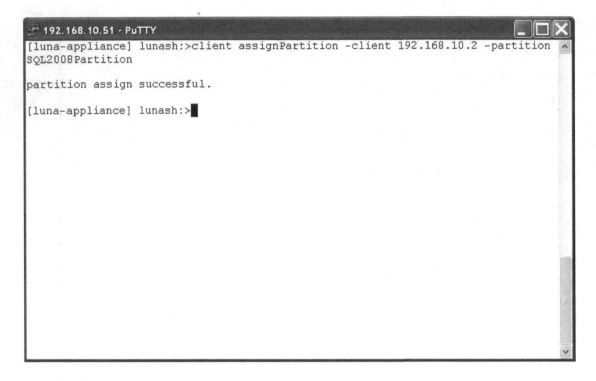

Figure C-12. Assigning a client to a partition on the HSM

Once you've completed the installation and configuration steps for the Luna SA and have set up the network trust link between the SQL Server computer and the HSM, you can verify the installation at the Windows command prompt with the vtl verify command. The vtl verify command will report the Luna SA partitions accessible to your client, as shown in Figure C-13.

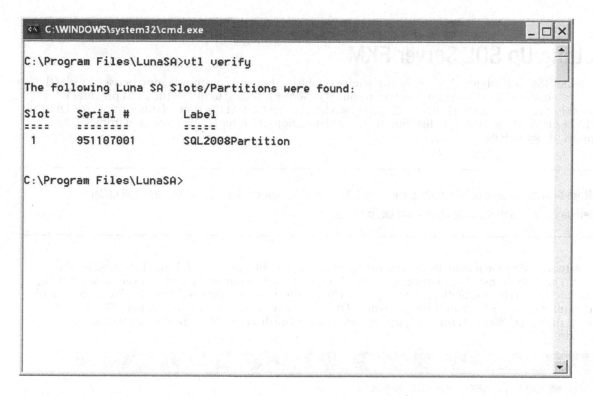

```
C:\WINDOWS\system32\cmd.exe                                    _ □ ×

C:\Program Files\LunaSA>vtl verify

The following Luna SA Slots/Partitions were found:

Slot     Serial #        Label
====     ========        =====
 1       951107001       SQL2008Partition


C:\Program Files\LunaSA>
```

Figure C-13. Verifying configuration and network trust link setup

Once you've completed the Luna SA and client configuration on your SQL Server computer, and established the network trust link between them, you're ready to configure SQL Server to communicate with the HSM.

Setting Up SQL Server EKM

Once the HSM is configured correctly and you've established secure communication between the SQL Server machine and the Luna SA, setting up your SQL Server instance to utilize the EKM provider is rather simple. The first step is to install the Luna SA EKM provider. At the time of this writing, the Luna SA EKM provider DLL was not distributed on the installation CD, it had to be requested from SafeNet support at www.safenet-inc.com.

■ **Note** Also at the time of this writing, the Luna SA 64-bit EKM provider for SQL Server was still under development and not available for general distribution.

After running the installation, the Luna SA EKM provider file, LunaEKM.dll, will be stored on the server. The default installation directory is LunaSA\EKM. From the command-line, run the LunaEKMConfig utility located in the installation directory. From inside the utility, execute the RegisterSlots command and enter the Luna SA slot number you want SQL Server to access, as shown in Figure C-14. This will update the LunaEKMConfig.ini configuration file in the same directory. Use the Quit command to exit the utility.

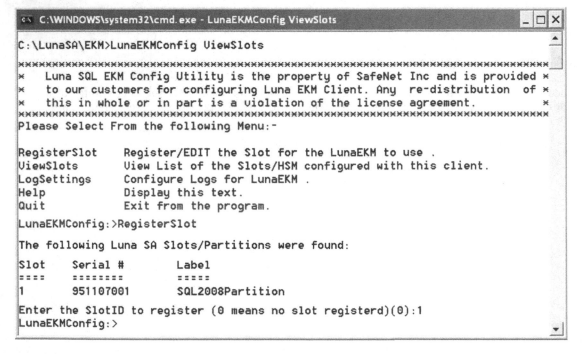

Figure C-14. Registering a Luna SA slot with the EKM provider

Configuring SQL Server

The remaining configuration is performed using T-SQL statements and can be performed from within Management Studio or sqlcmd. EKM is disabled by default in SQL Server 2008. To enable it, you must use the sp_configure system stored procedure to change the EKM provider enabled server configuration setting, as shown in Listing C-1.

Listing C-1. Enabling SQL Server EKM Provider Support

```
-- 'EKM provider enabled' is an advanced option in SQL Server
EXEC sp_configure 'show advanced options', 1;
GO
RECONFIGURE;
GO

EXEC sp_configure 'EKM provider enabled', 1;
GO
RECONFIGURE;
GO
```

■ **Note** The EKM provider enabled option is available only in the Enterprise and Developer editions of SQL Server 2008.

Once you've enabled the EKM provider capabilities of SQL Server, you need to register the EKM provider with the SQL Server instance to allow it to communicate with the HSM. Listing C-2 uses the LunaEKM.dll library to create a SQL Server cryptographic provider.

Listing C-2. Creating a Cryptographic Provider on SQL Server

```
CREATE CRYPTOGRAPHIC PROVIDER LunaEKMProvider
FROM FILE = N'c:\LunaSA\EKM\LunaEKM.dll';
```

The next step is to create a SQL Server credential for the cryptographic provider with the CREATE CREDENTIAL statement. You'll give this credential access to the client partition password you generated earlier in the HSM setup so that it can access the partition on the HSM. You'll also need to assign the credential to a login using the ALTER LOGIN statement, as shown in Listing C-3.

Listing C-3. Creating an EKM Credential

```
CREATE CREDENTIAL LunaEKMCredential
WITH IDENTITY = 'SQL2008\Michael',
SECRET = 'x9SP-PH9C-L/FK-q/TW'
FOR CRYPTOGRAPHIC PROVIDER LunaEKMProvider;
GO
```

```
ALTER LOGIN [SQL2008\Michael]
ADD CREDENTIAL LunaEKMCredential;
GO
```

At this point, you can verify that your cryptographic provider and its associated credential are properly set up with a query like the one shown in Listing C-4. Results are shown in Figure C-15.

Listing C-4. Verifying Cryptographic Provider and Credential

```
SELECT
  cp.provider_id,
  cp.name AS provider_name,
  cp.version,
  cp.dll_path,
  c.name AS credential_name,
  c.credential_identity
FROM sys.cryptographic_providers cp
INNER JOIN sys.credentials c
  ON cp.provider_id = c.target_id;
```

	provider_id	provider_name	version	dll_path	credential_name	credential_identity
1	65537	LunaEKMProvider	1.0.0.1	c:\LunaSA\EKM\LunaEKM.dll	LunaEKMCredential	SQL2008\Michael

Figure C-15. Verification that the EKM provider is properly registered

Verifying EKM Provider Functionality

After the EKM provider is registered as a cryptographic provider with SQL Server you can test the encryption and decryption functionality by creating a symmetric key and encrypting and decrypting data with it. Listing C-5 uses the EKM provider to create a symmetric key on the HSM, encrypt sample data from the spt_values system table in the master database, and decrypts the encrypted data. Partial results are shown in Figure C-16.

■ **Note** When you first initiate an EKM function after initializing the Luna SA, or after the HSM has been restarted, you'll need to use your black PED key and your assigned PIN to log into it with the PED.

Listing C-5. Use EKM to Create a Symmetric Key, Encrypt and Decrypt Data

```sql
-- Create an AES 128 symmetric key on the HSM
CREATE SYMMETRIC KEY Luna_AES128_Key
FROM PROVIDER LunaEKMProvider
WITH PROVIDER_KEY_NAME='Luna_AES128_Key',
CREATION_DISPOSITION = CREATE_NEW,
ALGORITHM = AES_128;
GO

--Create a temp table to hold results
CREATE TABLE #TestEncryption
(
  number int not null,
  name varbinary(120),
  type varbinary(120)
);

-- Encrypt some sample values from the dbo.spt_values
-- system table in the master database
INSERT INTO #TestEncryption
(
  number,
  name,
  type
)
SELECT
  number,
  EncryptByKey(Key_GUID(N'Luna_AES128_Key'), sv.name),
  EncryptByKey(Key_GUID(N'Luna_AES128_Key'), sv.type)
FROM master.dbo.spt_values sv
WHERE type = N'EOD';

-- Decrypt the previously encrypted values
SELECT
  number,
  CAST(DecryptByKey(te.name) AS nvarchar(35)) AS DecryptName,
  CAST(DecryptByKey(te.type) AS nvarchar(3)) DecryptType,
  te.name AS EncryptName,
  te.type AS EncryptType
FROM #TestEncryption te;

-- Clean up
DROP TABLE #TestEncryption;
GO

DROP SYMMETRIC KEY Luna_AES128_Key
REMOVE PROVIDER KEY;
GO
```

287

	number	DecryptName	DecryptType	EncryptName	EncryptType
1	8257	SERVER AUDIT	EOD	0x00F3E3D4C8686A49A74BA2DC9F88D9BC0...	0x00F3E3D4C8686A49A74BA2DC9F88D9BC0...
2	8259	CHECK CONSTRAINT	EOD	0x00F3E3D4C8686A49A74BA2DC9F88D9BC0...	0x00F3E3D4C8686A49A74BA2DC9F88D9BC0...
3	8260	DEFAULT	EOD	0x00F3E3D4C8686A49A74BA2DC9F88D9BC0...	0x00F3E3D4C8686A49A74BA2DC9F88D9BC0...
4	8262	FOREIGN KEY CONSTRAINT	EOD	0x00F3E3D4C8686A49A74BA2DC9F88D9BC0...	0x00F3E3D4C8686A49A74BA2DC9F88D9BC0...
5	8272	STORED PROCEDURE	EOD	0x00F3E3D4C8686A49A74BA2DC9F88D9BC0...	0x00F3E3D4C8686A49A74BA2DC9F88D9BC0...
6	8274	RULE	EOD	0x00F3E3D4C8686A49A74BA2DC9F88D9BC0...	0x00F3E3D4C8686A49A74BA2DC9F88D9BC0...
7	8275	TABLE SYSTEM	EOD	0x00F3E3D4C8686A49A74BA2DC9F88D9BC0...	0x00F3E3D4C8686A49A74BA2DC9F88D9BC0...
8	8276	TRIGGER SERVER	EOD	0x00F3E3D4C8686A49A74BA2DC9F88D9BC0...	0x00F3E3D4C8686A49A74BA2DC9F88D9BC0...
9	8277	TABLE	EOD	0x00F3E3D4C8686A49A74BA2DC9F88D9BC0...	0x00F3E3D4C8686A49A74BA2DC9F88D9BC0...
10	8278	VIEW	EOD	0x00F3E3D4C8686A49A74BA2DC9F88D9BC0...	0x00F3E3D4C8686A49A74BA2DC9F88D9BC0...
11	8280	STORED PROCEDURE EXTENDED	EOD	0x00F3E3D4C8686A49A74BA2DC9F88D9BC0...	0x00F3E3D4C8686A49A74BA2DC9F88D9BC0...

Figure C-16. Results of test EKM encryption and decryption

This is a very simple test that demonstrates the Luna's basic symmetric key creation, key deletion, and data encryption and decryption capabilities. Chapter 5 provides several additional code samples to demonstrate symmetric and asymmetric encryption as well as alternative methods to validate your EKM configuration and settings within SQL Server Management Studio.

Index

You Need the Companion eBook

Your purchase of this book entitles you to buy the companion PDF-version eBook for only $10. Take the weightless companion with you anywhere.

We believe this Apress title will prove so indispensable that you'll want to carry it with you everywhere, which is why we are offering the companion eBook (in PDF format) for $10 to customers who purchase this book now. Convenient and fully searchable, the PDF version of any content-rich, page-heavy Apress book makes a valuable addition to your programming library. You can easily find and copy code—or perform examples by quickly toggling between instructions and the application. Even simultaneously tackling a donut, diet soda, and complex code becomes simplified with hands-free eBooks!

Once you purchase your book, getting the $10 companion eBook is simple:

❶ Visit **www.apress.com/promo/tendollars/**.

❷ Complete a basic registration form to receive a randomly generated question about this title.

❸ Answer the question correctly in 60 seconds, and you will receive a promotional code to redeem for the $10.00 eBook.

233 Spring Street, New York, NY 10013

Offer valid through 4/10.